**Self-Scoring Study Guide
and Student Activities Manual
to accompany**

Adjustment and Growth: The Challenges of Life

Seventh Edition

by

Spencer A. Rathus

and

Jeffrey S. Nevid

prepared by

Gary W. Piggrem
DeVry Institute of Technology, Columbus, Ohio

Harcourt Brace College Publishers

Fort Worth • Philadelphia • San Diego • New York • Orlando • Austin • San Antonio
Toronto • Montreal • London • Sydney • Tokyo

Printed in the United States of America

8 9 0 1 2 3 4 5 6 7 202 9 8 7 6 5 4 3 2 1

ISBN: 0-15-507180-7

TO THE STUDENT
by Spencer A. Rathus and Gary W. Piggrem

This study guide is designed to accompany your ***Adjustment and Growth: The Challenges of Life Seventh Edition*** textbook. It will help you study the text material, review this material systematically, and check how well you've covered the material. The study guide covers all the important points covered in the corresponding chapters of the text, but it is **NOT** a substitute for reading and studying the text and attending class. If you read the text conscientiously, attend class regularly, and use the study guide to strengthen your learning, you should do very well in the course.

This study guide also contains two sections that will be of broader interest to you. They are intended not only to help you do well in psychology but in your other courses as well. They are "**Some Study Tips**" and "**Test Anxiety**." Many students who are motivated to do well in their courses are concerned that because they never had to study seriously before they entered college, they have not acquired the study skills they need to do well in college. By following the suggestions in this section on study tips these students can acquire and strengthen their study skills. Other students are concerned because they study hard and learn the material well, but are prevented from adequately demonstrating the depth and extent of their knowledge on tests because of test anxiety. Test anxiety is a cruel handicap for students who work hard to learn the material. The section on test anxiety will help the test-anxious student develop ways of coping with test anxiety and achieving higher grades.

HOW TO USE THIS STUDY GUIDE

Each chapter in this study guide corresponds to a chapter in your text. There are eighteen chapters in the text and in the study guide. Each chapter in the study guide contains a number of features: a chapter outline, learning objectives, key terms, a key terms review, a chapter review, and a sample test.

The Chapter Outline: A Preview of the Chapter

The outline serves to give you a feel for the general thrust of each chapter by highlighting chapter subheadings and topic areas. It is a skeleton outline which can serve as an "advance organizer" for you as you study the chapter.

The Chapter Overview: Putting Some "Meat" on the Bones

The overview gives you a brief description of each of the key topics and subheadings covered in the chapter. It is **not** a substitute for reading the chapter, but it provides you with a more detailed description of the various topics in the chapter than does the chapter outline.

Learning Objectives: What You Should Learn from the Chapter

This section will give you an idea of what you should know when you have finished your study of the chapter. You should read these objectives carefully **BEFORE** you read the chapter in your text, since they will help make you "ready" for the material by allowing you to recognize the main points. Once you have read the chapter in the text, it will be useful to reread the learning objectives in the study guide and ask yourself whether you have met them. If you have not, you may wish to return to the chapter and seek out the missing information before you proceed any further in your studying.

The learning objectives are varied, but tend to fall into a number of categories. Some ask you to define or compare and contrast important terms. Some ask you to describe or explain an experimental procedure or to summarize the results of a number of experiments. Others ask you to identify a number of items that may require memorization.

As you read these objectives, it will be helpful for you to write out your answers and to say them aloud. Try to be precise. This will be especially helpful if your instructor uses essay questions on the tests. Essay questions commonly involve comparing and contrasting important terms and describing research that may be used to support or contradict particular points of view. The learning objectives are easily converted into essay questions and many of your instructor's essay questions are likely to be similar, if not identical, to the learning objectives presented in this study guide.

Key Terms: Important Words and Phrases

Each chapter has a list of important or "key" terms. Many of these terms are found in the running glossary (the words and terms defined in the margins) of your text. All are found in the reading matter of the chapter. Some are repeated in a number of chapters. This indicates that these terms, such as psychoanalysis, social-cognitive theory, or self-actualization, have applications in a variety of areas studied by psychologists.

Ideally, you should be able to define each key term precisely and, often, provide an example of its use. The example may indicate how the term fits into psychological theory or how it relates to psychological research that has been conducted. Your definitions need not be in the exact words used in the text. However, the words must be similar enough in meaning so that it is clear that you have not confused the term with another term.

The Key Terms Review: Defining Your Terms

This section tests your knowledge of many of the key terms presented in the chapter. Since so much of your ability to do well in a course such as this depends on your mastery of the vocabulary, it is important that you be able to define accurately key concepts and ideas presented in the textbook material. In this section, key terms and phrases are presented from the original "Key Terms" section following the chapter outline. There are usually 20 key terms in a "Key Terms Review" exercise. You must write a definition for each of the terms listed in this section. ***Note:*** *Some chapters contain so many terms that more than one "Key Terms Review" is provided for those chapters. Chapter 2 contains three such exercises.*

The Chapter Review: A Step-by-Step Approach

This section summarizes the chapter in a fill-in-the-blank and matching question format. This permits you to test your knowledge of the chapter in a systematic way. The material is presented in the same sequence as it normally appears in the text. We suggest you try filling in the blank and matching questions after you first read the chapter and then reread any parts of the chapter which presented you with difficulties. Several challenging formats are presented in either "fill-in-the-blank" or "matching" questions.

The Practice Test: Taking a Stab at It

In each chapter, there is a sample test with twenty multiple-choice questions, five true-false questions, and an essay question. This test is designed to test your abilities to recognize accurately major principles as well as more detailed information from the chapter, such as names, statistics, etc. Your performance on these practice tests should be a relatively accurate predictor of how well you will perform on your instructor's tests, especially if she or he uses mostly multiple-choice items.

In grading your practice test, you should formulate a letter grade only for the 25 objective questions. You should compare the essay question with the answer outlined in the answer key (at the back of the study guide) and see if any required information was lacking, but grading these can be tricky and it will be easier to grade yourself just on the objective questions in the sample test. For the objective portion of the test, you will need to get the following number of items correct to achieve the letter grade indicated:

A	=	23, 24, or 25	(90 -100%)
B	=	20, 21, or 22	(80 - 89%)
C	=	18 or 19	(70 - 79%)
D	=	15, 16, or 17	(60 - 69%)
F	=	14 or below	(0 - 59%)

In answering multiple-choice items there are a few factors you might keep in mind in order to do as well as you can. First, carefully read the entire question, including **ALL** of the possible choices. Do **NOT** just focus on a single key word or term and jump to conclusions about what is being asked. Second, keep in mind that you must select the answer that **BEST** answers a questions or completes a sentence. Try to select a full, satisfying answer, not an inexact answer. If you have time, you may find it helpful to find a reason for eliminating each of the incorrect choices. If you cannot find a reason for eliminating a choice, it may be the correct answer.

Today, most professors prefer multiple-choice questions. However, some use a variety of types of questions and some others prefer fill-in-the-blank, matching, true-false, or essay questions. If your professor prefers the fill-in-the-blank or matching formats, you should probably spend more time on the chapter review section. If your professor prefers essay questions, pay attention to the essay question in your sample test and spend more time reviewing the learning objectives (converting them into essays and trying to answer them).

Student Activities: Critically Thinking About the Material

These activities are designed to help you apply the knowledge you have gained from the chapter and to help you further explore key issues raised in the chapter. They are often thought provoking, and in many cases, there is no single correct answer to the questions they pose. Many of the exercises are designed to help you explore your own feelings and experiences related to important issues raised by the text. Hopefully they will help you in your personal adjustment and growth process.

SOME STUDY TIPS

Imagine participating in a one-person experiment in which you first put some water in a bathtub and then sit in the tub. You wait a few moments and then look around. You notice that the water is still there, although you may have displaced a bit.

You may have been dry when you sat in the tub, but you are a person and not a sponge. You will not simply soak up the water. You would have to take rather active measures to get it inside you - perhaps a straw, patience, and a great deal of single-mindedness would help. It is also a task that must be accomplished gradually.

The problem of "soaking up" knowledge in psychology and in your other courses is not entirely dissimilar. You will not accomplish a great deal by sitting on your textbook, except perhaps looking an inch or so taller. It will not even help to flip through your textbook a dozen times unless you are doing some active searching for answers to questions.

Some tips on studying effectiveness follow. They involve taking an active approach to studying and using the SQ3R method.

An Active Approach to Studying

Begin your active approach to studying by assessing the amount of material you must master during the academic term and then measure the rate at which you plan to learn. How long does it take for you to read a chapter or a book in each of your courses? How much time must you spend studying each day? Does it add up correctly? Will you make it?

Once you have determined how much study time you will need for each of your courses for the academic term, try to space your study periods evenly. For most of us, spaced or distributed learning is more efficient than cramming or massed studying. Psychologists do not yet know exactly why, but it takes some time for learning to be "consolidated." Continuing to study when prior learning has not yet been consolidated may be less efficient than distributing, or breaking up, your study times. So try to outline a study schedule that will provide an approximately equal amount of study time each weekday. Leave weekends relatively free. Weekends will provide you with extra hours for reviewing notes and working on assignments that may be causing more difficulty than had been anticipated. If you have kept to your study schedule, you have probably earned some "reward" time for yourself and your friends.

Try to avoid studying psychology all day Monday, composition all day Tuesday, chemistry all day Wednesday, and so on. Psychology is so fascinating that you may have difficulty ripping yourself away from the text, but it may be more efficient to spend some time studying several subjects each day for at least two reasons. First, switching to a new subject may allow time for what you have learned in the previous subject to consolidate, so you will remember more of it later. Second, research indicates that old learning can interfere with new learning and new learning can interfere with old learning, particularly if it is all similar material. Switching subjects should reduce the amount of "interference" between old and new learning.

If you have difficulty pushing yourself to study for the required amount of time each day, begin with a more comfortable amount of time and build your study time gradually. Find a place to study that is relatively quiet, comfortable, and free from distractions. Try to do nothing but study in this place (that is, do not munch on chips, talk, listen to music, and fantasize about the weekend here), and try to remain in this place for the required amount of time. Then this place will come to mean studying to you.

Set specific goals for what you want to accomplish during your time in this study place and push yourself to achieve those goals. Your goals should focus on topics ***learned***, not just topics ***covered.*** After you have accomplished an immediate goal, such as studying and learning two topics, you may want to reward yourself with a break. In general, you should take a ten-minute break (not 15 or 20 minutes) each hour you study, just to get up, stretch your muscles, get a snack, or go to the bathroom, etc. This can relieve fatigue, help refresh you, and improve your concentration during the next hour. You should try to reward yourself somehow for meeting your daily study goals, even if only by putting off your dessert until after you have studied. Do not try to be a martyr and put off all pleasures until the end of the academic term. Some people are capable of doing this, but most of us are not, and if you have never spent much time in nonstop studying you may be demanding too much for yourself and setting yourself up for failure.

SQ3R: SURVEY, QUESTION, READ/WRITE, RECITE, REVIEW

Educational psychologist Francis Robinson (1970) of Ohio State University originated a method of studying called SQ3R - Survey, Question, Read/Write, Recite, Review - in which you are encouraged to become more active in soaking up academic material. Essentially, you phrase questions about the material as you first survey it. Then you answer these questions as you study. SQ3R has helped many college students study more effectively and raise their grades.

SURVEY: Some people short-circuit their pleasure in reading mystery novels by turning to the last pages of the novel to find out "whodunit" when their curiosity gets the best of them. While skipping through the pages of a novel may harm the dramatic impact by revealing information before the suspense has been adequately built, skipping through the pages can be an excellent prelude to learning textbook material. More and more textbooks are being written specifically to stimulate the student to survey the material before reading it.

Your adjustment and growth textbook and this study guide have chapter outlines at the beginning of each chapter. Your textbook also has "Truth or Fiction?" sections at the beginning of each chapter. These provide a preview of what is to come when you read the chapter. Familiarity with the outline of the chapter will provide you with a framework, or advance organizers, for learning the substance of the chapter as you later absorb it page by page.

QUESTION: Phrase questions for each of the major and minor headings in the chapter outline. If you were to do this for the headings in the beginning of Chapter 1, the beginning of a list of questions might look like this:

- What are psychology and adjustment and how are they related?
    - What is the difference between adjustment and personal growth?
    - How is nature different from nurture? Is biology/heredity destiny?
    - How is the clinical approach different from the healthy personality approach?
- Why is human diversity important to the study of adjustment?
    - Why is ethnic diversity important?
    - Why is gender important?
    - What other kinds of diversity are there?

You may have phrased the questions differently. Your method of phrasing may be more efficient for you. With some practice you will learn to form questions that work well for you.

Textbooks for your other courses may not begin with chapter outlines. Some may not have headings for clearly defined sections. If the book lacks headings, get into the material page by page and phrase relevant questions as you go along.

READ/WRITE

READ: Once you have phrased each question, read the relevant subject matter with the purpose of answering the question. This will help you attend to the central points of the section of the chapter. If the material is fine literature, such as a novel, you may wish to read it once to appreciate its poetic features fully. Then you may wish to skim it and phrase questions so that you may read it in order to answer those questions later on.

WRITE: As you read, write down your questions and write the answers to those questions. This helps you actively focus on important questions raised by the section or the chapter while at the same time providing you with a written record for later study.

A more formal way to do this is to wait until you have thoroughly read the chapter, then go back and take notes from it just as you would normally take notes in a classroom. It is better to take notes from a chapter after you have read it thoroughly because then you will know what is important and needs to be written down. If you take notes before you have thoroughly read the chapter, it is more difficult to know what is really important, and most students tend to write down too many irrelevant items, making it more difficult to study effectively later on.

If you prefer to highlight your text rather than to take notes from it, you should do it here, ***after*** having read the material thoroughly. Again, students who highlight their text as they read it for the first time tend to highlight too much, making it difficult to figure out what is really important when they are studying later on. In general, the rule of thumb is that you should highlight no more than 10 percent of the material in your text. Most study skills experts prefer that students take notes instead of highlighting because taking notes is more active and involves more concentration and focused thinking whereas highlighting can become mechanical, passive, and requires little focus or concentration. Taking notes may be more efficient than highlighting for gathering information from your text.

RECITE: Once you have read the appropriate section or chapter and highlighted it or taken notes from it, put it down and answer the question or questions you have phrased as clearly and briefly as possible. Jot down a few key words that will "telegraph" the answer to you when you review your notes. Recite your answer aloud if possible. Your willingness to recite aloud may depend on where you are, who is near you, and how you feel about the reaction you expect from those who are near you.

REVIEW: Review the material briefly at the conclusion of each study session, and then on a reasonable schedule - perhaps weekly - cover the key response words and read your questions like a quiz. Perhaps you can enlist friends to read them. Then recite the answers and check them for accuracy against the key response words. Reread the relevant subject matter if the key response words are not sufficiently meaningful to you. Forgetting the answers to too many questions may mean a number of things: that you are not phrasing your questions in an appropriate way, that you did not read the textbook material carefully, that you did not fully understand the textbook material, that you chose your key response words carelessly, or that you did not recite the material on a schedule that is efficient for you.

Once you have actively studied your material, you may feel less anxious about the prospect of taking quizzes and examinations. But if you suffer from test anxiety, you will find the following section useful.

TEST ANXIETY

In Chapter 11 of your text there is a discussion of test anxiety. As noted, there are few experiences more frustrating than test anxiety. When a student works diligently to prepare for a test, it can seem particularly unfair that concern about taking the test can be linked to poor performance. This section presents a lengthy treatment of methods that may be used to cope with test anxiety for students who have this problem.

Tests are practically inescapable. From achievement and intelligence tests in the elementary schools to SATs, GREs, and civil service examinations, tests seem built into every corner of our society. It is not entirely unusual for graduate students to boast about their test scores or even to introduce themselves by their test scores. We know of a statistics professor who said that one of the first pieces of information she and her future husband shared when they met were their scores on the Miller Analogies Test, a test often used for entry into graduate schools. Students who have done poorly on the SATs and GREs have often told us that they wonder whether they "have what it takes" for college work. They take their test scores very seriously. Unfortunately, their concern about the importance of tests often becomes part of the problem.

Is It All in Your Mind?

Why do some people become so upset about tests? Can it be explained through principles of classical conditioning (which you will learn about in Chapter 2)? That is, do a few bad experiences with tests lead a person to automatically experience a fear response at the thought of taking another test? Experiments in test anxiety suggest that what people tell themselves while they are taking tests may be a more important factor.

Psychologist Kenneth Holroyd of Ohio University and his colleagues (1978) recruited seventy-two women taking introductory psychology for an experiment in test anxiety. Thirty-six of the women showed high test anxiety as measured by Irwin Sarason's (1972) Test Anxiety Scale, and thirty-six showed low test anxiety. All the women were then given anagrams (jumbled words) to solve as quickly as they could. ATSR, for example, is an anagram for STAR, ARTS, or RATS. It had been shown earlier that high test anxiety interferes with the ability to solve anagrams, but how it did so was not entirely clear (Sarason, 1973).

In the Holroyd study, the high-test-anxious women were down on themselves regardless of how well they actually did. High-test-anxious women and low-test-anxious women showed similarity in bodily signs of anxiety as a result of the stress of the test-taking situation, as measured by heart rate and by sweat in the palms of their hands. This study and others (Bandura, 1977; Sarason, 1978) suggest that highly critical self-evaluation during the test situation may impede test performance.

It appears reasonable to conclude that persons who report themselves to be highly test anxious are more critical of themselves during tests and allow themselves to be somewhat distracted from their tasks by self-criticism and worry. It makes sense that there could be an interaction between self-criticism and high bodily arousal such that these two variables may cause each other to increase, perhaps in a vicious cycle. A standard method for coping with test anxiety focuses on changing highly critical self-evaluations and other troublesome thoughts.

Rational Restructuring of Test Taking

Psychologist Marvin Goldfried of the State University of New York at Stony Brook and his colleagues (1978) reported a technique that was successful in reducing test anxiety among college women and men attending either Stony Brook or Catholic University: rational restructuring. Essentially, these students were taught to restructure or reshape their thoughts while taking tests.

Participants in the study first selected fifteen anxiety-evoking situations taken from the Suinn Test Anxiety Behavior Scale (Suinn, 1971). Items from the Suinn scale (which is presented in Chapter 11 of the text) include the following:

waiting for the test to be handed out
studying for a quiz
hearing the announcement of the coming test
reading the first item on a final examination
discussing the approaching test with friends a few weeks before the test is due

Students then listed items in a hierarchy from least anxiety-inducing to most anxiety-inducing. Then, during each of the five clinical treatment sessions, three of the items were presented for four one-minute trials. During each trial, students did the following: they noted their self-defeating, anxiety-producing thoughts as they imagined themselves in the situation, and they attempted to replace each self-defeating thought with a rational alternative. For instance, one self-defeating thought was, "I'm going to fail this test, and everyone's going to think I'm stupid!" An example of rational restructuring of this thought is, "Chances are I probably won't fail. And even if I do, people probably won't think I'm stupid." Students noted their levels of anxiety before and after rational restructuring and discussed their problems and progress with other students.

You can rationally restructure test-taking situations with the following steps:

1. pinpoint your self-defeating thoughts
2. construct rational alternative thoughts
3. practice the rational alternatives ***before*** you take the test as well as during the test
4. reward yourself for your efforts

Pinpointing Self-Defeating Thoughts: Imagine yourself in a variety of test-taking situations. Sit back, relax, and fill in the details of the situation as vividly as possible. Search for any thoughts that cause you concern. Write down these thoughts after a minute or so. Perhaps some of the items on the Suinn scale cause you concern. Imagine yourself in these situations. Here are other situations that may cause you concern:

the proctor writing down the time left on the blackboard
students discussing their answers after class
not being able to think of the answer to an easy question immediately
a student who has completed the test leaving the room
not being able to answer the first question of a test

Constructing Rational Alternatives: Carefully examine each of your anxiety-producing thoughts. Note how they may distract you from focusing on the test items themselves. Construct rational alternatives for these thoughts, as in the following examples:

Self-Defeating Thoughts	**Rational Alternatives**
"I'm the only one who's going to go bananas over this thing!"	"Nonsense! Lots of people have test anxiety. Just don't let it distract you from the test itself!"
I'm running out of time!"	"Time is passing, but take it item by item and answer what I can. Panicking won't help."
"This is impossible! Are all the items going to be like this?"	"Just take it item by item. They're all different. There's no reason to assume the worst."
"I just can't remember a thing!"	"Just slow down and think about it for a moment. It may come back. If not, go on to the next item. Getting upset won't help.
"Everyone is smarter than I am!"	"That's an exaggeration, but they may not be distracting themselves from taking the test by worrying. Just do the best I can, item by item."
"I've got to get out of here. I can't take it any longer!"	"Even if I feel that way now and then, I don't have to act on it. Just focus on the items, one by one."

"I just can't do well on tests!"

"That's only true if I believe it's true! Now get back to the items. One at a time."

"There are a million items left!

"Quite a few, but not a million! Worrying about how many items are left just leaves me with less time to complete them. Now get back to the items and answer as many as I can, one by one."

"Everyone else is leaving. They're all finished before I am."

"Fast work does not guarantee correct work. The first people done do not usually get the best grades. I must work at my own pace taking each item one at a time, finishing what I can."

"If I flunk, everything is ruined!"

"I won't be happy if I fail but it's not the end of my life either. Distracting myself by worrying about failure just increase my chances of failure. My best chance to pass is to answer each item as best I can, one at a time!"

Practicing Rational Alternatives: Arrange practice tests in your courses that are as close to actual testing conditions as possible. Time yourself. If the tests are Graduate Record Exams, or civil service type exams, obtain practice tests and make the testing conditions as realistic as you can.

You may wish to use one of the practice tests in each chapter of this study guide to practice rational alternatives for the tests in your psychology course. If so, allow yourself as much time as your professor would permit you and try to take the test in the actual room (or a room similar to) where you take your psychology tests.

Pay close attention to the thoughts you experience as you take the practice test. For each self-defeating thought, think firmly of a rational alternative. Repeat the rational alternative aloud, firmly, and then return to working on the test items, item by item. If you feel anxious, you need not allow your anxiety to distract you from working on the test items.

When you have finished the first ten or fifteen items, you may wish to run through the list of self-defeating thoughts you had identified to see if you left any out. If so, you may think through them purposefully, then follow them with rational alternatives. Then return to the test and continue, item by item, as before.

Self-Reward: When you have firmly thought a rational alternative to a self-defeating thought, say to yourself, "That's better! Now I can return to the test," or "I don't have to allow anxiety to distract me after all." When you have completed the test, think something like, "Well, I did it! Regardless of the grade I get, I certainly got through that test feeling much better than I usually do. And I may have done better than usual as well! Now there's no reason why I can't do even better on my future tests!"

Now it's up to you. Psychology is the most exciting part of our lives, and we sincerely hope that you find it stimulating and rewarding. If you work your way through the sections of each chapter of the study guide, one at a time, you should thoroughly master the material for the course. Your performance on the practice test at the end of each chapter should serve as a relatively accurate predictor of how you will do in the actual tests in your course.

References

Bandura, A. Social Learning Theory. Englewood Cliffs, NJ. Prentice-Hall, 1977.

Doerr, H.O. and Hokanson, J.E. "A relation between heart rate and performance in children." *Journal of Personality and Social Psychology*, 1965, *2*, pp. 70-76.

Goldfried, M.R., Linchan, M.M., and Smith, J.L. "Reduction of test anxiety through cognitive restructuring." *Journal of Counseling and Clinical Psychology*, 1978, *46*, pp. 32-39.

Holroyd, K.A., Westbrook, T., Wolf, M., and Badhorn, E. "Performance, cognition, and physiological responding to test anxiety." *Journal of Abnormal Psychology*, 1978, *87*, pp. 442-451

Robinson, F.P. *Effective Study*, 4th ed. New York: Harper & Row, 1970.

Sarason, I.G. "Experimental approaches to test anxiety: Attention and uses of information." In C.D. Spielberger (ed.), *Anxiety and Behavior* (vol. 2). New York: Academic Press, 1972.

Sarason, I.G. "Test anxiety and cognitive modeling." *Journal of Personality and Social Psychology*, 1973, *28*, pp. 58-61.

Sarason, I.G. "The test anxiety scale: Concept and research." In C.D. Spielberger and I.G. Sarason (eds.), *Stress and Anxiety* (vol. 5). New York: Halstead-Wiley, 1978.

Suinn, R.M. *The Suinn Test Anxiety Behavior Scale*. Fort Collins, CO: Rocky Mountain Behavioral Science Institute, 1971.

Contents

1

What Is Adjustment?

Chapter Outline

I. Psychology and Adjustment

II. Controversies in Psychology and Adjustment

A. Adjustment versus Personal Growth
B. Nature versus Nurture: Is Biology Destiny?
C. The Clinical Approach versus the Healthy-Personality Approach
   1. Box: Adjustment in the New Millennium: Where Are We Headed?

III. Human Diversity and Adjustment

A. Ethnic Diversity
   1. Box: Adjustment in a World of Diversity: On Increasing Diversity in American Higher Education
B. Gender
C. Other Kinds of Diversity

IV. How Psychologists Study Adjustment

A. The Scientific Method
B. Samples and Populations: Representing Human Diversity
   1. Box: Adjustment in a World of Diversity: *Including* Women and Members of Diverse Ethnic Groups in Research
C. Methods of Observation: The Better to See You With
   1. Box: Adjustment in a World of Diversity: A Sex Survey That Addresses Sociocultural Factors
   2. Box: Self-Assessment: Dare You Say What You Think? The Social Desirability Scale
D. The Correlational Method: On What Goes Up and What Comes Down
E. The Experimental Method: Trying Things Out

V. Adjustment and Modern Life

A. Becoming a Successful Student

Harcourt Brace & Company

Chapter Overview

Psychology and Adjustment. Life is replete with challenges. Challenges are changes, events, and problems that require adjustment and provide us with the opportunity to grow. Some challenges, such as anxiety, obesity, or depression are personal. Other challenges involve intimate relationships and sexuality. Still others involve the larger social context - the workplace, prejudice and discrimination, natural and technological disasters, pollution, and urban life. Psychology, which is the scientific approach to the study of behavior and mental processes, is ideally suited to helping people meet the challenges of everyday life. One of the ways psychologists meet this challenge is through the study of adjustment. Adjustment is behavior that permits us to meet the challenges of life. Some adjustments are inferior, whereas others allow us to actively change self-defeating or troublesome behavior patterns so that they trouble us less.

Controversies in Psychology and Adjustment. There are several controversies relating to adjustment. One controversy regards the definition of adjustment itself. While adjustment is reactive, meeting the challenges of life, people are not merely reactors to their environment. They are proactive. Personal growth involves conscious, active self-development beyond merely reacting to the environment. Another controversy centers on how much of personality is biologically predestined. Research indicates that genes may determine the ranges for the expression of traits, but our chosen behavior patterns can minimize genetic risk factors and maximize genetic potential. There are also two major approaches to studying adjustment: the clinical approach and the healthy-personality approach. The clinical approach focuses on ways in which problems can be corrected, whereas the healthy personality approach focuses on optimizing our development along personal, social, physical, and vocational lines.

Human Diversity and Adjustment. It is important to study human diversity because awareness of the richness of human diversity enhances our understanding of the individual and enables students to appreciate the cultural heritages and historical problems of various ethnic groups. Knowledge of diversity helps psychologists understand the aspirations and problems of individuals from various groups so that they can successfully intervene to help group members.

One type of diversity is based on ethnic groupings. An ethnic group may share factors such as cultural heritage, common history, race, and language. Minority ethnic groups have frequently experienced prejudice and discrimination by members of the dominant culture. Another type of diversity is based on gender, the state of being male or female. There have been historic, gender-based prejudices against women. Much of the scientific research into gender roles and gender differences assumes that male behavior represents the norm. The careers of women have been traditionally channeled into domestic chores, regardless of women's wishes as individuals.

How Psychologists Study Adjustment. Psychology is a science and scientific statements must be supported by evidence. To gather evidence, psychologists use the scientific method. This method is a systematic approach to gathering scientific evidence. It involves formulating a research question, developing a hypothesis, testing the hypothesis, and drawing conclusions. Subjects who are studied in scientific research are referred to as a sample. A sample is a segment of a population. Samples must accurately represent the population they are intended to reflect. Women's groups and health professionals argue that there is a historic bias in favor of conducting research with men. Research samples have also tended to underrepresent minority ethnic groups in the population. Researchers use two ways to ensure that their samples represent the targeted populations: random and stratified samples. In a random sample, each member of a population has an equal chance of being selected to participate. In a stratified sample, identified subgroups in the population are being represented proportionately.

Psychologists use specific methods of observation that include the case-study, survey, testing, naturalistic-observation, and laboratory-observation methods. Case studies consist of information about the lives of individuals or small groups. The survey method employs interviews, questionnaires, or public records to provide information about behavior that cannot be observed directly. Psychological tests are used to measure various traits and characteristics among a population. The naturalistic-observation method observes behavior carefully and unobtrusively where it happens - in the "field." The laboratory-observation method observes behavior in a controlled environment created by psychologists

Psychologists also use correlational and experimental research to gather information. Correlational research reveals relationships between variables, but does not determine cause and effect. In a positive correlation, variables increase simultaneously. In a negative correlation, one variable increases while the other one decreases. Experiments are used to seek cause and effect, specifically, the effect of independent variables on dependent variables. Experimental subjects are given a treatment, whereas control subjects are not. Blinds may be used to control for the effects of expectations.

Learning Objectives

After studying this chapter you should be able to:

1. Explain what psychology is, what psychologists do and how psychology can be helpful in exploring adjustment and growth issues.
2. Compare and contrast adjustment and personal growth.
3. Explain what genes and chromosomes are and what they do. Also discuss why biology is not necessarily destiny.
4. Identify the differences between the clinical and healthy-personality approaches to adjustment.
5. Define "ethnic group" and discuss why it is important to study human diversity.
6. Define "gender" and discuss the various prejudices experienced by women historically and in scientific research.
7. Explain what the scientific method is and describe the various steps involved in it.
8. Describe the relationship between samples and populations and explain how researchers ensure that their samples represent target populations.
9. Explain and provide some examples of the various sampling bias problems present in scientific research in regard to women.
10. Identify and briefly explain the various methods of observation used by psychologists.
11. Explain the case study method of research in terms of its purposes and its limitations.
12. Describe the survey method of research in terms of its purposes and its limitations.
13. Describe the testing method of research in terms of its purposes and its limitations.
14. Describe the naturalistic-observation method of research in terms of its purposes and its limitations.

15. Describe the laboratory-observation method of research in terms of its purposes and limitations.

16. Describe the correlational method of research in terms of its purposes and limitations, and explain what a positive correlation, a negative correlation, and a correlation coefficient are.

17. Describe the experimental method of research in terms of its purposes and limitations, and explain what control subjects, experimental subjects, and placebo treatments are.

18. Identify and briefly explain at least five steps that are essential to taking an active approach to college.

19. Identify at least 6 specific actions you can take as part of planning ahead to get the most out of your studying.

20. Identify the steps involved in the SQ3R system and explain what can be done to maximize one's learning during each step of this system.

Key Terms

bulimia nervosa
psychology
adjustment
personal growth
genes
chromosomes
clinical approach
healthy-personality approach
the human genome
ethnic groups
Ebonics
bilingualism
gender
scientific method
hypothesis
operational definitions
subjects
selection factor
replicate
sample
population
generalize
random sample
stratified sample
volunteer bias
case study
survey
validity scales
naturalistic observation
unobtrusive
laboratory
correlational method
correlation coefficient
positive correlation
negative correlation
experiment
treatment
experimental subjects
control subjects
blind
placebo
SQ3R
advance organizers

Key Terms Review

Define each of the following terms:

1. Bulimia Nervosa: ________________________________

____

2. Psychology: __________________________________

____

3. Adjustment: ____

____

4. Personal Growth: ____

____

5. Clinical Approach: ____

____

6. Healthy-Personality Approach: ____

____

7. Scientific Method: ____

____

8. Hypothesis: ____

____

9. Operational Definition: ____

____

10. Sample: ____

____

11. Population: ____

____

12. Positive Correlation: ____

____

13. Negative Correlation: ____

____

14. Experiment: ____

____

15. Treatment: ____

____

16. Blind: ____

____

17. Placebo: ____

____

18. Random Sample: ____

____

19. Stratified Sample: ____

____

20. SQ3R: ____

____

Chapter Review

1. Most challenges offer us the opportunity to __________.
2. The science of __________ is ideally suited to helping people meet the challenges of contemporary life.
3. __________ is behavior that permits us to meet the demands of the environment.
4. __________ is essentially reactive, whereas __________ is active and creative.

5. __________ are segments of DNA which represent the basic units of heredity, and the stuff of which our __________ are composed.

6. Most psychology textbooks are written from either the __________ approach or the __________ __________ approach

7. The __________ __________ consists of all of our genes, the basic units of heredity.

8. __________ __________ are subgroups within the population that have a common cultural heritage.

9. The two fastest growing ethnic groups right now in the United States consist of __________ Americans and __________ Americans.

10. Three reasons for studying ethnic diversity are:

    a. ______________________________

    b. ______________________________

    c. ______________________________

11. In addition to race and gender, human diversity also touches upon differences in __________, __________ __________, and __________ __________.

12. The four basic steps of the scientific method are:

    a. ______________________________

    b. ______________________________

    c. ______________________________

    d. ______________________________

13. In surveys, naturalistic observation, and other research methods, the actual participants in a study are called the __________, and they represent a larger group of people called the __________.

14. Samples in which each member of a target population has an equal chance of being chosen to participate in an experiment are called __________ samples.

15. Historically there is a bias in favor of conducting research with __________, and there is a crucial deficiency of research into ________ health.

16. __________ scales are sensitive to misrepresentations and alert the psychologist when test results may be deceptive.

17. The naturalistic observation method provides __________ information, but it is not the best method for determining a behavior's __________.

18. A correlation coefficient is a number that varies between __________.

19. Ideally, experiments randomly assign people to be __________ subjects, who receive an experimental treatment, and __________ subjects, who do not.

20. **Matching:** Match the name of the psychological research method with its corresponding definition:

a. __________.	A method in which organisms are observed in their natural environments	1. the case study method
b. __________.	A biography compiled from interviews, questionnaires, and psychological tests	2. the survey method
c. __________.	A method in which people are observed in a carefully controlled environment	3. the correlational method
d. __________.	A method that studies the relationships between variables	4. the testing method
e. __________.	A method in which large numbers of people are questioned with verbal or written questionnaires	5. naturalistic observation
f. __________.	A method that seeks to discover cause and effect relationships	6. the experimental method
g. __________.	A method that measures individual differences in personality or in specific areas such as intelligence	7. laboratory observation

21. In many experiments, some subjects are given a "sugar pill," or __________ treatment, to control for the effects of their expectations.

22. The steps involved in taking an active approach to studying are:

a. ____

b. ____

c. ____

d. ____

e. ____

23. The steps in the SQ3R system are:

a. ____

b. ____

c. ____

d. ____

e. ____

Sample Test

Multiple-Choice Questions

1. Most challenges offer us the opportunity to ______.
   a. fail
   b. prove ourselves
   c. grow
   d. retrench

2. Behavior which permits people to meet the demands of the environment is called ______.
   a. prosocial behavior
   b. adjustment
   c. proactive behavior
   d. dysfunctional behavior

3. Which of the following is true of genetic factors and psychological adjustment?
   a. Genetic factors have been shown to have little or no effect on psychological development and adjustment.
   b. Genetic factors interact with environmental factors and self-determination to influence behavior.
   c. Genetic factors interact with prenatal conditions to influence neural development of the fetus, but cease affecting psychological adjustment and growth after birth.
   d. Psychological development and adjustment are almost completely predetermined by genetic factors.

4. The percentage of non-Hispanic white Americans in the United States will ______ of the total U. S. population by the year 2050.
   a. increase to about 95%
   b. decrease to about 75%
   c. decrease to about 53%
   d. decrease to about 33%

5. The state of being male or female is known as ______.
   a. sexuality
   b. sensuality
   c. sexual orientation
   d. gender

6. Which of the following ethnic groups comprises the largest percentage of female college students?
   a. African Americans
   b. Asian Americans
   c. Hispanic Americans
   d. Native Americans

7. An organized means of expanding and refining knowledge, consisting of a group of principles that generally guide scientists' research endeavors, is known as ______.
   a. a theory
   b. the scientific method
   c. a hypothesis
   d. a cognitive schema

8. A researcher knows that 12% of a target population is African American and 9% is Hispanic American. The researcher selects her sample so that she ends up with a sample containing exactly 12% African Americans and 9% Hispanic Americans. This researcher used a ______ sample.
   a. stratified
   b. control
   c. biased
   d. random

9. Scientists have found that people who agree to participate in research studies differ systematically from people who do not. This problem is known as ______.
   a. population bias
   b. volunteer bias
   c. control variance
   d. placebo effect

10. Which of the following is **NOT** listed by your text as a weakness of the case study method?
    a. Subjects' memories are often incomplete.
    b. Subjects' memories are often distorted.
    c. There are ethical issues regarding the inappropriate use of control groups.
    d. Researchers sometimes guide subjects to remember information in ways that are consistent with the researchers' theoretical perspectives.

11. A place in which scientific theories, techniques, and methods are tested and demonstrated is technically known as a(n) ______.
    a. office
    b. base
    c. laboratory
    d. enclave

12. A correlation coefficient is a number that varies between ______.
    a. -.50 and +.50
    b. -1.00 and +1.00
    c. -2.00 and +2.00
    d. -5.00 and +5.00

13. Most psychologists agree that the preferred method for determining cause and effect in human behavior is the ______ method.
    a. case study
    b. correlational
    c. laboratory observation
    d. experimental

14. In an experiment, if there are two groups being studied and one group is given alcohol to measure its effects, while the other group is not given alcohol, the alcohol would be considered ______.
    a. the experimental blind
    b. the experimental control
    c. the experimental treatment
    d. the dependent variable

15. A bogus treatment that has the appearance of being genuine is called ______.
    a. a placebo
    b. a control
    c. a schema
    d. a selection factor

16. For most people, spaced or distributed learning is ______.
    a. more efficient than massed learning
    b. about as efficient as massed learning
    c. less efficient than massed learning
    d. less efficient when memorizing concepts, but more efficient when memorizing facts

17. According to your text, you should question ______ of your instructor's assignments.
    a. none
    b. some
    c. most
    d. all

18. Chapter outlines, "Truth or Fiction?" questions, highlighted key terms, and chapter headings are all examples of ______.
    a. structural reactors
    b. advance organizers
    c. format reducers
    d. review implicators

19. According to your text, the best preparation for critical encounters with the cultures of others is ______.
    a. the critical study and mastery of knowledge about those other cultures
    b. a fair and objective attitude
    c. the critical study and mastery of knowledge of psychology
    d. the critical study and mastery of knowledge about one's own culture

20. According to your text, as many as one woman in ______ has been raped.
   a. two
   b. four
   c. six
   d. eight

True-False Questions

21. Adjustment is essentially proactive. ______

22. Ebonics is less complex than standard English. ______

23. Scientific research has shown that TV violence causes aggressiveness in children. ______

24. Research findings with men can usually be generalized to women. ______

25. Reciting material out loud as you study helps you remember it better. ______

Essay Question

26. Identify the differences between the clinical and healthy-personality approaches to adjustment.

Student Activities

Name ________________________________ Date ____________

1.1 What Is Challenging?

Rathus and Nevid begin their first chapter with several examples of individuals facing challenges. They illustrate the nature of challenge for Beth, John, Maria, Lisa, and David, and they also review a litany of problems and opportunities that could serve as a checklist. Have you considered which ones apply to you? Some can be regarded as concerns, some as hassles, some as crises, and some as openings for growth. Try this: skip any issues that do not concern you, but count the number of issues in the list below that are (1) issues you have had to adjust to and are examples of your growth, and (2) issues that remain a challenge.

Interpersonal relations
Family
Health
Economics
Career
Self-worth
School
Environmental pollution
Sex
Politics
Ethics
Emotions
Concern for others
Constraints of time
Sexual orientation
AIDS and/or safe-sex practices
Alcohol
Divorce
Exercise
Heart disease
Cigarette smoking
Job interviews
Tranquilizer use
Social approval
Gender issues in the workplace

Test taking
Premarital living arrangements
Career goals
Child care
Life goals conflicts
Grades
Moral decisions
Food and eating
Insomnia
Motivation
Depression
Suicide
Role conflicts
Self-esteem
Changing technology
Religion
Personal budget
Aging
Drug abuse
Marriage
Values
Studying
Family planning
Mental health
Cultural diversity

How many issues fit category (1)?______ How many issues fit category (2)?______

Pat yourself on the back for each issue you have faced and managed. For those issues you still must face, consider the following possibility. Look in the index of the text and see if this text promises to discuss issues relevant to you. You may wish to look ahead, or even to visit the library or bookstore for references to supplement your reading.

It might be valuable to ask your classmates how many issues they recorded in each case. Everyone could submit their results anonymously, so it could be made apparent that everyone has some challenge to face. That might help your instructor to recognize which directions to take a class.

Activity continued on the back

Follow-Up Questions:

1. Which of the above issues were **not** faced by your parents?

2. Which of the above issues were **not** faced by people 150 years ago?

3. How are these issues more (or less) difficult than those faced by your parents or by people 150 years ago?

4. In what way were some of the issues faced by your parents or by people 150 years ago more difficult than those you face today?

5. What classes on your campus address any of these challenges?

Name ________________________________ **Date** ______________

1.2 A Learning Theory Assessment of Your Studying

Learning theorists encourage us to analyze how reinforcers and punishments affect our behavior, and Chapter 1 recommends we use self-rewards for encouraging studying. It might be useful to attempt a "behavioral assessment" of studying behavior by asking ourselves these questions and recording our answers:

1. What are my rewards for studying and how powerful are they?

2. How soon after studying do I receive these rewards?

3. What behaviors do I do instead of studying (to avoid it)?

4. What are my rewards for these incompatible behaviors, and how soon do they get rewarded?

5. Which comes first, studying or other behaviors? Why?

Activity continued on the back

Now consider these general principles from learning theories:

1. Rewards are more effective when they are immediate.
2. Bigger rewards are more effective and weak rewards are less effective.
3. If we engage in less rewarding behavior before a more rewarding behavior, we may grow to like the less rewarding behavior and do it more and more.

In other words, if our main rewards for studying are grades, graduation, and maybe the approval of others, all of which are delayed, we can choose to follow studying with entertainment or socializing which are immediate and attractive rewards. Now if you will create a simple plan for organizing activities that can serve as immediate rewards for studying, you will have taken your first step as a behavioral technician. Write your plan here:

Name ______________________________ **Date** ____________

1.3 Research: A Way of Knowing

Chapter 1 explains the value of the scientific approach, and especially the role of research. Being able to do research can put you on the leading edge of knowledge, which is a valuable position in our "information age," whether your career takes you into business, human services, science, or industry.

To explore research as a tool for knowledge, follow the outline for research in Chapter 1, and pick one of the issues mentioned in the chapter.

1. First, what is the nature of the problem?

2. Formulate a research question.

3. Form a hypothesis.

4. Design an experiment to test your hypothesis. Present your experimental design here:

Activity continued on the back

Harcourt Brace & Company

5. Imagine the hypothesis is supported, what can you conclude?

6. How can you be sure that the results are due to the factors you are studying, instead of outside variables that you could not control for in your experiment?

Name ______________________________ Date ___________

1.4 Gender Issues in Challenges to Adjustment

Fifty years ago, the expectations for what men and women should become in our society were very clear cut, and often very different from each other. Today, many of those expectations have changed, while some have remained remarkably similar.

1. Identify three major expectations for men that you believe have substantially changed since the 1950s and briefly explain what impact you believe that has had on males growing up in our society today.

   a.

   b.

   c.

2. Identify three major expectations for women that you believe have substantially changed since the 1950s and briefly explain what impact you believe that has had on females growing up in our society today.

   a.

   b.

   c.

3. Identify two major expectations for men that you believe have remained similar to those of the 1950s and briefly explain what impact you believe they have on males growing up in our society today.

   a.

   b.

4. Identify two major expectations for women that you believe have remained similar to those of the 1950s and briefly explain what impact you believe they have on females growing up in our society today.

   a.

   b.

5. Many people in our culture still have somewhat different expectations for males and females and how they should fulfill social roles. Given this, who do you think has the more difficult task in adjusting in our society today, males or females? Why?

Name ________________________________ **Date** ____________

1.5 Planning Your Study Time

Taking an active rather than passive approach to studying can begin with the mastery of the material in this text. To organize your study plans, use a chart such as the one below to fill in the planned amount of study time and the planned number of pages to read at the beginning of the week. Fill in the **actual** amount of study time and the **actual** number of pages read each day. At the end of the week, compare the totals from the "planned" columns and the "actual" columns.

Adjust next week's plans according to how much leftover and new material remain to be studied. Each day that your "actual" total is equal to or greater than your "planned" column, you have met your study goals for that day and are entitled to reward yourself.

	Planned Amount of Study Time	Planned Number of Pages Read	Actual Study Time	Actual Number of Pages Read	Reward?
Monday					
Tuesday					
Wednesday					
Thursday					
Friday					
Saturday					
Sunday					

2

Personality and Behavior: Understanding People

Chapter Outline

I. Psychodynamic Theory

A. Sigmund Freud's Theory of Psychosexual Development
B. Other Psychodynamic Views
C. The Healthy Personality

II. Trait Theory

A. The Healthy Personality

III. Learning Theories

A. Behaviorism
B. Social-Cognitive theory
   1. Box: Self-Assessment: Will You Be a Hit or a Miss? The Expectancy for Success Scale
A. The Healthy Personality

IV. Phenomenological Theory

A. Abraham Maslow and the Challenge of Self-Actualization
   1. Box: Self-Assessment: Do You Strive to Be All That You Can Be?
B. Carl Rogers' Self-Theory
   1. Box: Adjustment in the New Millennium: Do You Strive to Be All That You Can Be?
C. The Healthy Personality

V. Sociocultural theory

A. The Healthy Personality
   1. Box: Adjustment in a World of Diversity: One Nation Under Gods

VI. Adjustment and Modern Life

A. Understanding Yourself: Will the One True Theory of Human Nature Please Stand Up?
B. Taking Charge of Your Fears
C. Getting in Touch With the Untouchable Through Biofeedback Training
D. Controlling Bad Habits Through Aversive Conditioning

Chapter Overview

Psychodynamic Theory. Freud's psychodynamic view of human nature suggests that our behavior is determined by the outcome of internal and largely unconscious conflict. Conflict is inevitable as the primitive instincts of sex and aggression come up against social pressures to follow laws, rules, and moral codes.

Psychic Structures and Their Functions. The unconscious id represents psychological drives and operates on the "pleasure principle." The mostly conscious ego represents the sense of self or "I," and seeks realistic ways for gratifying the desires of the id. The superego acts like a conscience, handing out judgments of right and wrong.

The Stages of Psychosexual Development. People undergo psychosexual development as psychological energy, or libido, is transferred from one erogenous zone to another. There are five stages of psychosexual development: the oral, anal, phallic, latency, and genital stages. Each stage has an inherent conflict which must be resolved or the person's personality may become fixated.

The Oedipus Complex. The Oedipus complex is a conflict of the phallic stage. In this conflict, children long to possess the parent of the other gender and resent the parent of the same gender. Under normal circumstances, these complexes eventually become resolved by identifying with the parent of the same gender.

Neoanalysts' Views. Most neoanalysts downplay the importance of the sexual instinct. Jung believed in the Self, a unifying force in the personality that provides us with direction and purpose. Adler believed that people are basically motivated by an inferiority complex, and that this complex gives rise to a compensating drive for superiority. Horney was more optimistic than Freud about children's ability to overcome early emotional hardships. Erikson highlights the importance of early social relationships rather than the gratification of childhood sexual impulses and extended Freud's five developmental stages to eight, which extend across the entire lifespan, rather than just childhood.

Trait Theory. Trait theory catalogs human traits and assumes that they are largely inherited. Eysenck theorized that there are two key personality dimensions: introversion-extraversion and emotional stability. More recent research adds another three basic traits: conscientiousness, agreeableness, and openness to new experience.

Behavioral Theory. John B. Watson, the father of modern behaviorism, rejected notions of mind and personality altogether. Watson and B. F. Skinner discarded notions of personal freedom and argued that environmental contingencies can shape people into wanting to do the things that the physical environment and society require of them. Behaviorists explain behavior in terms of conditioning. The two major types of conditioning are classical conditioning, based upon the work of Ivan Pavlov, and operant conditioning, based upon the work of B. F. Skinner.

Social-Cognitive Theory. Social-cognitive theory focuses on the importance of person variables in individual differences: competencies, encoding strategies, expectancies, subjective values, and self-regulatory systems and plans. Two major social-cognitive theorists are Albert Ellis, the founder of rational emotive therapy, and Aaron Beck.

Phenomenological Theories. These theories focus on the personal, or subjective, experiencing of events and postulate that this is the most important aspect of human nature. They also propose that we each have unique ways of perceiving the world. Two major phenomenological theorists are Carl Rogers, the developer of person-centered therapy, and Abraham Maslow, who developed the concepts of self-actualization and a hierarchy of needs.

Rogers believed that the self is an innate, organized, and consistent way in which a person perceives his or her "I" to relate to others and the world. The self attempts to develop its unique potential when the person receives unconditional positive regard.

Maslow believed that we are motivated by self-actualization - the urge to become everything we are capable of being. He stated that people travel up through a hierarchy of five levels of needs: biological, safety, love and belongingness, esteem, and self-actualization needs.

Sociocultural Theory. Sociocultural theory focuses on the roles of ethnicity, gender, culture, and socioeconomic status in personality formation, behavior, and mental processes. Sociocultural theorists are interested in issues such as individualism versus collectivism and the effects of discrimination and acculturation on the sense of self.

Learning Objectives

After studying this chapter, you should be able to:

1. Discuss the major features and concepts of the psychodynamic view of human nature.
2. Explain Freud's "iceberg" view of consciousness, identifying each level of consciousness and explaining its functions.
3. Identify the three psychic structures in Freud's personality theory and how each structure functions.
4. Identify the stages of Freud's theory of psychosexual development and describe what happens at each stage.
5. Briefly explain the views of the various neo-Freudians in terms of their major concepts and how they differed from Freud.
6. Explain Erikson's view of development, identifying each of his stages of development and the life crisis characterizing that stage.
7. Summarize the elements that psychodynamic theorists feel are essential for a person to have a healthy personality.
8. Discuss the views of trait theorists in terms of their focus and how they differ from the other personality perspectives.
9. Summarize the elements that trait theorists feel are necessary for a person to have a healthy personality.
10. Discuss the views of the behaviorists in terms of their focus and how they differ from the other personality perspectives.
11. Explain how classical conditioning works. In your explanation, be sure to briefly discuss what extinction and spontaneous recovery are.
12. Explain how operant conditioning works and discuss the differences among positive and negative reinforcers, primary and secondary reinforcers, and punishment.

13. Describe the views of social-cognitive theorists in terms of their focus, concepts, and how they differ from the other personality perspectives.

14. Summarize the elements that social-cognitive theorists believe are necessary for a person to have a healthy personality.

15. Describe the views of phenomenological theorists in terms of their focus and common features, and how they differ from the other personality theories.

16. Explain the major ideas of Abraham Maslow's phenomenological theory.

17. Explain the major ideas of Carl Rogers' self theory.

18. Summarize the elements that phenomenological theorists believe are essential for a person to have a healthy personality.

19. Describe the views of sociocultural theorists in terms of their focus and common features, and how they differ from the other personality theories.

20. Summarize the elements that sociocultural theorists believe are essential for a person to have a healthy personality.

21. Identify and briefly explain the various fear-reduction methods developed by behavioral therapists.

Key Terms

psychodynamic
conscious
preconscious
unconscious
repression
psychoanalysis
self-insight
resistance
psychic structure
id
ego
superego
defense mechanism
identification
eros
libido
erogenous zones
psychosexual development
oral stage
fixation
anal stage
anal retentive
anal expulsive
phallic stage
Oedipus complex
displaced
latency stage
genital stage
pregenital fixation
the Self
inferiority complex
drive for superiority
creative self
psychosocial development
ego identity
traits
introversion
extraversion
neuroticism
behaviorist
classical conditioning
stimuli
response
unconditioned stimulus
unconditioned response
conditioned stimulus
conditioned response
extinction
spontaneous recovery
operant conditioning
reinforcement
reward
positive reinforcers
negative reinforcers
primary reinforcers
secondary reinforcers
punishment
socialization
social-cognitive theory
reciprocal determinism
person variables
modeling
situational variables
competencies
encode
expectancies
self-efficacy expectations
self-regulatory systems
phenomenological
existential
self-actualization
hierarchy of needs
self theory
frames of reference
self-esteem
unconditional positive regard
conditional positive regard
conditions of worth
person-centered therapy
self-ideals
Bokanovsky's process
individualists
collectivists
acculturation
flooding
systematic desensitization
counterconditioning
biofeedback training
aversive conditioning
rapid smoking

Key Persons

Sigmund Freud
Carl Jung
Alfred Adler
Karen Horney
Erik Erikson
Hippocrates
Gordon Allport
Hans Eysenck
John B. Watson
Ivan Pavlov
Little Albert
B. F. Skinner
Albert Bandura
Abraham Maslow
Carl Rogers

Key Terms Reviews: Due to the complexity of this chapter, there are three different exercises in this section. The first exercise deals with terms related to psychodynamic and biological theories. The second exercise presents terms related to behavioral, social-cognitive, and phenomenological theories. The third exercise presents the people associated with the various theories discussed in this chapter.

Key Terms Review #1

Define each of the following terms:

1. Conscious: ______________________________

   ____

2. Preconscious: ______________________________

   ____

3. Unconscious: ______________________________

   ____

4. Resistance: ______________________________

   ____

5. Psychic Structure: ______________________________

   ____

6. Id: ______________________________

   ____

7. Ego: ______________________________

   ____

8. Superego: ______________________________

   ____

9. Libido: ______________________________

   ____

10. Psychosexual Development: ______________________________

____

11. Fixation: ______________________________________

____

12. Anal Retentive: __________________________________

____

13. Anal Expulsive: __________________________________

____

14. Inferiority Complex: ______________________________

____

15. Creative Self: ___________________________________

____

16. Drive for Superiority: _____________________________

____

17. Psychosocial Development: ___________________________

____

18. Ego Identity: ____________________________________

____

19. Traits: ____

____

20. Neuroticism: ____________________________________

____

Key Terms Review #2

Define each of the following terms:

1. Behaviorist: ____________________

2. Classical Conditioning: ____________________

3. Unconditioned Stimulus: ____________________

4. Unconditioned Response: ____________________

5. Conditioned Stimulus: ____________________

6. Conditioned Response: ____________________

7. Extinction: ____________________

8. Spontaneous Recovery: ____________________

9. Operant Conditioning: ____________________

10. Reinforcement: ____________________

11. Reward: ____

____

12. Punishment: ____

____

13. Person Variable: ____

____

14. Situational Variable: ____

____

15. Phenomenological: ____

____

16. Existentialism: ____

____

17. Self-Actualization: ____

____

18. Hierarchy of Needs: ____

____

19. Frames of Reference: ____

____

20. Unconditional Positive Regard: ____

____

Key Persons Review

Identify the theory, technique, or ideas most closely associated with each of the following people:

Example: Sigmund Freud: Psychoanalysis, psychodynamic theory, and the influence of unconscious urges and sexuality on personality.

1. Alfred Adler: ____________________

2. Abraham Maslow: ____________________

3. Erik Erikson: ____________________

4. B. F. Skinner: ____________________

5. Albert Bandura: ____________________

6. Carl Jung: ____________________

7. Carl Rogers: ____________________

8. Ivan Pavlov: ____________________

9. John Watson: ____________________

10. Karen Horney: ____

____

Chapter Review

1. Each psychodynamic theory owes its origins to the thinking of __________.

2. Freud was trained as a __________.

3. Freud pictured the human mind as similar to a(n) __________.

4. Freud divided the mind into three levels of awareness: the __________, the __________, and the __________.

5. Freud labeled the three psychic structures that control personality the __________, the __________, and the __________.

6. Freud believed that there is a major life instinct called __________, which contains a certain amount of energy called __________.

7. The five stages of psychosexual development postulated by Freud are the __________ stage (age 0-1), the __________ stage (1-2), the __________ stage (3-5), the __________ stage (6-11), and the __________ stage (12 and over).

8. Freud believed that indadequate or excessive gratification in any stage can lead to __________ in that stage.

9. Four psychodynamic theorists other than Freud are __________, __________, __________, and __________.

10. Carl Jung believed in a unifying force of personality called the __________.

11. Adler believed that children develop a drive for __________ to overcome an __________ __________.

12. Erik Erikson described eight stages of __________ development.

13. **Matching:** Match the conflict with the stage of development in which Erikson thought it would occur.

_______	a. Infancy	1. Identity vs. role diffusion
_______	b. Early childhood	2. Initiative vs. guilt
_______	c. Preschool years	3. Integrity vs. despair
_______	d. Grammar school years	4. Industry vs. inferiority
_______	e. Adolescence	5. Generativity vs. stagnation
_______	f. Young adulthood	6. Trust vs. mistrust
_______	g. Middle adulthood	7. Intimacy vs. isolation
_______	h. Late adulthood	8. Autonomy vs. shame and doubt

14. For Erikson, the goal of adolescence is the attainment of __________.

15. The five elements of a healthy personality according to the psychodynamic model are:

a. ____

b. ____

c. ____

d. ____

e. ____

16. Reasonably stable elements of personality that are inferred from behavior are __________.

17. Trait theory can be traced back to the Greek physician __________, who believed that personality was dependent on the balance of __________ bile, __________ bile, __________, and __________.

18. Gordon Allport cataloged about __________ human traits.

Harcourt Brace & Company

19. Recent research on traits suggests that there are five basic personality factors:

__________, __________, __________, __________, and __________

to new experiences.

20. John Watkins was the founder of the __________ movement.

21. **Matching:** Match the term on the left with the appropriate definition on the right.

________ a.	Extinction	1. a reinforcer that increases the frequency of a behavior when it is presented
________ b.	Spontaneous recovery	2. a pleasant stimulus that increases the frequency of a behavior
________ c.	Flooding	3. an unlearned reinforcer, such as food or water
________ d.	Systematic Desensitization	4. repeated presentation of a conditioned stimulus in the absence of the unconditioned stimulus, leading to suspension of the conditioned response
________ e.	Counterconditioning	5. a technique for extinguishing fear in which a person is continuously exposed to fear-evoking, but harmless, stimulation
________ f.	Classical conditioning	6. an unpleasant stimulus that supresses behavior
________ g.	Operant conditioning	7. a simple form of learning in which the frequency of behavior is increased by means of rewards or reinforcement
________ h.	Reinforcement	8. a stimulus that gains a value as a reinforcer as a result of being associated with established reinforcers (i.e., money)
________ i.	Primary reinforcer	9. a form of conditioning in which previously desirable objects become repugnant as a result of being paired with unpleasant stimulation
________ j.	Secondary reinforcer	10. the eliciting of an extinguished response by a conditioned stimulus after some time has elapsed
________ k.	Positive reinforcer	11. the pairing of a pleasant stimulus with a fear-evoking stimulus to eliminate the fear response
________ l.	Negative reinforcer	12. a method for reducing fears in which images of fear-evoking stimuli are presented while a person is deeply relaxed, thus leading to a cessation of the fear response
________ m.	Punishment	13. a simple form of learning in which one stimulus brings about a response usually brought forth by a second stimulus as a result of being paired repeatedly with the second stimulus
________ n.	Aversive conditioning	14. a reinforcer that increases the frequency of a behavior when it is removed
________ o.	Reward	15. a stimulus that increases the frequency of a behavior

22. **Matching:** Match the term on the left with its appropriate descriptor on the right taken from Pavlov's research with dogs.

_______ a. Unconditioned stimulus	1. A bell
_______ b. Unconditioned response	2. A piece of meat
_______ c. Conditioned stimulus	3. Salivation to a bell
_______ d. Conditioned response	4. Salivation to a piece of meat

23. To social-cognitive theorists, whether a person behaves in a certain way depends on __________ variables, ___________ variables, as well as the person's __________ concerning the outcome of the behavior.

24. Social-cognitive theory emphasizes the role of __________ learning.

25. Five person variables that account for individual differences in social-cognitive theory are:

    a. ______________________________

    b. ______________________________

    c. ______________________________

    d. ______________________________

    e. ______________________________

26. Social-cognitive theorists see the following six elements as essential to a healthy personality:

    a. ______________________________

    b. ______________________________

    c. ______________________________

    d. ______________________________

    e. ______________________________

    f. ______________________________

27. Maslow's views are largely rooted in the European philosophy of __________.

28. According to Maslow, the eight characteristics of a self-actualizing individual are:

    a. ______________________________

    b. ______________________________

    c. ______________________________

    d. ______________________________

    e. ______________________________

    f. ______________________________

    g. ______________________________

    h. ______________________________

29. Maslow's hierarchy of needs, from lowest to highest within the hierarchy, include __________, __________, __________, __________, and __________-__________ needs.

30. Carl Rogers' views of personality are labeled __________ theory.

31. When parents show children __________ positive regard, they learn to disown the thoughts and behaviors rejected by the parents and may develop __________ __________ __________, which make them feel as if they are acceptable **ONLY** if they behave in certain ways. However, if parents show children __________ positive regard, it can help them develop high __________-__________.

32. In Aldous Huxly's novel ***Brave New World***, children are bred through a technique known as __________ __________.

33. Phenomenological theorists see the following seven qualities as essential to a healthy personality:

a. ______________________________

b. ______________________________

c. ______________________________

d. ______________________________

e. ______________________________

f. ______________________________

g. ______________________________

34. Cross-cultural research indicates that people in the United States and many northern European countries tend to be __________, whereas people from Africa, Asia, and Central and South America tend to be __________.

Sample Test

Multiple-Choice Questions

1. Freud concluded that the human mind was like ______.
   a. an elephant
   b. an iceberg
   c. seaweed
   d. a computer

2. According to Freud, biological instincts and urges such as hunger, thirst, sexuality and aggression all originate in the ______.
   a. conscious mind
   b. semi-conscious mind
   c. preconscious mind
   d. unconscious mind

3. Which of the following is **NOT** one of Freud's psychic structures?
   a. the ego
   b. the libido
   c. the id
   d. the superego

4. A college student spends an entire evening trying to logically sort out the pros and cons of a job offer she has just received. According to Freud, the psychic structure responsible for this type of mental activity is the ______.
   a. id
   b. ego
   c. libido
   d. superego

5. According to Freud, the superego incorporates the moral standards of parents and significant others through ______.
   a. identification
   b. repression
   c. subliminal perception
   d. projection

6. Freud theorized ______ stages of psychological development.
   a. 3
   b. 4
   c. 5
   d. 6

7. Jack is dependent, gullible, and overly optimistic. He is ______, according to Freud.
   a. orally fixated
   b. an anal expulsive
   c. an anal retentive
   d. fixated in the phallic stage

8. Jung and Adler both believed that Freud placed too much emphasis on ______.
   a. free will
   b. sexual impulses
   c. lifelong development
   d. psychodynamic principles

9. The conflict which Erikson felt characterized the preschool years (ages 4-5) was ______.
   a. initiative versus guilt
   b. autonomy versus shame and doubt
   c. industry versus inferiority
   d. trust versus mistrust

10. Camille is best described as "choleric." She has, to say the least, a "short fuse." She is very quick-tempered and her temper flares at just about anything that doesn't go her way. Hippocrates would argue that her disposition is due to an excess of ______.
    a. yellow bile
    b. blood
    c. phlegm
    d. black bile

11. The term "neuroticism" refers to ______.
    a. introversion
    b. sexual obsession
    c. emotional instability
    d. extraversion

12. Learning which occurs through repeatedly pairing a neutral stimulus to a response-eliciting stimulus is called ______.
    a. classical conditioning
    b. vicarious learning
    c. self-actualization
    d. operant conditioning

13. In Pavlov's research with dogs, the bell was ______.
    a. the unconditioned stimulus
    b. the unconditioned response
    c. the conditioned stimulus
    d. the conditioned response

14. In classical conditioning, the reappearance of a CR in response to a CS, when some time has elapsed since the extinction of the CR, is called ______.
    a. transference
    b. generalization
    c. reactivation
    d. spontaneous recovery

15. A pigeon learns to peck at buttons because it receives food each time it pecks at the buttons. This learning is due to ______.
    a. classical conditioning
    b. flooding
    c. observational learning
    d. operant conditioning

16. Nagging someone to do something until he or she does it is an example of ______.
    a. flooding
    b. punishment
    c. positive reinforcement
    d. negative reinforcement

17. According to learning theorists, ______ is the preferable method of teaching young children new behavior.
    a. positive reinforcement
    b. aversive conditioning
    c. negative reinforcement
    d. punishment

18. According to Maslow, which needs were at the **TOP** of his needs hierarchy? (the last needs to be satisfied)
    a. biological needs
    b. esteem needs
    c. love and belongingness needs
    d. self-actualization needs

19. The process of adaptation in which immigrants and native groups identify with a new, dominant culture by learning about that culture and making changes in their behaviors and attitudes is called ______.
    a. acculturation
    b. actualization
    c. congruence
    d. ingratiation

20. The idea of pairing a pleasant stimulus with a fear-evoking object in order to block the fear response is called ______.
    a. flooding
    b. negative reinforcement
    c. counterconditioning
    d. aversive conditioning

True-False Questions

21. Most of the ego is unconscious. ______

22. Skinner is noted to have equated psychological health with the abilities to love and work. ______

23. Punishment can rapidly suppress undesired behavior. ______

24. Rogers, unlike Maslow, saw each of us as having a unique potential. ______

25. Aversive conditioning is a method based on classical conditioning. ______

Essay Question

26. Describe the views of phenomenological theorists in terms of their focus and common features, and how they differ from the other personality theories.

Student Activities

Name ______________________________ **Date** ____________

2.1 What Is Your Theory of Human Nature?

In the second chapter, Rathus and Nevid describe some of the most important theories of personality developed in this century by psychologists. We all have our own theories of human nature, whether they are explicit or implicit. Just as the people who construct such theories for a living, we tend to begin with observations and then hypotheses. What theories are we working with? Explore this by simply asking yourself if you think humans are more inclined to be kind and benevolent or more inclined to be egotistical, selfish, and only interested in "number one." To provoke some thinking here, decide which description of people you think is more accurate.

Sigmund Freud said:

". . . men are not gentle friendly creatures wishing for love, who simply defend themselves if they are attacked, but . . . a powerful measure of desire for aggressiveness has to be reckoned with as part of their instinctual endowment. The result is that their neighbor is to them not only a helper or sexual object, but also a temptation to them to gratify their aggressiveness . . . to seize his possessions, to humiliate him, to cause him pain, to torture and to kill him . . . Anyone who calls to mind the atrocities of the early migrations of the invasions of the Huns or by the so-called Mongols under Ghengis Khan and Tamurlane, of the sack of Jerusalem by the pious crusaders, and even the horrors of the last world war, will have to bow his head humbly before the truth of this view of man . . . We see man as a savage beast to whom the thought of sparing his own kind is alien" (***Civilization and Its Discontents,*** 1930).

Carl Rogers wrote:

"I have little sympathy with the rather prevalent concept that man is basically irrational, and that his impulses, if not controlled, will lead to destruction of others and self. Man's behavior is exquisitely rational, moving with subtle and ordered complexity toward the goals his organism is endeavoring to achieve" (***Journal of Consulting Psychology,*** 1957).

Questions:

1. Which position do you think is more accurate? Why?

Activity continued on the back

Questions (continued)

2. Since Freud cited historical cases to support his view, what examples could be used to refute him?

3. How could either of the arguments use case histories, correlated observations, or research findings to support the theories (provide some specific examples)?

4. Is there any way to resolve this debate? If so, how? If not, why not?

5. What would the consequences be should the followers of each theorist, Freud and Rogers, be placed in charge of education? What if each point of view were represented by presidential candidates? Where else in society might big differences be created by the applications of these different models?

Name ________________________________ Date ______________

2.2 Researching Human Nature

We have been much encouraged to think that research is an important and powerful tool for answering questions about ourselves and others. If we use case histories to support one side or the other, it seems it will become a draw. There are lots of nice people in the world and lots of dangerous people. A tougher test of theories is to create hypotheses and to test them.

What hypotheses could address such basic issues as those raised by Freud and Rogers? Consider the following possibility as we engage in each of the four basic steps to the scientific method:

1. **Formulate a research question.** When people are given a chance to be helpful, are they as ruthless as Freud says, or as benevolent as Rogers pictures? What do you think? Why?

2. **Developing a hypothesis.** When people find a wallet with identification and money in it, they are in a position to be helpful. What hypothesis would Freud and Rogers likely create to predict if we were purposely to drop wallets at various locations around campus? Also, what is your prediction? Express your predictions as percentages of wallets returned intact with money and identification inside. Explain why you feel the way you do?

3. **Testing a hypothesis.** Where will you place or drop the wallets? How much money would you place in each, or would you choose different amounts? How will finders be able to return wallets if they choose to do so, and can they be returned anonymously?

Activity continued on the back

4. **Drawing conclusions about the hypothesis.** Since this is speculation, unless you have vast resources upon which to draw, just imagine the outcomes fit your own predictions even better than Freud's and/or Rogers'. What could you conclude about the alternative theories? What other hypotheses and tests could you now create?

5. While your experiment has done a good job of explaining the "what" of your hypothesis (how many people picked up the wallet and returned it), has it been able to explain the "why"? One drawback of many psychological research studies is that they do little to reveal why people act as they do. Is there any way you could empirically discover the "why" in your study? If so how? If not, why not?

Name ________________________________ Date ____________

2.3 Creating Classical Conditioning

It is useful to start this exercise by reading about Pavlov's work on classical conditioning, described in Chapter 2. He used dogs in his research, but we can use roommates and friends to explore classical conditioning. Simply ask a friend to hold out his or her hands with the palms turned up. Tell your subject to resist the moderate pressure you exert downward on his or her hands with your own hands. Each time, before you push down, say the word "Now!" then immediately press down. Repeat this four times. On the fifth occasion, sharply say "Now!" without pressing down. Did the hands rise up to meet yours? (If not, pronounce your friend less than a dog, and try another.) Now tell your subject that you will continue to place your hands just above his or hers and sharply say "Now!" until he or she no longer responds by raising the hands upward. Note how many trials until you "extinguish" his or her hand response. Finally, ask your friend to explain what happened and to write down what he or she tells you.

Follow-Up Questions:

1. Using the above exercise and the textbook, identify the:

    a. Conditioned stimulus: ______________________

    b. Unconditioned stimulus: ______________________

    c. Conditioned response: ______________________

    d. Unconditioned response: ______________________

2. If the hand response extinguishes immediately after telling the subject not to respond to the stimulus "Now!", how would you explain the extinction? However, if it takes more than one trial to extinguish the response, what explanation would you use?

Activity continued on the back

3. What results did your classmates get?

4. How did your subject explain what happened? Is it a behavioral, social-cognitive, phenomenological, or psychodynamic explanation, or some combination of them?

5. What theory is best supported by your results? Why?

Name ______________________________ **Date** ____________

2.4 Nature versus Nurture?

Various psychological theories conceptualize people as being inherently "good" or "evil." They also have different views about how much of personality is learned (nurture) as opposed to being genetically inherited (nature). Given what is discussed in Chapter 2 of your text, state where you think each of the following theories falls on the issue of nature versus nurture and then briefly explain why you feel as you do:

a. Freudian Psychodynamic Theory:

b. Trait Theory:

c. Phenomenological Theory:

d. Social-Cognitive Theory:

e. Behavioral Theory:

Activity continued on the back

f. Sociocultural Theory:

Which of the above theories' views makes the most sense to you? Why?

Name ______________________________ Date ____________

2.5 Free Will or Not?

The various theories of personality have widely opposing views of whether or not people have free will. Freud's theory implies that we are basically prisoners of our unconscious instincts, drives, and impulses with little conscious control (or free will) over our actions. Learning theorists are nearly as pessimistic in that many of them see us as prisoners of the conditioning imposed on us by the environment, with little or no ability to rise above that conditioning. Phenomenological theorists and cognitive theorists are somewhat more optimistic, arguing that we do have the ability to rise above biological needs and social conditioning. How do you feel about this?

1. Do you believe that people have free will? Why or why not?

2. If people do have free will, what implications does this have for society in areas such as education, religion, politics, and the criminal justice system? Explain why you feel as you do.

3. If people do not have free will, what implications does this have for society in areas such as education, religion, politics, and the criminal justice system? Again, explain why you feel as you do.

3

Social Perception: How We See Others and Ourselves

Chapter Outline

I. On Perception and Schemas: Processing Social Information

II. Perception of Others
A. Primacy and Recency Effects: The Importance of First Impressions
B. Body Language
C. Prejudice

III. Self-Perception
A. The Self as a Guiding Principle of Personality
B. The Parts of the Self
   1. Box: Adjustment in a World of Diversity: African-American Women - Happier with Themselves
   2. Box: Self-Assessment: How Content Are You With Your Physical Self?
   3. Box: Adjustment in a New Millennium: Are Pills for Self-Improvement in the Offing?
C. Aspects of the Self-Schema: Names, Values, and Self-Concept
   1. Box: Self-Assessment: Values Clarification - What Is Important to You?
   2. Box: Self-Assessment: Are You One of Your Favorite People? The Self-Acceptance Scale

IV. Attribution Theory
A. Dispositional and Situational Attributions
B. The Fundamental Attribution Error
C. The Actor-Observer Effect
D. The Self-Serving Bias
   1. Box: Adjustment in the New Millennium: Can Psychologists Use Attribution Theory to Enhance International "Adjustment"?

V. Adjustment and Modern Life
A. Managing First Impressions
B. Using Body Language to Foster Adjustment and Enhance Social Relationships
C. Coping With Prejudice and Discrimination
D. Enhancing Self-Esteem

Chapter Overview

Schemas. Schemas are expectations that influence our perceptions of other people (person schemas), social roles (role schemas), and ourselves (self-schemas). Schemas bias us to see things in certain ways.

First Impressions. First impressions matter. According to the primacy effect, we tend to interpret people's behavior in terms of our first impressions of them. However, we may also focus on our most recent impressions of people, the so-called recency effect, especially when we are advised to weigh all the evidence in impression formation.

Body Language. People who are anxious are usually rigid in posture, whereas people who are relaxed usually "hang loose." When people lean toward one another they are usually interested in each other. Gazing is a sign of interest, and sometimes of love; hard staring is usually interpreted negatively.

Prejudice. Prejudice is an attitude toward a group that leads us to evaluate that group negatively. Prejudice is associated with negative feelings and discrimination. Discrimination is behavior that results in the denial of privileges or basic rights to a person or group on the basis of prejudice. Possible sources of prejudice include attitudinal differences (real or assumed) between groups, social conflict, authoritarianism, and social learning. Prejudices in the form of stereotypes also make it easier to process information about unknown individuals.

The Self. The self is the guiding principle of personality. The self is an organized, consistent way of perceiving our "I" and our perceptions of the ways in which we relate to the world. The self has physical, social, and personal aspects. Our social selves are the masks and social roles we don to meet the requirements of our situations. Our personal selves are our private, inner identities.

Names and Self-Identities. Names are linked to expectations by parents and society at large. People with common names are usually rated more favorably, but people with unusual names often accomplish more. People of higher status often sign their names larger and less legibly.

Values. Our values indicate the importance we place on objects and behavior. Values give rise to goals and set limits on behavior. We are more subject to social influences when we do not have personal values or when our values are in flux.

The Self-Concept, the Ideal Self, and Self-Esteem. Our self-concept is our self-description, or our impression of ourselves, in terms of bipolar traits or dimensions. Our ideal self is our vision of what we "should" or "ought" to be in a perfect world. Our self-esteem is our sense of self-worth. Our self-esteem rests on our approval of our placement along the dimensions we use to describe ourselves. The smaller the discrepancy between our self-concept and our ideal selves, the higher our self-esteem.

Attributions. The attribution process refers to our inferences of the motives and traits of others through observing their behavior. There are two types of attribution: dispositional and situational. When using dispositional attributions, we attribute people's behavior to internal factors, such as personality traits and choice. When using situational attributions, we attribute people's behavior to their circumstances, or external forces.

There are three major types of errors people commonly make in the attribution process: the fundamental attribution error, which is the tendency to attribute too much of other people's behavior to dispositional factors; the actor-observer effect, which is the tendency to attribute the negative behavior of others to internal, dispositional factors, while attributing our own shortcomings to situational factors; and the self-serving bias, which is the tendency to attribute our successes to dispositional factors, such as hard work or talent, while attributing our failures to situational factors.

Learning Objectives

After studying this chapter you should be able to:

1. Identify the various types of schemas and explain how they influence our perceptions of others.
2. Compare and contrast the primacy and recency effects, and explain how important these effects are in our relationships with others in the long run.
3. Explain what body language is and why it is important.
4. Compare and contrast prejudice and discrimination, and identify several sources of prejudice.
5. Describe the various parts of the self and discuss how, together, these parts meld together to form the "self."
6. Explain the relationship between one's name and one's self-identity, and summarize what the research has found about people with unusual names as compared to people with common names.
7. Explain what values are and discuss what they imply about us.
8. Compare and contrast the self-concept, the ideal self, and self-esteem, and explain how each contributes to our overall self-perception.
9. Identify the various types of attributions and discuss the attribution process in terms of the fundamental attribution error, the actor-observer effect, and the self-serving bias.
10. Briefly explain the ways in which psychologists might be able to mediate international conflicts.
11. Identify and briefly describe at least five different ways to manage first impressions.
12. Identify and briefly describe at least three different ways to use information about body language to foster adjustment and social relationships.
13. Identify and briefly describe at least three different ways to cope with prejudice.
14. Identify and briefly describe five ways one can boost one's self-esteem.

Key Terms

schema
Procrustean bed
role schema
person schema
self-schema
primacy effect
recency effect
body language
prejudice
affective
racism
sexism
ageism
discrimination
stereotypes
self
physical self
social self
personal self
ethics
ideal self
self-concept
self-esteem
attribution
attribution process
dispositional attribution
situational attribution
fundamental attribution error
actor-observer effect
self-serving bias

Key Terms Review

Define each of the following terms:

1. Schema: ______________________________

____

2. Primacy Effect: ______________________________

____

3. Recency Effect: ______________________________

____

4. Prejudice: ______________________________

____

5. Affective: ______________________________

____

6. Discrimination: ______________________________

____

7. Self: ______________________________

____

8. Physical Self: ______________________________

____

9. Social Self: ______________________________

____

10. Personal Self: ______________________________

____

Harcourt Brace & Company

11. Ethics: ____

____

12. Self-Concept: ____

____

13. Self-Esteem: ____

____

14. Ideal Self: ____

____

15. Attribution: ____

____

16. Dispositional Attribution: ____

____

17. Situational Attribution: ____

____

18. Fundamental Attribution Error: ____

____

19. Actor-Observer Effect: ____

____

20. Self-Serving Bias: ____

____

Chapter Review

1. We all carry different kinds of schemas such as __________ schemas, about how people in certain roles (husbands, wives, bosses, teachers) are expected to behave, __________ schemas, about how particular individuals are expected to behave, and __________ schemas, the generalizations, beliefs, and feelings we have about ourselves.

2. The tendency to evaluate others in terms of first impressions is called the __________ effect, whereas the tendency to evaluate others in terms of the most recent impression is called the __________ effect.

3. Various combinations of __________ __________, __________, and __________ between people provide cues as to their moods and feelings toward their companions.

4. When people __________ us, and lean __________ us, we may assume that they like us or are interested in us.

5. Hard stares are interpreted as __________ or signs of __________.

6. Racism, sexism, and ageism are all examples of __________, which often results in biased treatment toward minorities, women, or older persons, known as __________.

7. Five sources of prejudice are:

   a. ____

   b. ____

   c. ____

   d. ____

   e. ____

8. The three parts of the self are the __________ self, the __________ self, and the __________ self.

9. Models, who tend to represent the female ideal, are __________ and __________ than the average woman.

10. Unusual names are linked to __________ in childhood but __________ in adulthood.

11. The importance we place on objects and things, called __________, is closely related to our standards of conduct or behavior, called __________.

12. Your impression of yourself is your __________ __________.

13. Self-approval, or one's favorable opinion of oneself, is called __________.

14. One's concept of what one ***ought*** to be is called one's __________.

15. A belief concerning why people behave in a certain way is called a(n) __________.

16. An assumption that a person's behavior results from internal causes is called a __________ attribution, whereas an assumption that a person's behavior results from external sources is called a __________ attribution.

17. **Matching:** Match the following terms on the right with their corresponding definitions on the left.

_______ a. The tendency to attribute our own behavior to external factors but to attribute the behavior of others to internal factors	1. Dispositional attribution
_______ b. An assumption that a person's behavior is motivated by external forces	2. Fundamental attribution error
_______ c. The tendency to view one's success as stemming from internal factors and one's failures from external factors	3. Situational attribution
_______ d. An assumption that a person's behavior is motivated by internal forces	4. Self-serving bias
_______ e. The tendency to assume that others act primarily because of internal causes even when there is evidence that their behavior is due to external factors	5. The actor-observer effect

18. Four ways that psychologists can use attribution theory to mediate international conflicts are:

a. ____________________

b. ____________________

c. ____________________

d. ____________________

19. At least five ways to manage first impressions are:

a. ____________________

b. ____________________

c. ____________________

d. ____________________

e. ____________________

20. Three ways of using information about body language to foster adjustment and social relationships are:

a. ____________________

b. ____________________

c. ____________________

21. Four methods of coping with prejudice and discrimination are:

a. ____________________

b. ____________________

c. ____________________

d. ____________________

22. Four methods of improving self-esteem are:

a. ______________________________

b. ______________________________

c. ______________________________

d. ______________________________

Sample Test

Multiple-Choice Questions

1. A career woman is much more aggressive at work than her male boss thinks women should be. She has violated his ______ schema.
   a. person
   b. situation
   c. self-
   d. role

2. People wear their best suits to interviews and lawyers dress their clients to look like the "all-American" girl or boy in court in an effort to take advantage of the ______.
   a. primacy effect
   b. recency effect
   c. fundamental attribution error
   d. actor-observer effect

3. Which of the following is **MOST** likely to be interpreted as being assertive, direct, interested, and open?
   a. looking someone "squarely in the eyes"
   b. averting someone's gaze
   c. giving someone a "hard stare"
   d. closing your eyes while someone talks to you

4. Ellsworth's 1972 study found that when drivers who were stopped at intersections were subjected to "hard stares" from drivers of neighboring motor scooters, they ______.
   a. stared back until the motor scooter drove away
   b. drove off more rapidly than drivers who did not receive the stares
   c. drove off more slowly than drivers who did not receive the stares
   d. ignored the stares

5. Jack believes that all women are illogical and should not be allowed in the workplace. His beliefs about women are examples of ______.
   a. prejudice
   b. discrimination
   c. subjugation
   d. gender constancy

6. Which of the following theorists did **NOT** view the "self" as a central architect or guiding principle of personality?
   a. Carl Jung
   b. Sigmund Freud
   c. Alfred Adler
   d. Carl Rogers

7. According to the text, roles and masks are ______ responses to the social world.
   a. reactive
   b. adaptive
   c. maladaptive
   d. inferior

8. According to your text, unusual names ______.
   a. are linked to psychological problems in both childhood and adulthood
   b. are linked to depression in adulthood
   c. are linked to high levels of popularity in childhood
   d. seem linked to success in adulthood

9. A system of beliefs from which one derives standards of conduct or behavior is collectively known as ______.
   a. mores
   b. ethics
   c. recriminations
   d. values

10. Your self-concept is comprised of each of the following **EXCEPT** ______.
   a. self-esteem
   b. psychological self
   c. ideal self
   d. self-efficacy expectations

11. According to your text, parents of boys with high self-esteem were likely to be ______.
   a. extremely lenient; rarely, if ever, disciplining their sons
   b. generally lenient, but harsh when they did decide to discipline their sons
   c. strict, but not harsh or cruel
   d. rigid and harsh when dealing with most disciplinary situations

12. Coopersmith found that low self-esteem ______.
   a. tends to disappear with a few successful experiences in adolescence or adulthood
   b. tends to increase with age
   c. may become a self-fulfilling prophecy
   d. tends to decrease with age

13. Examples of ______ include explaining behavior in terms of extermal pressures such as lack of time.
   a. the fundamental attribution error
   b. dispositional attribution
   c. situational attribution
   d. psychogenic attribution

14. After hearing a story of how a man was forced to steal food because his children were starving, Terri says that he was stupid, irresponsible, and probably dishonest anyway. Terri's comments reflect ______.
   a. the fundamental attribution error
   b. a self-serving bias
   c. a psychogenic attribution
   d. a situational attribution

15. The actor-observer effect involves _____.
   a. the tendency to see our own behavior as being situationally motivated while attributing the behavior of others to dispositional motivations
   b. the tendency to see our own behavior as being internally motivated while attributing the behavior of others to situational causes
   c. the tendency to see our own behavior as more important than it really is
   d. the tendency to see out own behavior as less important than it really is

16. Which of the following is **NOT** one of the ways recommended by your text for raising your self-esteem?
   a. self-improvement
   b. substitute real, attainable goals for unattainable goals
   c. build self-efficacy expectations
   d. increase the standards of your ideal self

17. The degree to which you believe your efforts will bring about a positive outcome is your ______.
   a. self-concept
   b. self-esteem
   c. ideal self
   d. self-efficacy expectancies

18. Which of the following groups is **LEAST** likely to be satisfied with their physical selves?
   a. white women
   b. African-American women
   c. African-American men
   d. white men

19. In the ***Psychology Today*** poll on people's satisfaction with their body parts, ______ percent of men expressed dissatisfaction with their sexual organs.
   a. 15
   b. 25
   c. 35
   d. 45

20. According to Rokeach's study, the value least important to Americans was ______.
   a. social recognition
   b. salvation
   c. national security
   d. pleasure

True-False Questions

21. People have condemned billions of other people without ever meeting them. ______

22. An average person has many social selves. ______

23. We get along best with people whose values resemble our own. ______

24. Self-concept is based on the discrepancy between our ideal selves and our self-esteem. ______

25. Women are more likely than men to interpret a man's friendliness toward women as flirting. ______

Essay Question

26. Describe the various parts of the self and discuss how these parts meld together to form the "self."

Student Activities

Name ______________________________ **Date** ____________

3.1 Testing Our Perceptions

If there is a consistency in the theories of Freud, Erikson, Rogers, and Maslow, it may be the idea that adjustment depends on the accuracy of the perception of reality. It would seem that accurate perception would increase the likelihood of correct choices, reduce or eliminate anxieties from unnecessary worry, provide feedback for change, and so on and so on. In Chapter 3, Rathus and Nevid portray the virtues of accurate social perception. If only we could see others more accurately without prejudice! If only others could see us the same way!

Select a classmate, or roommate, for this exercise which tests your perceptiveness. It will be a tough test so be prepared to encounter your limitations.

Ask a friend to recall or answer as well as possible and write down:

1. The last two magazines read and circle the one he or she liked best.

2. The last two movies seen and circle the one he or she liked best.

3. Two television shows watched regularly and the one he or she prefers.

4. Would the erson quit school or work if he or she won a $5,000,000 lottery? Why?

5. Would the person sacrifice his or her life to save anyone in the world? Why or why not?

6. Did he or she vote in the last election?

7. Would the person choose the sex of his or her first child?

Activity continued on the back

You can make up and ask many more such questions. Now tell your subject what you think his or her answer will be on the first question and your rationale for it. Proceed through all the questions to test your accuracy. Maybe you would be willing to let your friend try the same thing with you as a target.

Follow-Up Questions:

1. What, if any, are the bases for predicting people's responses in advance?

2. What leads you to make correct predictions?

3. What leads you to make incorrect predictions?

Name ______________________________ **Date** ____________

3.2 Testing the Accuracy of Social Perceptions

Which labels in the list created for the last activity would you assign to yourself and your classmates? Can you correctly guess each other's assignments? Students have often found this exercise to be one of the most revealing and interesting activities in this course.

1. Each person has access to the master list created in Activity 3.2, which might be on the blackboard or another handy place.

2. Assign a label to yourself from the list created by the class. Do not tell others what label you have chosen.

3. Each person then prepares two response sheets. On the first sheet write down the names of everyone in the class and beside each name assign a stereotype from the master list you think best fits them. On the second sheet, write only your name.

4. Pass the second sheet around the room systematically so each person can record the label or stereotype they chose for the named individual in question 3. When everyone has responded, each paper is returned to the person named at the top of the page.

5. Students then reveal the label they originally chose to describe themselves. They can then check the accuracy of their label assignments against other students' perceptions of themselves.

Follow-Up Questions:

1. Do people perceive you the way you thought they would? If not, in what way were their perceptions different?

2. How do you feel about the way that others perceived you? Has it made you think about changing some aspect of your public "persona"? If so, what would you change and how would you do it?

3. How accurate were ***your*** perceptions? What percentage of your labels did your classmates assign themselves?

4. If your perceptions were incorrect, in what way were they incorrect, and what could you do to increase their accuracy?

5. Look again at the text discussion regarding how to cope with prejudice and discrimination. Is it possible that this activity could alter the way we discriminate?

Name ______________________________ **Date** ____________

3.3 Perceiving How Others Dress to Impress

Does your school require you to wear a uniform? Probably not, but it may be possible for students to choose some rather uniform ways to dress, which may be their attempt to make a statement about what they want us to think about them. How do you believe that people use their clothing, hairstyles, and even facial expressions to help themselves achieve an identity?

This activity asks you to sit in the student union or another suitable location and catalog the different social identities you perceive others are trying to project. You might categorize some as Greek, some as Athletes, some as Art Students, and so on. List your proposed labels here:

Questions:

1. How can you do this without being negative? For example, are any of the labels you use derogatory, such as "nerds," "frat rats," or "animals"? How can you avoid labels such as this?

2. Beside each label write the degree of confidence you have in assigning people you see in this category as a percentage from 0 to 100 percent. How does this idea alter the way you see this task?

3. With classmates, create a single list of labels that will be useful for the next project. Assign a number to each label as a code. How many labels have you created?

Harcourt Brace & Company

4

Social Influence: Being Influenced By - and Influencing - Others

Chapter Outline

I. Persuasion

A. The Persuasive Message: Say What? Say How? Say How Often?
B. The Persuasive Communicator: Whom Do You Trust?
C. The Context of the Message: Get 'Em in a Good Mood
D. The Persuaded Audience: Are You a Person Who Can't Say No?
E. The Foot-in-the-Door Technique
   1. Box: Self-Assessment: Do You Speak Your Mind or Do You Wimp Out? The Rathus Assertiveness Schedule
F. Lowballing
   1. Box: What Do You Say Now? Responding to "Lowballing"

II. Obedience to Authority

A. The Milgram Studies: Shocking Stuff at Yale
B. On Truth at Yale
C. On Deception at Yale
D. The Big Question: Why?

III. Group Behavior

A. Mob Behavior and Deindividuation
B. Conformity
C. Helping Behavior and the Bystander Effect

IV. Adjustment and Modern Life

A. How to Become an Assertive Person (How to Win Respect and Influence People)
   1. Box: Adjustment in a World of Diversity: "But You're Not in Hong Kong": Asian Americans Fight a Stereotype Through Assertiveness Training

Chapter Overview

Routes of Persuasion. People can be persuaded to change attitudes by central and peripheral routes. The central route involves change by consideration of arguments or evidence. The peripheral route involves associating the objects of attitudes with positive or negative cues, such as attractive communicators.

Other Factors in Persuasion. Repeating messages makes them more persuasive. Messages that are too discrepant with audience views, however, may fail to persuade. We also tend to be persuaded by communicators who appear to have expertise, trustworthiness, and attractiveness. Emotional appeals are more effective with most people than are logical presentations. We are more likely to be persuaded by people who compliment and agree with us. Food and music also create an atmosphere in which we are more compliant. Finally, some people are more readily persuaded than others. People who feel inadequate, or who believe that it is awful to earn the disapproval of others, show less sales resistance.

The Foot-in-the-Door Technique. This is a method for inducing compliance in which a person makes a small request to which you are likely to accede. Having gotten his or her "foot in the door," he or she follows with a larger request. Since you have already acceded to the first request, you are now more likely to accede to the second, more intrusive request.

Lowballing. This is a persuasive, or sales, technique in which you are induced to make a commitment (such as to buy a product) by being offered extremely generous terms (the "bait"). Then the persuader, or salesperson, alters the terms (the "switch") in hopes that you will retain your commitment.

The Milgram Studies. In the Milgram studies, most subjects gave electric shocks to an innocent person in obeying an authority figure. Factors that heighten the tendency to obey other people include socialization, lack of social comparison, perception of a legitimate authority figure, the foot-in-the-door technique, inaccessibility of values, and buffers between the actor and the victim.

Crowd Behavior versus Individual Behavior. As members of crowds, many people engage in behavior they would find unacceptable if they were acting alone, to some degree because of high arousal and anonymity. In doing so, they set aside their own values and adopt the norms of the group. The adoption of group norms is called deindividuation, and once people have become deindividuated, their sense of responsibility for their own behavior becomes diffused.

Groups and Helping Behavior. When we are members of groups or crowds, we may ignore people in trouble because of diffusion of responsibility. We are more likely to help others when we think we are the only ones available to help, when we understand the situation, when we believe that our efforts will succeed, and when we feel responsible for helping.

Assertive Behavior. Assertive behavior helps us withstand social influence. It is assertive to express our genuine feelings and stand up for our legitimate rights. It is aggressive, not assertive, to insult, threaten, or attack verbally or physically. We can become more assertive through techniques such as self-monitoring, challenging irrational beliefs that prevent us from speaking up, modeling, and behavior rehearsal. In doing so, we should attend to nonverbal communications such as eye contact, posture and gestures, and distance from others, as well as to the things we say.

Learning Objectives

After studying this chapter you should be able to:

1. Define "social influence" and discuss the "routes" involved in the social influence process.
2. Identify and briefly discuss the factors involved in making a message persuasive.
3. Identify and briefly discuss the factors involved in making a communicator persuasive.
4. Discuss how the context of a message influences its persuasiveness and briefly describe the audience factors involved in the persuasiveness of a message.
5. Explain the "foot-in-the-door" technique and lowballing. Give an example of each and discuss methods of coping with these techniques.
6. Describe what happened in the Milgram studies on obedience and identify the factors thought to be responsible.
7. Explain why people behave differently in groups than they do as individuals.
8. Define conformity and social norms and briefly discuss the factors that influence conformity.
9. Explain what the bystander effect is and the various factors that determine or influence helping behavior.
10. Compare and contrast assertive behavior with nonassertive and aggressive behavior in terms of what each is and how such behavior affects our self-esteem.
11. Identify and describe various methods of becoming more assertive.

Key Terms

social influence
persuasion
emotional appeal
central route
peripheral route
two-sided argument
emotional appeal
selective avoidance
selective exposure

foot-in-the-door technique
lowballing
obedience
deindividuation
diffusion of responsibility
conform
social norms
the bystander effect
altruism

assertive behavior
unassertive behavior
aggressive behavior
self-monitoring
irrational beliefs
modeling
behavioral rehearsal
fogging
broken-record technique

Key Terms Review

Define each of the following terms:

1. Social Influence: ______________________________

   ____

2. Emotional Appeal: ______________________________

   ____

3. Selective Avoidance: ______________________________

   ____

4. Selective Exposure: ______________________________

   ____

5. Foot-in-the-Door Technique: ______________________________

   ____

6. Lowballing: ______________________________

   ____

7. Obedience: ______________________________

   ____

8. Deindividuation: ______________________________

   ____

9. Diffusion of Responsibility: ______________________________

   ____

10. Conform: ______________________________

    ____

11. Social Norms: ____

____

12. Bystander Effect: ____

____

13. Altruism: ____

____

14. Aggressive Behavior: ____

____

15. Assertive Behavior: ____

____

16. Nonassertive Behavior: ____

____

17. Self-monitoring: ____

____

18. Behavioral Rehearsal: ____

____

19. Fogging: ____

____

20. Broken-Record Technique: ____

____

Chapter Review

1. Puritan minister Jonathan Edwards used the persuasion technique of __________ __________, playing on people's __________, to persuade people to follow his advice.

2. Petty and others point out that persuasive messages use two routes, the __________ route and the __________ route, to change people's opinions and behavior.

3. The one central factor and three peripheral factors in persuasion are:

   a. ______________________________

   b. ______________________________

   c. ______________________________

   d. ______________________________

4. Four techniques for increasing the likelihood that a message will be persuasive are:

   a. ______________________________

   b. ______________________________

   c. ______________________________

   d. ______________________________

5. Four personal characteristics that make a person's message more persuasive are __________, __________, __________, and __________ to the audience.

6. Two viewer behaviors that limit the impact of biased news reports on public attitudes and behavior are __________ __________ and __________ __________.

7. Persuasive messages are most likely to be accepted when the person is in a __________ mood.

8. People with __________ self-esteem and __________ social anxiety are least likely to resist social pressure.

9. Two common sales techniques designed to persuade you to buy something you may not really want are the __________-__________-__________-__________ technique, and the __________ technique.

10. Stanley Milgram compared the Watergate cover-up to the ____________________ ____.

11. In the Milgram studies, subjects were told that they were taking part in a study on ___ ____.

12. Of the 40 men who took part in Milgram's original "learning" study, __________ refused to go beyond the 300-volt level, and __________ percent delivered the full 450-volt shock.

13. Six reasons why people obey the commands of others, even when asked to commit immoral acts, are:

    a. ____

    b. ____

    c. ____

    d. ____

    e. ____

    f. ____

14. Two key factors which prompt conformity to social norms when we are in groups are __________, which is made likely by anonymity and arousal of the crowd, and __________ __________ __________.

15. Personal factors that contribute to social norms are __________ self-esteem, __________ self-consciousness, __________ __________, __________, and __________ with the task. Situational factors include __________ __________ and __________ __________.

16. The Kitty Genovese case is a classic example of the __________ __________.

17. Six factors that increase the chances that bystanders will come to the aid of people in distress are:

a. ______________________________

b. ______________________________

c. ______________________________

d. ______________________________

e. ______________________________

f. ______________________________

18. Behavior that is expressive of genuine feelings and maintains social rights is called __________ behavior. This compares to submissive, passive __________ behavior in which one's feelings are not expressed, and __________ behavior in which one expresses feelings in a way that does not respect the rights of others.

19. Four techniques which can be helpful in an attempt to become more assertive are:

a. ______________________________

b. ______________________________

c. ______________________________

d. ______________________________

20. Two techniques which can help you remain assertive in the face of someone who is resisting your efforts to stand up for your rights are __________ and the __________ __________ technique.

Sample Test

Multiple-Choice Questions

1. Jonathan Edwards, the Puritan minister whose sermon is presented in the beginning of the chapter, used which emotion in his sermon to persuade his parishioners to rededicate themselves to the church?
   a. fear
   b. hope
   c. love
   d. embarrassment

2. A famed politician decides that the only way to convince voters to support her controversial political views is to carefully explain to them the facts lending support to those views. Her approach utilizes the ______ route.
   a. primary
   b. peripheral
   c. central
   d. tertiary

3. In regard to repeated exposure, research indicates that familiarity breeds ______.
   a. contempt
   b. boredom
   c. antipathy
   d. content

4. Two-sided arguments are most effective when ______.
   a. the communicator is considered unattractive
   b. the audience is already sure of its position on the issue being presented
   c. the audience is uninterested in the position being presented
   d. the audience is uncertain of its position on the issue being presented

5. Each of the following is more likely to make a fear appeal more effective **EXCEPT** ______.
   a. appeals that involve deep personal sacrifice
   b. appeals that are strong
   c. appeals that involve believable dire consequences
   d. appeals that offer practical recommendations

6. Studies indicate that when people watch the news, they will deliberately seek out a television newscast that covers the news in a way that supports their beliefs. This is an example of ______.
   a. cognitive dissonance
   b. selective perception
   c. selective exposure
   d. selective avoidance

7. Which of the following people are **LEAST** likely to resist social pressure?
   a. people with high self-esteem and low social anxiety
   b. people with high self-esteem and high social anxiety
   c. people with low self-esteem and high social anxiety
   d. people with low self-esteem and low social anxiety

8. A salesperson promises you the item you want at a low price and you make a commitment to buy it. Then, the salesperson comes back and tells you that the item you committed to buy is no longer in stock, but that you can have a more expensive item at a "special" price that is still much more expensive than you had originally committed to spend. You have just been victimized by the ______ technique.
   a. lowball
   b. fool's gold
   c. foot-in-the-door
   d. "bandwagon"

9. According to Stanley Milgram, Watergate was made possible through the compliance of people who were concerned about ______.
   a. morality
   b. political freedom in the U. S.
   c. their salaries
   d. the approval of their supervisors

10. In Milgram's studies, how did the "teacher" punish the "learner's" errors?
   a. verbal castigation
   b. electric shock
   c. a painfully loud buzzer
   d. the learner had to drink a foul-tasting liquid

11. Of the 40 men in Milgram's study, how many complied with the scientist throughout the study, believing they were delivering the maximum voltage shocks?
   a. 2 (5%)
   b. 10 (25%)
   c. 18 (45%)
   d. 26 (65%)

12. Which of the following would **NOT** increase the likelihood that a person would obey an illegal, immoral, or unethical order?
   a. the foot-in-the-door technique
   b. inaccessibility of values
   c. removal of buffers
   d. perception of legitimate authority

13. According to your text, factors such as anonymity, diffusion of responsibility, emotional arousal, and the focusing of attention on group processes lead to ______.
   a. fogging
   b. rebellion
   c. deindividuation
   d. cognitive dissonance

14. The **MAXIMUM** probability of conformity to group judgments is achieved when a group reaches ______ members in size.
   a. 4
   b. 6
   c. 8
   d. 10

15. Which of the following persons would be **MOST** likely to help someone in distress?
   a. someone in a good mood
   b. someone with a low need for approval
   c. someone who does not fully understand the situation of the person in distress
   d. someone who fears making social blunders or looking foolish

16. A person is **MOST** likely to help someone else if he or she is ______.
   a. the only one around and knows the person in distress
   b. the only one around and doesn't know the person in distress
   c. is with several other people and they all know the person in distress
   d. is with several other people and none of them knows the person in distress

17. An accountant deserves a raise, but when it comes time to ask his boss he waits quietly, hoping she will offer him the raise without being asked. His behavior is best described as ______.
   a. submissive
   b. assertive
   c. argumentative
   d. aggressive

18. The text describes early socialization messages received by many women about passivity and submissiveness to be harmful because they deny women ______.
   a. choice
   b. protection
   c. a traditional sex role
   d. security

19. Joan goes to a therapist to learn how to become more assertive. The therapist teaches Joan a therapeutic technique in which a person paraphrases someone else's words to show that feelings are understood, then disagrees with those feelings. This therapeutic technique is called ______.
   a. behavioral rehearsal
   b. role-playing
   c. fogging
   d. the broken-record technique

20. In the United States, many groups of Asian Americans are stereotyped as ______.
   a. aggressive
   b. poor decision-makers
   c. autocratic
   d. highly assertive

True-False Questions

21. We are more likely to find attractive people persuasive. ______

22. Giving money to door-to-door charities will tend to cause them to leave you alone for a while. ______

23. People tend to obey authority figures even when the figures' demands contradict their own values. ______

24. The tendency to conform to social norms is rarely a good thing. ______

25. Assertive people do not need to use social influence techniques to achieve their ends. ______

Essay Question

26. Identify and briefly discuss the factors involved in making a communicator persuasive.

Student Activities

Name ______________________________ **Date** ______________

4.1 Who's Listening?

No one has ever lost money by underestimating the intelligence of the American people.

P. T. Barnum

I am confident that Mr. Barnum didn't have us in mind when he was estimating people's gullibility. But researchers repeatedly question how mindfully we handle attempts to influence us. Consider what you would predict people would do in response to these experimental conditions set forth by Harvard's Ellen Langer and her research group.

Imagine you have positioned yourself at a library table very near the photocopy machine. Each time someone starts to use the machine and **before** he or she puts money in it, you approach with one of three requests to use the machine without waiting. Estimate what percent of people will comply with each type of request:

1. "Excuse me, I have five pages. May I use the Xerox machine?"

   Compliance estimate = _______ %

2. "Excuse me, I have five pages. May I use the Xerox machine because I have to make copies?"

   Compliance estimate = _______ %

3. "Excuse me, I have five pages. May I use the Xerox machine, because I am in a rush?"

   Compliance estimate = _______ %

Follow-Up Questions:

1. What reasons would you give for any differences in your predictions?

Activity continued on the back

2. What real value is there in the reason given for request number 2?

3. Now try to explain the results Langer reported for approaches 1, 2, and 3 respectively: 60, 93, and 94 percent.

4. What do Langer's results say about people's attempts to organize incoming information?

5. The researchers also tested the same requests except they changed the number of pages from 5 to 20. These requests resulted in compliance rates of 24, 24, and 42 percent. How do you explain the differences from the first set of results, including a general decline in compliance, and the similar results for approaches 1 and 2? Langer has used the concepts "mindlessness" and "mindfulness" to account for these outcome differences. How do you think she used them?

Name ______________________________ **Date** ____________

4.2 A Simple Question

Compared to Britain and other nations, people in the U.S.A. watch more TV and, on the average, sets are switched on for seven hours a day. This would expose some of us to a considerable amount of effort to influence us through advertising.

For this activity please watch your favorite commercial TV show this week. (Sorry about the hard assignment, but it will be a good lesson.) While watching, use a watch, clock, or calendar to keep track of the total time devoted to advertising and take some notes on your favorite ad. If you are not quite fast enough to catch it all, you might watch for the ad again. It is bound to be repeated, especially if it is interesting and well done. You will be able to identify some of the strategies used in the ad to persuade the audience by analyzing the characteristics of the communicator, the central and peripheral routes of the message, and the audience.

1. Is the communicator an expert, attractive, familiar, or similar to the intended listener? Why do you think he or she was chosen?

2. It is not uncommon for people strong in some of these qualities to be weak in others, and yet still be chosen. For example, ex-athletes often represent brands of beer, and actresses explain why it is good to use buffered aspirin. Since they are not experts, why are they chosen?

3. Would the use of music, dance, song, beautiful people or scenery (all known as production values) take advantage of the central or the peripheral route of influencing discussed in Chapter 4? What route was used in the ad you have chosen to analyze? How do you think it affected the ad's persuasiveness? Why?

Activity continued on the back

4. What information used the central route? How memorable or effective was this information? Why?

5. What audience do you think this ad is aimed at? Can you characterize the intended audience as to age, gender, and motivation to be mindful? What other audiences do you think this ad could be targeted toward, if any? Why?

6. Would you evaluate the ad as successful or not? Why or why not?

7. In general, which influences you more? The communicator, the central message, or the peripheral messages? Why?

Name ________________________________ **Date** ______________

4.3 Another Simple Question

For this activity please watch your favorite commercial TV show this week. (Sorry about the hard assignment, but it will be a good lesson.) While watching, use a watch, clock, or calendar to keep track of the total time devoted to advertising and take some notes on your ***least*** favorite ad. If you are not quite fast enough to catch it all, you might watch for the ad again. It is bound to be repeated, and you are bound to notice it, especially if it is annoying to you. You will be able to identify some of the strategies used in the ad to persuade the audience by analyzing the characteristics of the communicator, the central and peripheral routes of the message, and the audience.

1. Is the communicator an expert, attractive, familiar, or similar to the intended listener? Why do you think he or she was chosen, and could they have chosen someone better? If so, who, and why would your choice have been better than theirs?

2. What information in the ad used the central or the peripheral route? How do you think it could have been better used to affect the ad's persuasiveness? Why?

3. What audience do you think this ad is aimed at? Can you characterize the intended audience as to age, gender, and motivation to be mindful? What other audiences do you think this ad could be targeted toward, if any? Why?

Activity continued on the back

4. What biases, positive or negative, do you have about the product being advertised in this ad. Do you think any negative biases about the product or the spokesperson in the ad could have affected your reaction to the ad? If so, how? And what could the ad have done differently to help prevent your biases from interfering with the persuasiveness of the message it wanted you to accept?

5. Some advertisements are used even when market research indicates that a large percentage of the public finds the ad annoying. This is because the same research indicates that the more annoying some ads are, the more likely it is that viewers will buy that product when they shop, despite the annoying qualities of the ad. Why do you think this happens? Has this ever happened to you? If so, what was the ad and the product being advertised?

Name ______________________________ **Date** ____________

4.4 What Would You Predict?

1. Consider for a moment the next presidential election. What would influence you to become highly involved in the campaign of your choice for president? List your ideas here:

2. Now suppose you want to persuade someone who does not know whom he or she wants to support to help you with the very big job of handing out leaflets for your candidate in public places on campus and elsewhere. Which techniques in the chapter can you use to influence this person to help? Why would he or she help?

3. Predict your helper's attitude toward your favorite candidate if: you only thank the helper for the help he or she gave you, or you pay more than the usual amount students can earn in such jobs. Under which condition do you think your helper's attitude would change more? Why?

Name ______________________________ **Date** ____________

4.5 Will We Be Willing to Help?

We are disturbed by the Kitty Genovese story, and probably ask ourselves what we would do in similar situations. After the discussions of helping behavior in Chapter 4, we realize that circumstances and even our mood may influence our willingness to help or remain a bystander. If we chose to be more helpful, we can consider ideas already discussed earlier in the text, and organize our thoughts to increase helping. Consider your answer to these questions:

1. How do you create a schema of yourself as a helper? What would be your ideal?

2. How do you practice being helpful? What are some common opportunities to use? What are some opportunities you could create for yourself, with a little effort?

3. Are you comfortable that you can assert yourself when the occasion warrants it? Why or why not? If the answer is no, what changes can you make so that eventually the answer will be yes?

4. Social psychologists, who have led the work on helping research, are prone to investigate the situational variables that affect behavior - that's why it's called social psychology. While they may not emphasize enduring traits of persons as factors, we can speculate what traits might be worth investigating. What traits do you think would be worth studying? Why?

Name ______________________________ **Date** __________

4.6 Are Our Attitudes Being Manipulated by Madison Avenue?

It appears to me to be a very clever advertising campaign when I see a beer pegged as the choice of **real** mountain men. The ads are replete with implied similes about appreciating the "wildlife," and carrying six-packs instead of six-shooters. Of course, we could not have expected advertisers to be so truthful as to include the possibilities of beer bellies, belches, and hangovers. Instead, we are exposed to promises that the good life is a function of our beverage choice, with popularity and sex as bonuses if we choose wisely. To begin questioning the possible influence advertising could have we might start with our own experience.

1. During this week, keep a diary of all alcohol and tobacco ads you encounter. Record the products and the total number of ads. You are likely to encounter ads in newspapers, television, radio, billboards, and points of purchase in stores. How many did you record total? For each specific item?

2. Would you include T-shirts, sponsorship of sports or music events, and insignias on equipment as ads also? Why or why not?

3. Which ones were the most effective? Why?

4. Which ones were the least effective? Why?

Activity continued on the back

5. Also record some information about the actors and models in the ads with particular attention to such details as their age, gender, appearance, and behavior. Other information includes to whom the ads are addressed (the target audience), what implicit rewards are promised for using the product, and what kinds of behavior are encouraged by the ads. What conclusions can you draw from what you have seen, giving specfic reasons to support your conclusions?

5

Stress: Sources and Moderators

Chapter Outline

I. Stress

II. Sources of Stress

A. Daily Hassles
B. Life Changes: "Going Through Changes"
  1. Box: Self-Assessment: Have You Been Going Through Changes? The Social Readjustment Rating Scale
C. Criticisms of the Research Links Between Hassles, Life Changes, and Illness
D. Pain and Discomfort
E. Frustration
F. Conflict
G. Type A behavior
  1. Box: Self-Assessment: Are You Type A or Type B?
H. Environmental Stressors
  1. Box: Adjustment in a World of Diversity: One Quake, Two Worlds

III. Moderators of the Impact of Stress

A. Self-Efficacy Expectancies
B. Psychological Hardiness
  1. Box: Self-Assessment: Who's in Charge Here? The Locus of Control Scale
C. Sense of Humor: "Doeth a Merry Heart Good Like a Medicine?"
D. Predictability
E. Social Support
  1. Box: Adjustment in a World of Diversity: Stress and Ethnic Pride among African Americans

IV. Adjustment and Modern Life

A. Using a Balance Sheet to Make Decisions

Chapter Overview

What Is Stress? Stress is the demand made on an organism to adjust. Whereas some stress is desirable ("eustress") to keep us alert and occupied, too much stress can tax our adjustive capacities and contribute to physical illness. Sources of stress include daily hassles, life changes, pain, frustration, conflict, Type A behavior, and environmental stressors such as noise, natural disasters, technological disasters, and crowding.

Daily Hassles and Life Changes. Daily hassles are regularly encountered sources of aggravation and annoyance. Life changes occur on an intermittent basis and may be positive (such as a major achievement or a vacation) as well as negative. Hassles and life changes require adjustment, although negative life changes are more taxing than positive life changes. People who earn more than 300 life-change units within a year, according to the Holmes and Rahe scale, are at higher risk for medical and psychological disorders. The data on these relationships are correlational, however, and not experimental. It is possible that people about to develop illnesses encounter more hassles or lead lifestyles with more life changes. Also, the degree of stress associated with an event is linked to one's appraisal of that event.

Pain and Discomfort. Pain originates at a source of body injury and is transmitted to the brain. Pain and discomfort impair our ability to perform, especially when severe demands are made on the heels of a traumatic experience. There are several psychological methods for pain management. These include provision of accurate information about the source, intensity, and duration of the pain; distraction and fantasy; hypnosis; relaxation training; coping with irrational beliefs; and social support.

Frustration. Frustration results from having unattainable goals or from facing barriers to reach our goals.

Conflict. Conflict results from opposing motives. We often vacillate when we are in conflict. Approach-approach conflicts are least stressful. Multiple approach-avoidance conflicts are most complex and tend to be the most stressful. Making decisions is often the way out of conflict. We can use a balance sheet to help resolve conflicts because balance sheets tend to improve decision-making by listing and weighing the pluses and minuses for the alternatives available to us.

Type A Behavior. Type A behavior is characterized by aggressiveness, a sense of time urgency, and competitiveness. Type A people are more aggressive and are more reluctant to relinquish control or power than are Type Bs. Type A people also respond to challenge with higher blood pressure than Type Bs. Evidence is mixed concerning whether Type As are at greater risk for heart attacks.

Environmental Stressors. Environmental stressors include natural disasters, technological disasters, high noise levels, air pollution, extremes of temperature, and crowding.

Self-Efficacy Expectations. Self-efficacy expectations encourage us to persist in difficult tasks and to endure pain and discomfort.

Psychological Hardiness. Psychological hardiness is characterized by commitment, challenge, and control. People with an internal locus of control ("internals") endure stress more successfully than people with an external locus of control ("externals"). Internals seek information about their situation, and are more likely to engage in active methods of coping, which increases their chances of coping successfully with stressors. The ability to produce and enjoy humor when under stress also seems to buffer its impact.

Seeking Stress. There may be times when we actually seek stress. When we are in a goal-directed mode of functioning, we tend to be serious-minded and try to decrease the stress impinging upon us by lowering our levels of arousal. However, when we are in a playful mode, we may seek to increase the amount of arousal we experience.

Predictability. Predictability buffers stress by allowing us to brace ourselves and to plan ways of coping.

Social Support. Social support buffers the impact of stress in five ways: expression of emotional concern, instrumental aid, provision of information, appraisal, and socialization activities.

Learning Objectives

After studying this chapter you should be able to:

1. Define stress and identify nine different sources of stress.
2. Compare and contrast daily hassles and life changes and explain how each of them affects us.
3. Discuss what pain and discomfort are, how they are transmitted to the brain, and how they affect us.
4. Identify and briefly discuss physiological and psychological methods of pain management.
5. Compare and contrast frustration and conflict, identifying the four types of conflict discussed in the text.
6. Compare and contrast Type A and Type B behavior, and explain how Type A behavior affects us.
7. Identify and briefly discuss the various environmental stressors and how they affect us.
8. Discuss what self-efficacy expectations are and how they affect us.
9. Explain what psychological hardiness is and discuss how it helps us cope with stress.
10. Explain how control, predictability, humor, and social support can help people cope with stress.

Key Terms

stress
daily hassles
uplifts
life changes
eustress
prostaglandins
analgesic
endorphins
relaxation training
frustration
emotional barriers
tolerance for frustration
conflict
approach-approach conflict
avoidance-avoidance conflict
approach-avoidance conflict
multiple approach-avoidance conflict
Type A behavior
Type B behavior
environmental stressors
serum cholesterol
decibel
crowding
tripling effect
self-efficacy expectations
adrenaline
psychological hardiness
commitment
challenge
control
locus of control
internal locus of control
external locus of control
balance sheet

Key Terms Review

Define each of the following terms:

1. Stress: ______________________________

   ____

2. Daily Hassles: ______________________________

   ____

3. Uplifts: ______________________________

   ____

4. Life Changes: ______________________________

   ____

5. Prostaglandins: ______________________________

   ____

6. Analgesic: ______________________________

   ____

7. Endorphins: ______________________________

   ____

8. Frustration: ______________________________

   ____

9. Conflict: ______________________________

   ____

10. Approach-Approach Conflict: ______________________________

    ____

11. Avoidance-Avoidance Conflict: ______________________________

____

12. Approach-Avoidance Conflict: ______________________________

____

13. Multiple Approach-Avoidance Conflict: ______________________

____

14. Type A Behavior: ____

____

15. Decibel: ____

____

16. Crowding: ____

____

17. Tripling Effect: ____

____

18. Psychological Hardiness: ____________________________________

____

19. Self-Efficacy Expectations: ___________________________________

____

20. Locus of Control: ____

____

Chapter Review

1. In psychology, stress is the demand made on an organism to __________, __________, or __________.

2. Eight types of daily hassles are:

   a. ______________________________

   b. ______________________________

   c. ______________________________

   d. ______________________________

   e. ______________________________

   f. ______________________________

   g. ______________________________

   h. ______________________________

3. Five criticisms of the research links between hassles, life changes, and illness are:

   a. ______________________________

   b. ______________________________

   c. ______________________________

   d. ______________________________

   e. ______________________________

4. __________ facilitate transmission of pain messages to the brain and heighten blood circulation to an injured area.

5. __________ drugs such as aspirin and ibuprofen work by inhibiting the production of __________ and thus decreasing fever, inflammation, and pain.

6. A neurotransmitter that is functionally similar to morphine is an __________.

7. Six methods for improving pain management are:

   a. ______________________________

   b. ______________________________

   c. ______________________________

   d. ______________________________

   e. ______________________________

   f. ______________________________

8. The emotion produced by the thwarting of a motive is called __________.

9. Anxiety and fear can serve as __________ __________ that prevent us from effectively meeting our goals.

10. Four types of conflict which can contribute to stress are:

    a. the __________-__________ conflict (the least stressful)

    b. the __________-__________ conflict

    c. the __________-__________ conflict

    d. the __________ __________-__________ conflict (the most stressful)

11. People with __________ behavior pattern are competitive, highly driven, impatient, and aggressive, in contrast to __________ people who are more laid back and relaxed and focus on the quality of life.

12. Type A personalities perceive time as passing more __________ than do Type B personalities.

13. Six types of environmental stressors are:

a. ______________________________

b. ______________________________

c. ______________________________

d. ______________________________

e. ______________________________

f. ______________________________

14. High levels of __________ are stressful and can lead to illnesses such as hypertension, neurological and intestinal disorders, and ulcers.

15. __________ __________, a colorless, odorless gas found in cigarette smoke and auto fumes, decreases the oxygen-carrying capacity of the blood and impairs learning ability.

16. High temperatures are connected to __________ behavior.

17. In Calhoun's study, __________ was the snake in rat paradise.

18. When three students live together, a coalition frequently forms between two of them so that the third feels isolated. This phenomenon is called the __________ __________.

19. Social-cognitive theorists argue that __________ __________ expectations have important influences on our abilities to withstand stress.

20. Kobasa's research found that psychologically hardy individuals were high in __________, __________, and __________.

21. Examples from everyday life suggest that a sense of __________ - a sense of making choices - fosters healthy adjustment.

22. Researchers have found that students who react with __________ in difficult situations are less affected by negative life events than other students.

23. Five types of social support that may serve to buffer the effects of stressors are:

    a. ____

    b. ____

    c. ____

    d. ____

    e. ____

24. Among many ethnic groups, self-esteem is connected to ethnic __________.

25. Balance sheets help us to identify the __________ and __________ of any situation.

26. To use a balance sheet, one must jot down the following information for each choice:

    a. projected ____________________________________

    b. projected ____________________________________

    c. projected ____________________________________

    d. projected ____________________________________

Sample Test

Multiple-Choice Questions

1. In psychology, the demand made on an organism to adapt is called ______.
   a. pressure
   b. stress
   c. anxiety
   d. coercion

2. "Uplifts" refer to ______.
   a. little padded devices short people put in their shoes to look taller
   b. positive life changes
   c. regularly occurring enjoyable experiences
   d. religious conversion experiences

3. Which of the following is true of daily hassles and life changes?
   a. Both daily hassles and life changes may involve positive and negative experiences.
   b. Both daily hassles and life changes involve only negative experiences.
   c. Hassles involve both positive and negative experiences, whereas life changes involve only negative experiences.
   d. Hassles involve only negative experiences whereas, life changes involve both positive and negative experiences.

4. Which of the following is true of daily hassles and life changes?
   a. Both daily hassles and life changes occur on a daily basis.
   b. Both daily hassles and life changes are relatively infrequent events.
   c. Hassles are relatively infrequent events, whereas life changes occur on a daily basis.
   d. Hassles occur on a daily basis, whereas life changes are relatively infrequent events.

5. According to Holmes and Rahe, people who scored below 150 points. on their scale had a ______ chance of developing medical problems within the next year.
   a. one-in-twelve
   b. one-in-nine
   c. one-in-six
   d. one-in-three

6. Substances that facilitate the transmission of pain messages to the brain and heighten circulation to injured areas of the body are called ______.
   a. endorphins
   b. prostaglandins
   c. analgesics
   d. corticosteroids

7. In water at room temperature, Richter found that rats could swim to stay afloat about 80 hours. When Richter made the water uncomfortably hot or cold or blew noxious streams of air into their faces the rats remained afloat for ______.
   a. only a few minutes
   b. 1 - 20 hours
   c. 20 - 40 hours
   d. 40 - 60 hours

8. According to your text, the process of being torn in two or more directions at the same time by opposing motives is called ______.
   a. frustration
   b. conflict
   c. state anxiety
   d. trait anxiety

9. Greg is fearful of visiting the dentist, but he is also fearful of having his teeth decay if he does not visit the dentist. He is experiencing a(n) ______ conflict.
   a. approach-approach
   b. approach-avoidance
   c. multiple approach-avoidance
   d. avoidance-avoidance

10. People who are highly driven, competitive, rushed, perfectionistic, and impatient are ______ personalities.

a. hyperencephalic
b. Type A
c. Type B
d. hypoencephalic

11. Blizzards, hurricanes, tornadoes, etc., are all examples of ______.

a. ecological imbalances
b. technological disasters
c. natural disasters
d. human neglect of nature

12. How long after the Three Mile Island incident were psychological and physical effects of stress found among the residents?

a. 1 - 3 weeks
b. 1 - 6 months
c. up to 1 year
d. up to 2 years

13. Which of the following is **NOT** true of high levels of noise?

a. Angry people are more likely to behave aggressively when exposed to high levels of noise.
b. High levels of noise can lead to an assortment of stress-related disorders.
c. Attraction increases between partners in dating couples when exposed to high levels of unpleasant noise.
d. People are less concerned with the distress of others in areas of high noise.

14. Which of the following is true of **BOTH** hot and cold temperatures?

a. They cause you to sweat.
b. They increase your arousal.
c. They cause your metabolism to increase.
d. They cause restriction of the blood vessels in the skin.

15. Which of the following best describes what happened in "rat city" once a critical population was reached?

a. The rats learned to get along with each other.
b. The mortality rate declined.
c. Females built sturdier nests and spent more time nurturing their young.
d. Family structure broke down.

16. Research indicates that with humans, it is ______ that is aversive where crowding is concerned.

a. the social contact that comes with crowding
b. the lack of control which accompanies crowding
c. the crowding itself
d. the lack of free space which accompanies crowding

17. Which of the following is **NOT** a way in which psychologically hardy individuals differ from non-hardy individuals?

a. Hardy individuals are higher in commitment.
b. Hardy individuals have more of an external locus of control.
c. Hardy individuals are high in challenge.
d. Hardy individuals are more resistant to stress.

18. Research on humor and stress indicates that ______.

a. attempts at humor, when people are already under stress, seem to increase the stress
b. humor has little or no effect on people's stress levels
c. people who are under stress are less able to effectively generate or appreciate humor
d. humor serves to buffer the effects of stress

19. Which of the following is **NOT** true of social support?
    a. Social support is less important to the well-being of men than it is to the well-being of women.
    b. People who receive social support may live longer than those who do not.
    c. Women are more likely to form supportive social networks than men.
    d. People with strong social support networks report less stress from disasters than those without such networks.

20. A technique which allows one to weigh the pluses or minuses of any situation or potential decision is called ______.
    a. response-cost tracking
    b. a positive/negative diary
    c. cue-controlled planning
    d. a balance sheet

True-False Questions

21. Some stress is necessary to keep us alert and occupied. ______

22. Analgesics are similar to the narcotic morphine. ______

23. High concentrations of carbon monoxide can contribute to highway accidents. ______

24. Psychological hardiness removes buffers between individuals and stressful life events. ______

25. People who receive social support live longer than those who do not. ______

Essay Question

26. Compare and contrast frustration and conflict, identifying the four types of conflict discussed in the text.

Student Activities

Name ____________________________________ Date ______________

5.1 Sources of Stress: Hassles

In Chapter 5, we learned that stress can be associated with emotional distress, physical illness, poorer performance, and behavioral problems. Among the several sources of stress are the big changes in life, like graduation or marriage, and the daily hassles like broken shoestrings and snarled traffic. The Social Readjustment Rating Scale in Chapter 5 has us consider some of the major life changes that increase health risks and are associated with stress. In addition to your score on this scale, consider the possible effects of daily hassles by keeping a "hassles diary" for one week.

Follow-Up Questions:

1. Which hassles occur at a frequent rate such as daily or several times daily?

2. For each hassle identified, decide what would be best changed: 1) the hassle or 2) your response. For example, a more scenic route might eliminate the hassle of a difficult commute, while a problem with rainy weather might require a "change in attitude," or more precisely, challenging an irrational idea. Why?

Name ______________________________ **Date** ____________

5.2 Where Can You Find "Merry Heart Medicine"?

When Norman Cousins tried to take some control over his own painful medical condition, he asked friends to bring funny films and videos to the hospital. His choices included Laurel and Hardy and Candid Camera. Where would you turn if you wanted to select humorous material? What are at least five specific source of comedy material you would use if you were in Cousins' situation?

Follow-Up Questions:

1. If you wanted evidence that your humorous material was having a "medicinal" effect, how could you empirically measure any benefits?

2. What are three kinds of humorous programs you could envision for a pediatric ward at a local hospital? Why would you choose these programs?

Name ________________________________ Date ____________

5.3 A Moderator of Stress: Hardiness

Sources of stress do not automatically cause stress-related problems. Moderators of stress, which can include our personal strengths, might mean that we can have a healthier and more productive life in spite of life's challenges, or maybe even because of them. As the text mentions, Suzanne Kobasa and others have studied people who have successfully handled much stress without becoming ill. Kobasa and others have listed some of the strengths for moderating stress, which have been paraphrased below to illustrate the concept of hardiness, and to give us a chance to evaluate ourselves. For each strength, write one change that you could **realistically** make for personal improvement, and how (if applicable) you would make that change.

1. Having a clear sense of goals, values, capabilities, and their importance.

2. Active involvement to promote change.

3. Finding personal meaning in stressful life events.

4. Having a sense of control.

5. Having a good support system.

Activity continued on the back

6. Seeking stimulation.

7. Having a stable and even disposition.

8. Having a Type B personality.

Critical Thinking

Could any of the characteristics of hardy people be **results** of health, rather than **causes** of health? Select one characteristic and describe how it might be a result rather than a cause.

Name ______________________________ **Date** _____________

5.4 Why Do Married Men Live Longer Than Single Men?

Some of the studies mentioned in the text, which support the relationship between social support and health, are correlational. Consider the observation that married men live longer than single men. What alternative explanations can you offer to the explanation that social support is the **cause** of longer living?

You might begin by thinking of what else is often different about being married and not being married.

Follow-Up Questions:

1. How could you test the alternative you generated?

2. How could men who prefer to remain bachelors gain the benefits of longevity and/or health that married men enjoy?

3. Do you believe that marriage has the same effect for women? Why or why not?

Name ________________________________ Date ____________

5.5 A Balance Sheet

Pick an issue in your life in which you are, or have been, struggling with what to decide to do about it. Use the following balance sheet, as descussed in your text, to help weigh the "pros" and "cons" of at least one of the alternatives for your decision.

1. Alternative A

	Positive Anticipation	Negative Anticipation
Tangible gains and losses for me		
Tangible gains and losses for others		
Self-approval or self-disapproval		
Social approval or social disapproval		

Make photocopies of this sheet to fill out and make similar evaluations of other alternatives in your decision.

6

Psychological Factors and Health

Chapter Outline

I. Health Psychology

1. Box: Self-Assessment: How Optimistic Is Your Outlook? The Life Orientation Test
2. Box: Adjustment in the New Millennium: Psychology and Health in the New Millennium

II. Biological, Emotional, and Cognitive Effects of Stress

A. Effects of Stress on the Body
B. Emotional Effects of Stress
C. Cognitive Effects of Stress

III. The Immune System

A. Functions of the Immune System
B. Effects of Stress on the Immune System

IV. Factors in Physical Health and Illness

A. Human Diversity and Health: A Land of Many Nations
   1. Box: Adjustment in the World of Diversity: Health and Socioeconomic Status: The Rich Get Richer and the Poor Get . . . Sicker
B. Headaches
C. Menstrual Problems
D. Coronary Heart Disease
E. Cancer
   1. Box: Self-Assessment: The Eating Smart Quiz
   2. Box: What Do You Say Now? Encouraging a Friend to Seek Help

V. Adjustment and Modern Life

A. Choosing a Physician

Chapter Overview

Health Psychology. Health psychology studies the relationships between psychological factors, (for example, behavior, emotions, stress, beliefs, and attitudes) and the prevention and treatment of physical illness.

The General Adaptation Syndrome (GAS). Hans Selye suggested that the general adaptation syndrome is triggered by perception of a stressor and consists of three stages: the alarm reaction, resistance, and exhaustion stages.

The Role of the Endocrine System. In response to stress, the hypothalamus and the pituitary glands secrete hormones that stimulate the adrenal cortex to secrete cortisol and other corticosteroids. Corticosteroids help the body resist stress by fighting inflammations and allergic reactions. Adrenaline and noradrenaline are also secreted by the adrenal medulla, and adrenaline arouses the body by activating the sympathetic division of the autonomic nervous system.

The Role of the Autonomic Nervous System (ANS). The sympathetic division of the ANS is highly active during the alarm and resistance stages of the GAS, and is characterized by rapid heartbeat and respiration rate, release of stores of sugar, muscle tension, and other responses that spend the body's stores of energy. The parasympathetic division of the ANS predominates during the exhaustion stage of the GAS and is characterized by responses such as digestive responses that help restore the body's reserves of energy.

Emotional Responses to Stress. Emotional responses to stress include anxiety, anger, and depression. Anxiety involves sympathetic ANS activity. Anger is a response to frustration and social provocations. Depression involves predominantly parasympathetic ANS activity and is a response to loss, to failure, and to prolonged stress.

Cognitive Responses to Stress. Stress can also distract us from focusing on the tasks at hand.

The Functions of the Immune System. The first function of the immune system is to engulf and kill pathogens, worn-out body cells, and cancerous cells. The second function of the immune system is to "remember" pathogens to facilitate future combat against them. The third function is inflammation, which increases the number of white blood cells brought to a damaged area. By stimulating the release of corticosteroids, stress depresses functioning of the immune system because steroids counter inflammation.

Headaches. The most common kinds of headaches are muscle-tension headaches and migraine headaches. Stress causes and compounds muscle headache pain by stimulating muscle tension. It also plays a role in the development of some migraine headaches.

PMS. Premenstrual syndrome is a combination of psychological (for example, mood changes) and physical symptoms (for example, bloating, cramping) that afflicts many women for a few days prior to menstruation. In most cases the symptoms are mild to moderate.

Risk Factors for Cardiovascular Disorders. The seven major risk factors for cardiovascular disorders are: family history; physiological conditions such as hypertension and high levels of serum cholesterol, behavior patterns such as smoking and eating fatty foods, Type A behavior, work overload, chronic fatigue, emotional strain, and physical inactivity.

Behavioral Measures to Prevent and Treat Cardiovascular Disorders. The following measures can be helpful: stopping smoking, controlling one's weight, reducing hypertension, lowering serum cholesterol, and modifying Type A behavior.

Risk Factors for Cancer. Risk factors for cancer include: family history, smoking, drinking alcohol, eating animal fats, sunbathing, and stress.

Behavioral Measures to Prevent and Treat Cancer. The following measures can be helpful: controlling exposure to behavioral risk factors for cancer, going for regular medical checkups, regulating the amount of stress impacting upon us, and vigorously fighting cancer if we are afflicted.

Learning Objectives

After studying this chapter you should be able to:

1. Explain what health psychology is and the types of things it studies.

2. Identify five areas which are likely to become the focus of research for health psychologists in the 21st century.

3. Describe the stages of the general adaptation syndrome and discuss the role of the endocrine system in this process.

4. Identify the various parts of the autonomic nervous system and explain their role in the body's response to stress.

5. Identify our emotional and cognitive responses to stress and explain the effects of those reactions on our mind and body.

6. Describe the functions of the immune system and explain the effects of stress on the immune system.

7. Explain how ethnicity, gender, and socioeconomic status affect people's reactions to stress and vulnerability to stress-related disorders.

8. Identify the various type of headaches and their symptoms, and discuss how they are related to stress.

9. Discuss the causes of menstrual problems, their effects, and ways to cope with them.

10. Describe the risk factors for cardiovascular disorders and the various behavioral measures that can contribute to the prevention and treatment of these disorders.

11. Identify the risk factors for cancer and discuss the various behavioral measures that can contribute to the prevention and treatment of cancer.

12. Summarize research findings on stress and cancer.

13. Briefly describe the suggestions presented in your text for choosing a physician. Explain, in your answer, why each suggestion is important.

Key Terms

health psychology
general adaptation syndrome
alram reaction
fight-or-flight response
endocrine system
hormones
corticosteroids
autonomic nervous system
sympathetic division
parasympathetic division
resistance stage
exhaustion stage
trait anxiety
state anxiety
immune system
pathogens
leukocytes
antigens
antibodies
inflammation
psychoneuroimmunology
muscle-tension headache
socioeconomic status
migraine headache
dysmenorrhea
prostaglandins
amenorrhea
premenstrual syndrome
coronary heart disease
hypertension
cancer
metastasize
carcinogen
osteoporosis

Key Terms Review

Define each of the following terms:

1. General Adaptation Syndrome: ____________________

____

2. Alarm Reaction: ____________________

____

3. Endocrine System: ____________________

____

4. Autonomic Nervous System: ____________________

____

5. Sympathetic Division: ____________________

____

6. Parasympathetic Division: ____________________

____

7. Resistance Stage: ____________________

____

8. Exhaustion: ____

____

9. Trait Anxiety: ____

____

10. State Anxiety: ____

____

11. Immune System: ____

____

12. Pathogen: ____

____

13. Leukocytes: ____

____

14. Antigen: ____

____

15. Antibodies: ____

____

16. Inflammation: ____

____

17. Psychoneuroimmunology: ____

____

18. Muscle-Tension Headache: ____

____

19. Migraine Headache: ____

____

20. Carcinogen: ____

____

Chapter Review

1. __________ psychology studies the relationships between psychological factors and the prevention and treatment of illness.

2. __________ can set the stage for, or exacerbate, physical illness.

3. Five trends in health psychology that are likely to become even more prominent in the 21st century are:

   a. ____

   b. ____

   c. ____

   d. ____

   e. ____

4. Hans Selye labeled the body's response to stress as the __________ __________ __________. This response can be broken down into three parts: the __________ __________ stage; the __________ stage; and the __________ stage.

5. The __________ system consists of a number of ductless glands that release a number of hormones called __________ which help the body respond to stress by fighting inflammation and allergic reactions.

6. The __________ nervous system has two branches, or divisions, the __________ division, which is most active when the body is expending reserves of energy, and the __________ division, which is most active when the body is restoring its energy reserves.

7. Two types of anxiety are __________ anxiety, a personality variable, and __________ anxiety, a temporary condition of arousal triggered by external events.

8. Three types of negative emotional responses to stress that can motivate us to behave in maladaptive ways are:

   a. ____

   b. ____

   c. ____

9. We are motivated to seek __________ levels of arousal at which we feel best and function most efficiently.

10. White blood cells, called __________, routinely engulf and kill __________, and destroy __________, by producing __________ which bind to foreign substances in the body and mark them for destruction.

11. The relationship between psychological factors and the immune system is studied by the field of __________.

12. The life expectancy of African Americans is __________ shorter than that of white Americans.

13. Men's life expectancy is __________ shorter, on average, than women's.

14. People with higher socioeconomic status have __________ health and lead __________ lives.

15. __________ are the most common stress-related ailments.

Harcourt Brace & Company

16. Two types of headaches are __________ __________ headaches, the most frequent kind, and __________ headaches, which result from changes in blood supply to the head.

17. Three types of menstrual problems are __________, __________, and __________ __________.

18. Menstrual cramps are triggered by heavy secretion of hormones called __________.

19. The prevailing view today is that premenstrual syndrome has a primarily __________ basis.

20. Women with menstrual problems seem to be extremely sensitive to the hormones __________ and __________. They also show imbalances in neurotransmitters such as __________.

21. Your text describes eleven ways to handle menstrual discomfort. Five of them are:

a. ____

b. ____

c. ____

d. ____

e. ____

22. Your text describes nine risk factors for cardiovascular disease. Five of them are:

a. ____

b. ____

c. ____

d. ____

e. ____

23. Six modifications one can make to reduce the risk of developing cardiovascular disease are:

a. ______________________________

b. ______________________________

c. ______________________________

d. ______________________________

e. ______________________________

f. ______________________________

24. The term __________ refers to a number of disorders that involve the development of mutant cells that reproduce rapidly and rob the body of nutrients.

25. The inherent __________ of cancer alone determines the prognosis, overriding the potentially mitigating influence of __________ factors.

26. Four things we can do to reduce our risk of dying of cancer are:

a. ______________________________

b. ______________________________

c. ______________________________

d. ______________________________

27. Three things you should do when choosing a physician are:

a. ______________________________

b. ______________________________

c. ______________________________

Sample Test

Multiple-Choice Questions

1. Health psychology studies ______.
   a. the effects of illness on a person's psychological functioning
   b. psychological methods for helping people with psychosomatic illnesses learn to overcome their disorders
   c. the relationships between the psychological factors and the prevention and treatment of physical illnesses
   d. the psychological qualities of mentally healthy individuals

2. Scheier and Carver (1985) found that optimistic people ______.
   a. tend to ignore symptoms of serious health problems
   b. tend to live longer than other people
   c. tend to report fewer symptoms of physical illness than do other people
   d. tend to have more physical illnesses than do other people

3. The general adaptation syndrome has ______ stages.
   a. 5
   b. 4
   c. 3
   d. 2

4. The hypothalamus secretes ______ during the alarm reaction.
   a. corticosteroids
   b. neurotransmitters
   c. CRH
   d. ACTH

5. The amounts of ______ in the body serve as an objective measure of stress.
   a. adrenaline and thyroxin
   b. cortisol and thyroxin
   c. adrenaline and cortisol
   d. noradrenaline and thyroxin

6. The two branches of the autonomic nervous system are the ______.
   a. central branch and the peripheral branch
   b. afferent division and the efferent division
   c. somatic branch and the pulmonary branch
   d. the sympathetic division and the parasympathetic division

7. A person who is calmly eating a meal probably has a(n) ______ that is active at that point in time.
   a. sympathetic nervous system
   b. parasympathetic nervous system
   c. afferent nervous system
   d. efferent nervous system

8. Continued stress after the body has reached the exhaustion stage of the general adaptation syndrome leads to ______.
   a. diseases of adaptation
   b. hypochondriasis
   c. a second alarm reaction
   d. a reaction formation

9. On a biological level, ______ involves predominantly sympathetic nervous system arousal.
   a. neither trait nor state anxiety
   b. state anxiety but not trait anxiety
   c. trait anxiety but not state anxiety
   d. both state and trait anxiety

10. Biologically, the exhaustion stage of the general adaptation syndrome is dominated by ______.
   a. neither sympathetic nor parasympathetic arousal
   b. sympathetic, but not parasympathetic arousal
   c. parasympathetic, but not sympathetic arousal
   d. both sympathetic and parasympathetic arousal

11. A substance, usually found on the surface of foreign agents, that stimulates the body to mount an immune-system response to it is called a(n) ______.
   a. pathogen
   b. antigen
   c. antibody
   d. platelet

12. Prolonged stress appears to impair immune system functioning because stress stimulates the production of ______ which suppress(es) immune system functioning.
   a. acetylcholine
   b. steroids
   c. antigens
   d. thyroxin

13. A study of dental students found which of the following to be true?
   a. Students with many friends showed significantly more immune system suppression than students with few friends.
   b. Students showed increased immune system functioning in times of increased stress.
   c. Students' immune system functioning was unimpaired by stress levels and levels of social support.
   d. Students with many friends showed significantly less immune system suppression than students with few friends.

14. African Americans make up 12 percent of the American population but African-American men account for ______ percent of AIDS cases.
   a. 21
   b. 31
   c. 41
   d. 51

15. African Americans are ______ likely than white Americans to contract most forms of cancer and are ______ likely to die from it.
   a. less, less
   b. less, more
   c. more, less
   d. more, more

16. Roger has a severe headache. He is sensitive to light, feels nauseous, and has trouble maintaining his balance. His mood has deteriorated rapidly since the onset of the headache. His headache is characterized by a throbbing pain on one side of his head and is best described as a ______.
   a. muscle-tension headache
   b. sinus headache
   c. migraine headache
   d. cluster headache

17. Which of the following is **NOT** one of the three clusters of symptoms associated with menstrual complaints discussed in your text?
   a. menstrual pain
   b. physiological discomfort during menstruation
   c. premenstrual syndrome
   d. postmenstrual depression

18. The absence of menstruation is known as ______.
   a. menarche
   b. amenorrhea
   c. dysmenorrhea
   d. mastalgia

19. About ______ percent of women report premenstrual symptoms severe enough to impair their social, academic, or occupational functioning.
   a. 2.5
   b. 12.5
   c. 22.5
   d. 32.5

20. Hypertension refers to ______.
   a. prolonged, excessive muscle tension
   b. prolonged, excessive nervous tension
   c. abnormally high levels of anxiety
   d. abnormally high blood pressure

True-False Questions

21. The "fight or flight" reaction occurs during the resistance stage of the general adaptation syndrome. ______

22. Many organs and glands are stimulated by both the sympathetic and parasympathetic branches of the autonomic nervous system. ______

23. Most of us seek dominance of the parasympathetic branch of the autonomic nervous system. ______

24. Stress increases our susceptibility to the common cold. ______

25. Less well-educated people are more likely to smoke cigarettes. ______

Essay Question

26. Discuss the causes of menstrual problems, their effects, and ways to cope with them.

Student Activities

Name ________________________________ **Date** ____________

<u>6.1 How Much Do We Value Health?</u>

Ask yourself and as many others as you care to, the following questions to obtain some idea of our values about health. Before you finish, consider what additional questions you could ask.

1. If you could achieve your ideal in only one of the following respects, while only achieving mediocrity in the others, which would you choose?

   a. Perfect health
   b. Perfect psychological well-being
   c. Perfect financial success
   d. Perfect career success
   e. Perfect spiritual success

   Why did you choose this one over the other ones?

2. If a new drug were to be made legally available that increased happiness by ten percent, but reduced the length of life, how many years would you be willing to forfeit to use the drug? How did you decide upon this number? What if the drug were illegal?

3. If you could sell years of your life to people willing to buy them, would you sell any? Why or why not? If you would sell some, how many would you sell and for how much money?

Name ______________________________ **Date** ______________

6.2 Health-Related Attitudes and Habits

Some good health habits are easier to acquire than others. Just as some bad health habits are more difficult to eliminate than others. Make a list of some of your current health-related attitudes and behaviors. When you have completed the list, answer the following questions:

1. Which of your health-related attitudes or behaviors is causing you the most stress or discomfort? Why?

2. What might you do to change this attitude or behavior? Identify at least three possible changes you could make.

3. What is the most difficult health-related habit for you to acquire and why is it such a problem for you?

4. What are at least two health-related attitudes or habits you would like to acquire and what can you do to help yourself acquire them?

Name ________________________________ Date ____________

6.3 The Physiology of Stress

As we learn about the autonomic nervous system and its role in our response to stress, we can create a demonstration of the response of two involuntary reactions, one in our heart rate, and one in our rate of perspiration. Changes in heart rate and perspiration are two of the physiological changes observed in stress research and also in so-called "lie detection" testing. If you can do these with a friend or classmate, you will be able to create a "balance order" of effects.

1. Alone, or together, take your resting heart rate and record the number of beats for one minute (BPM).

   Your BPM Friend's BPM

   _________ _________

2. To create a mild, temporary stressor, cough hard three times in a row. Your partner, if included, can skip the coughing this time for comparison.

   Your 2nd BPM Friend's 2nd BPM

   _________ _________

3. If applicable, change roles with your friend, and let the friend cough hard three times in a row while you relax. Then immediately count the heart rates after he or she coughs.

   Your 3rd BPM Friend's 3rd BPM

   _________ _________

4. After your heart rate(s) return to their original level, both of you cough hard three times and count BPMs until they recover to within two beats of the original level. How long does it take to recover?

   Minutes for you Minutes for your friend

   _________ _________

5. You can create a similar demonstration showing the response of the skin to a stressor. In bright light, or outside on a sunny day, look at the pad of your index finger. As you turn or tilt your finger, you will probably see it sparkle from the oils and sweat on it. These can be seen even better with slight magnification. If you wipe the finger on a cloth, the sparkle will be removed. How long does it take to return to this sparkling state if you cough as above? How long does it take if you just wait?

Activity continued on the back

Follow-Up Questions

1. Who responds stronger to the coughing?

2. How could you measure the recovery from the coughing?

3. What branch of the autonomic nervous system have you just witnessed?

4. According to the text, what other physical changes took place in response to the coughing and how could they be measured?

5. What stage or stages of the General Adaptation Syndrome have you demonstrated?

Name ______________________________ **Date** ____________

6.4 Demonstrating the Stress/Health Relationship

If you want to examine the effects of stress on health, you could ask people to record their physical ailments long before and shortly before a stressor such as final examinations. To actually do so would require that you investigate your school's human research guidelines and follow them to protect the rights and well-being of the subjects. Even if you do not attempt any actual data collection, you can design a research proposal. You will have to decide such issues as how many subjects, how health complaints can be recorded, which times recording takes place, and, if possible, how control subjects can be used to help verify any effects of stress.

1. Where can you recruit subjects and how many do you believe you will need?

2. How can your subjects' physical complaints be assessed?

3. When can you test the subjects to illustrate any effects of stress?

4. What kinds of differences, and how much in the way of differences, are necessary to verify stress effects?

7

Issues in Personal Health: Nutrition, Fitness, and Sleep

Chapter Outline

I. Nutrition

- A. Nutrients
- B. Nutrition and Health
- C. Obesity
- D. Eating Disorders
    1. Box: Adjustment in a World of Diversity: Eating Disorders: Why the Gender Gap?
    2. Box: Adjustment in the New Millennium: Will We Be Competing with Virtual Babes and Hunks in the New Millennium?

II. Fitness: Run for Your Life?

- A. Types of Exercise
- B. Effects of Exercise
    1. Box: Adjustment in the New Millennium: Will We See Gender Differences in Fitness Evaporate in the New Millennium?
    2. Box: Self-Assessment: Check Your Physical Activity and Heart Disease IQ
- C. Starting an Exercise Program
    1. Box: Adjustment in a World of Diversity: Exercise Is for Everyone: Exercise and the Physically Disabled

III. Sleep

- A. Functions of Sleep
- B. Dreams
- C. Insomnia: "You Know I Can't Sleep at Night"

IV. Adjustment and Modern Life

- A. How to Take It Off and Keep It Off - Weight, That Is
    1. Box: What Do You Say Now? Resisting an Invitation to Eat

Chapter Overview

Essential Food Elements. People need to eat proteins, carbohydrates, fats, vitamins, and minerals. Americans tend to eat too much protein and fats. Complex carbohydrates (starches) are superior to simple carbohydrates (sugars) as sources of nutrients. Cholesterol, fats, and obesity heighten the risk of cardiovascular disorders. Salt raises blood pressure. Fats and preservatives heighten the risk of cancer. Diets high in fiber, vitamins, fruit and vegetables, and fish are apparently healthful.

Factors That Contribute to Obesity. Risk factors for obesity include family history, overeating, and a low level of activity. Obese people have more fat cells, or adipose tissue, than normal-weight people.

Anorexia Nervosa. Anorexia nervosa is an eating disorder characterized by dramatic weight loss and intense fear of being overweight. Anorexic females also show amenorrhea, that is, they stop menstruating. Anorexic women have a distorted body image in which they view themselves as overweight when others perceive them as dangerously thin.

Bulimia Nervosa. In bulimia nervosa, the individual also fears becoming overweight, but goes on eating binges, especially of carbohydrates. Binge eating is followed by severe weight-loss methods such as fasting or self-induced vomiting.

Activity Patterns and Health. Physical inactivity is a risk factor for cardiovascular disease. Exercise has the benefits of promoting muscle strength, muscle endurance, flexibility, cardiorespiratory fitness, and a higher muscle-to-fat ratio. Exercise also appears to alleviate depression and anxiety and boost self-esteem.

Sleeping Patterns and Health. Sleep appears to serve a general restorative function, although the mechanisms are unclear. Sleep deprivation over a few days does not appear particularly harmful, although some cognitive lapses and drowsiness occur during the day.

Insomnia. Insomnia is a disorder in which sufferers either cannot fall asleep, cannot remain asleep, or wake up early. Many people use sleeping pills to cope with insomnia. Psychologists oppose the use of sleeping pills because people develop a tolerance for them and need progressively larger doses for them to work. Moreover, people taking sleeping pills attribute the sleep to the pills, not their own self-efficacy, making many people psychologically dependent on the pills once they've used them. Psychological methods for coping with insomnia are preferred by most psychologists. They include: lowering arousal, challenging irrational beliefs (such as the thought that something awful will happen if you don't get enough sleep tonight), using fantasy to distract yourself from the "task" of getting to sleep, and using stimulus control so that your bed comes to mean sleep to you.

Psychological Methods of Weight Control. Psychologists focus on improving nutritional knowledge (for example, substituting healthful foods for fattening, harmful foods), decreasing calorie intake, exercise in order to raise the metabolic rate, and behavior modification to help us avoid temptations and eat less.

Learning Objectives

After studying this chapter you should be able to:

1. Identify the essential food elements and discuss how nutritional patterns influence our health.

2. Describe the various factors that contribute to obesity.

3. Compare and contrast anorexia nervosa and bulimia nervosa in terms of their sufferers, symptoms, and effects.

4. Compare the various theoretical views regarding the causes of eating disorders such as anorexia nervosa.

5. Discuss the differences between aerobic and anaerobic exercise and explain the physical and psychological effects of exercise on health.

6. Discuss how exercise can be helpful to the physically disabled, explaining the types of exercises that are best for disabled people and the physical and psychological benefits exercise provides them.

7. Discuss how sleeping patterns influence our health, and summarize the research and current theories on dreams and nightmares.

8. Explain why psychologists are opposed to using sleeping pills to help people get to sleep and describe various psychological methods for coping with insomnia.

9. Identify and describe the various psychological methods for controlling your weight.

Key Terms

nutrients
proteins
carbohydrates
fats
vitamins
minerals
obesity
fat cells
adipose tissue
set point

anorexia nervosa
amenorrhea
bulimia nervosa
menarche
prepubescent
aerobic exercise
anaerobic exercise
fitness
REM sleep

activation-synthesis model
insomnia
calories
restricting the stimulus field
response prevention
chain breaking
response cost
covert reinforcement
covert sensitization

Key Terms Review

Define each of the following terms:

1. Nutrients: ____

____

2. Vitamins: ____

____

3. Minerals: ____

____

4. Adipose Tissue: ____

____

5. Set Point: ____

____

6. Anorexia Nervosa: ____

____

7. Amenorrhea: ____

____

8. Bulimia Nervosa: ____

____

9. Menarche: ____

____

10. Aerobic Exercise: ____

____

11. Anaerobic Exercise: ____

____

12. Fitness: ____

____

13. REM Sleep: ____

____

Harcourt Brace & Company

14. Activation-Synthesis Model: ____

____

15. Insomnia: ____

____

16. Calories: ____

____

17. Restricting the Stimulus Field: ____

____

18. Chain Breaking: ____

____

19. Response Cost: ____

____

20. Covert Sensitization: ____

____

Chapter Review

1. Foods provide __________, which furnish energy and the building blocks of muscle, bone, and other tissue.

2. Essential nutrients include __________, __________, __________, __________, and __________.

3. Proteins are __________ acids that serve as __________, __________, and __________.

4. Carbohydrates consist of __________, __________, and __________ and provide the body with __________.

5. Fats provide __________, nourish the __________, and store __________.

6. Vitamins are essential __________ compounds that need to be eaten regularly.

7. Vitamins like A,C, and E are __________-__________; that is, they deactivate substances in some foods (called __________ __________) that may contribute to the development of cancer.

8. __________, __________, __________ and __________, appear to reduce the risk of cancer.

9. Food is a symbol of __________ __________ and __________.

10. Research suggests that in obese people a so-called __________ gene may fail to signal the brain when one has eaten enough to satisfy one's nutritional needs.

11. Obese people and formerly obese people tend to have more __________ tissue than people of normal weight.

12. Two types of eating disorders are __________ __________, which is characterized by maintenance of abnormally low body weight and intense fear of weight gain, and __________ __________, which is characterized by recurrent episodes of binge eating followed by purging.

13. Fashion models are __________ and __________ than the average woman.

14. Two types of exercise are __________ exercise, which does not require sustained increases in oxygen consumption, and __________ exercise, which does require sustained increases in oxygen consumption.

15. The major physiological benefit of aerobic exercise is __________.

16. Exercise raises __________ rate and burns more __________ than we burn in a resting state.

17. The average man has an advantage over the average woman in muscle __________, especially in the __________ body.

18. Compared to the average woman, the average man has a heart that beats at a __________ rate and has higher levels of __________ in his bloodstream.

19. Research suggests that aerobic exercise may help alleviate feelings of __________.

20. The apparent benefits of exercise might also be attributed to:

    a. ______________________________

    b. ______________________________

    c. ______________________________

    d. ______________________________

    e. ______________________________

    f. ______________________________

21. Five suggestions you should consider when starting an exercise program are:

    a. ______________________________

    b. ______________________________

    c. ______________________________

    d. ______________________________

    e. ______________________________

22. Janet Reed's workout tape is aimed at users of __________.

23. Swimming is a low impact activity that fosters __________, __________, and __________ conditioning.

24. We spend about _________ of our adult lives sleeping.

25. Dreams are most common and vivid during _________ sleep.

26. According to the activation-synthesis model, dreams reflect primarily _________, not _________ activity.

27. Nightmares are generally the products of _________ sleep.

28. Our most common method of fighting insomnia is ____.

29. Four methods for coping with insomnia are:

a. ______________________________

b. ______________________________

c. ______________________________

d. ______________________________

30. Six methods for controlling weight are:

a. ______________________________

b. ______________________________

c. ______________________________

d. ______________________________

e. ______________________________

f. ______________________________

31. **Matching:** Match the behavior modification technique for reducing weight on the left with the appropriate example on the right.

_______ a. Restricting the stimulus field

_______ b. Avoiding triggers for eating

_______ c. Response prevention

_______ d. Using competing responses

_______ e. Chain breaking

_______ f. Successive approximations

_______ g. Making rewards contingent on desired behavior

_______ h. Response cost

_______ i. Covert sensitization

1. put your utensils down between bites
2. imagine reaching for something fattening and stopping
3. send a dollar to your least favorite cause each time you binge
4. keep fattening foods out of the house
5. eat in the dining area only
6. stuff your mouth with celery rather than ice cream or candy
7. do not eat dinner unless you have exercised during the day
8. shop from a list and stay out of the kitchen
9. eliminate fattening foods from your diet one by one

Sample Test

Multiple-Choice Questions

1. Which of the following people is **MOST** likely to have the **WORST** eating habits?
   a. a 45-year-old woman
   b. a 62-year-old man
   c. an 18-year-old woman
   d. a 25-year-old man

2. ______ are complex carbohydrates that provide vitamins, minerals, and a steady flow of energy.
   a. Sugars
   b. Salts
   c. Starches
   d. Fibers

3. Most Americans should eat ______ fat and ______ protein.
   a. less, less
   b. more, less
   c. less, more
   d. more, more

4. Fruits and vegetables are both rich in vitamin ______.
   a. A
   b. B
   c. C
   d. D

5. About one out of ______ Americans is obese.
   a. two
   b. three
   c. four
   d. five

6. Obese people have ______ than nonobese people.
   a. more adipose cells
   b. fewer adipose cells
   c. fatter adipose cells
   d. thinner adipose cells

7. The average female has ______.
   a. more than twice as much fat as muscle
   b. slightly more fat than muscle
   c. slightly more muscle than fat
   d. more than twice as much muscle as fat

8. Nicole's day is dominated by cycles of binge eating of foods rich in carbohydrates, then purging the food she has eaten to avoid getting fat. Her behavior is typical of someone with ______.
   a. anorexia nervosa
   b. Turner's syndrome
   c. Huntington's chorea
   d. bulimia nervosa

9. Jill enjoys baseball, bowling, and weight training. All of these activities are ______.
   a. aerobic
   b. anaerobic
   c. anabolic
   d. isometric

10. Activities such as weight training, push-ups, and chin-ups promote muscle ______.
    a. strength
    b. endurance
    c. fitness
    d. flexibility

11. A study comparing men who walked less than a mile a day to those who walked more than 2 miles a day found that those who walked had a ______ risk of dying from heart disease and a ______ risk of dying from cancer.
    a. lower, lower
    b. lower, higher
    c. higher, lower
    d. higher, higher

12. Research shows that sleep deprivation mainly affects ______.
   a. attention
   b. memory
   c. mood
   d. impulsivity

13. Most dreams ______.
   a. are simple extensions of the activities and problems of the day
   b. involve fantastic adventures
   c. involve attempts to resolve unconscious conflicts
   d. involve attempts to make unconscious fantasies come true

14. According to the activation-synthesis model, the neurotransmitter crucial to stimulating responses that lead to dreaming is ______.
   a. norepinephrine
   b. serotonin
   c. acetylcholine
   d. dopamine

15. Sleep preparations, such as sleeping pills, work by ______.
   a. enhancing REM sleep
   b. increasing central nervous system arousal
   c. increasing the production of neurotransmitters associated with sleep
   d. reducing arousal

16. One pound of body weight roughly equals ______ calories.
   a. 500
   b. 1,500
   c. 2,500
   d. 3,500

17. In her efforts to lower her calorie intake, Yvette now uses smaller plates, stays out of the kitchen as much as possible, shops from a list (and sticks to it), and pays attention only to her own plate while eating. These efforts are examples of ______.
   a. restricting the stimulus field
   b. avoiding powerful triggers for eating
   c. response prevention
   d. chain breaking

18. ______ to control their weight through intense exercise.
   a. Neither men nor women are likely
   b. Men are more likely than women
   c. Women are more likely than men
   d. Both men and women are equally likely

19. Lara Croft's persona is most similar to that of ______.
   a. Betty Boop
   b. Shirley Temple
   c. Barbie
   d. Indiana Jones

20. With weight training, women can develop upper body strength that is ______ that of men.
   a. superior to
   b. similar to
   c. within 20 percent of
   d. within 40 percent of

True-False Questions

21. Obesity runs in families. ______

22. College men actually prefer women to be heavier than most women expect. ______

23. The major physiological effect of aerobic exercise is increased muscle mass. ______

24. Students who pull "all nighters" rarely perform well on tests the following day. ______

25. Men complain of insomnia more frequently than women. ______

Essay Question

26. Explain why psychologists are opposed to using sleeping pills to help people get to sleep, and describe various psychological methods for coping with insomnia.

Student Activities

Name ________________________________ Date ____________

7.1 Personal Attitudes Toward Some Health-Related Issues

While considering the health-related problems below, which do you think would be the most difficult to experience? What would be next, and so forth? Rank from 1 to 5, the worst to the least troubling:

1. Type A behavior pattern _________
2. Inactive lifestyle _________
3. Obesity _________
4. Insomnia _________
5. Heart disease _________

Follow-Up Questions:

1. Considering these problems, which one is the object of the most ridicule? What defense could be offered for bashing these people?

2. Which of the problems do you think is the most difficult to correct? Why?

Activity continued on the back

3. How can one change from a Type A behavior pattern to more of a Type B behavior pattern? What social or psychological obstacles are likely to interfere with this change?

4. How much do you weigh, and what is your ideal weight? How much do you believe your ideal weight has been shaped by media influences, and, to the extent that they have, why have you let these influences determine your ideal weight?

5. How much sleep is ideal and how much do you prefer? How does it compare to how much sleep you are actually getting? What effect is it having on your daily energy levels and performance?

You will learn a great deal about health and health-related issues in this chapter. When you finish, you may find that you need to reconsider some of your answers. As always, you could ask others to reconsider their ideas about the above questions.

Name ________________________________ Date ____________

7.2 New Weight Guidelines

We can often turn to the government and other institutions for good information about nutrition, weight, and health. It might be interesting to compare your ideal weight from question 4 in activity 7.1 with a fairly new set of tables for healthy weight from the U. S. Departments of Agriculture and Health and Human Services. In comparison to previous tables and guidelines, these are more forgiving and allow a wider range of weights at each height. The source is the ***1990 Dietary Guidelines for Americans.***

Height	**Weight (in Lbs.)**	
	19 to 34 years	35 years and over
5'0"	97-128	108-138
5'1"	101-132	111-143
5'2"	104-137	115-148
5'3"	107-141	119-152
5'4"	111-146	122-157
5'5"	114-150	126-162
5'6"	118-155	130-167
5'7"	121-160	134-172
5'8"	125-164	138-178
5'9"	129-169	142-183
5'10"	132-174	146-188
5'11"	136-179	151-194
6'0"	140-184	155-200
6'1"	144-189	159-205
6'2"	148-195	164-210

Name ______________________________ **Date** ____________

7.3 Testing Our Aerobic Fitness

The text offers many reasons to exercise and quite a few guidelines for beginning and maintaining an aerobic training program. You might find the following test a challenging and rewarding way to chart your progress. Please observe the standard health precautions discussed in Chapter 7 before attempting this test if you are not already exercising, you smoke, have a family history of heart disease, are overweight, or are over 40. Time yourself and perhaps a friend or date if you care to, for a 1.5-mile run/walk. Your aerobic fitness rating can then be compared to the standards in the chart below (for all ages 13 and over).

Aerobic Fitness of Males and Females Estimated from 1.5-Mile Run*

	High (in minutes)	Low (in minutes)	Average (in minutes)
Males	9:29	12:39	11:29
Females	13:38	18:50	16:57
Sailing Team	9:54	11:49	10:43

*Source: Sharkey (no date)

You can use the 1.5-mile run to assess your status and your progress. You could also choose to repeat and time almost any similar task to measure progress. You do not have to compare yourself to any other people or a set of arbitrary standards to be motivated.

Name ______________________________ **Date** ___________

7.4 Sleep: The Gentle Tyrant or Benign Dictator?

Samuel Johnson called sleep the gentle tyrant because we cannot resist it, but we could also call sleep a benign dictator because it serves the body and mind as a clock that helps to organize the hundreds of functions that cycle through the 24-hour period. Sleep is only one of the clocks for controlling patterns that influence almost everything about us, including our moods, our intelligence, and most bodily functions. Without these clocks we might experience permanent jet lag. They seem to interact and help each other organize so we are generally at our best during the day.

One of the other clocks for controlling our body and mind is our core temperature, which is higher during our wake time and lower when we sleep. Even if we stay up all night, our temperatures still drop to their lowest levels at night and begin rising as our normal wake-up time approaches. Those functions that use core temperature for their timing go on as normal. Not so those functions that use sleep as a timer for control. Such desynchronization is largely responsible for discomfort and poor performance following a sleepless night. Usually one or two nights of sleep restores synchronization, and we feel better.

Occasionally specialists are asked to help people who have slept so poorly or inconsistently that their patterns and body clocks are confused. We often rely on oral temperature records to let us know where these people stand. Typically, if we take our temperature with an oral thermometer first thing in the morning, it will be several tenths of a degree cooler than just a few hours later. Then, in the late evening, as the day wanes, the pattern reverses and our temperature drops as our sleep time approaches. Sleep medicine specialists can use this pattern to study jet lag, depression, and other problems that seem to be highly related to the coordination of the patterns. For example, many depressed people show little or no pattern of core temperature changes.

You may find it interesting to graph your oral temperatures over the course of several days to verify this pattern, and also to see if it tends to correlate with your tendencies to be a morning person, otherwise known as a "Lark," or an evening person, known as an "Owl," or something inbetween (see activity 7.5). Morning temperatures tend to rise faster for Larks and more slowly for Owls. Knowing our own pattern can help us choose class times or design our own schedules.

With an oral thermometer, sample your temperature several times each day for one week. Plot the temperatures on the following graph. Estimate the curving lines that run through the points and best fit your data. You will find a prepared graph on the back of this page.

Activity continued on the back

Daily Oral Temperatures

Temperature	
-	
-	
-	
-	
-	
100.0	--
-	
-	
-	
-	
99.0	--
-	
-	
-	
-	
98.0	--
-	
-	
-	
-	
97.0	--
-	
-	
-	
-	
96.0	--

6AM 8AM 10AM 12PM 2PM 4PM 6PM 8PM 10PM 12AM 2AM 4AM

Time of Day

Name ______________________________ **Date** ____________

7.5 Are You a "Lark" or an "Owl"?

Some of us hit the floor running when we get up in the morning. We usually eat breakfast, prefer morning classes, and do not care to stay up too late "past our bedtime" without some very good reason. This is the pattern of "Larks," or morning people. Others of us hate getting up in the morning, avoid breakfast, and do not need an excuse to stay up late, even to watch a television show that has little attraction. This is the pattern of "Owls," or evening people. Still more of us fit neither extreme case, and fall somewhere in between. Use the questions below to create a better idea of your patterns.

1. Estimate the number of breakfasts you skip each week (0-7):

2. Estimate how often you sleep in each week (0-7):

3. Estimate how often you stay up past your best sleep time each week (0-7):

4. Estimate what time you feel and respond your very best (AM/PM):

Total the scores on questions 1 - 3: Total = __________

The higher your score, the more you are like an "owl" in your waking/sleeping pattern. Conversely, the lower your score, the more you are like a "lark."

Name ______________________________ **Date** ____________

7.6 Taming the Tyrant

Even gentle tyrants are at times unable to get their way, and so many people suffer a range of sleep-related difficulties. In addition to insomnia, as discussed in Chapter 7, some people sleep too long, some suffer from pattern disruption caused by shift work, and some people even create their own difficulties by keeping irregular sleep schedules. If we want to feel our best during the day and sleep better at night, we are told that it is best to maintain regular sleep patterns. To assess the regularity of your sleep, or lack of it, keep the following simple diary. You may want to do this exercise at the same time you keep track of your daily oral temperature (activity 7.4).

Date	Wake-Up Time	Sleep Start Time

Follow-Up Questions:

1. How much do you vary your sleep start? Various studies indicate that more than two hours' variation daily can have detrimental effects on daytime performance.

2. Do you sleep in after late nights? Research suggests that this will also decrease daytime abilities.

3. Did you experience any "Sunday night insomnia"? If we stay up later on weekends, we may delay our biological clocks and create problems, possibly including "Monday blues." It is best to keep to our regular patterns as much as possible by waking at our usual times even when we stay up late. While there is little trouble if we lose some sleep, there can be a problem if we disrupt our schedules.

8

Substance Abuse and Adjustment

Chapter Outline

I. Substance Abuse, Dependence, Intoxication, and Withdrawal

II. Alcohol

1. Box: Adjustment in a World of Diversity: Alcoholism, Gender, and Ethnicity
2. Box: Self-Assessment: Why Do You Drink?

III. Cigarettes (Nicotine)

1. Box: Self-Assessment: Why Do You Smoke?
2. Box: Adjustment in the New Millennium: Will We Find Ways to Make Nicotine (Gasp!) Good for You?

IV. Cocaine

V. Marijuana

VI. Opioids

VII. Sedatives: Barbiturates and Methaqualone

VIII. Amphetamines

IX. LSD, PCP, and Other Hallucinogenics

X. Getting There Without Drugs: Don't Just Say No, *Do* Something Else

XI. Adjustment and Modern Life

A. How to Use Self-Control Strategies to Quit and Cut Down on Smoking

Harcourt Brace & Company

Chapter Overview

Substance Abuse and Substance Dependence. Substance abuse is use of a substance despite the fact that the use is causing social, occupational, and other problems. Dependence is characterized by inability to control use, tolerance, and withdrawal symptoms.

Alcohol. Alcohol is a depressant that can induce feelings of euphoria, lead to cirrhosis of the liver, Korsakoff syndrome, cardiovascular disorders, and cancer.

Cigarettes. The active ingredient in cigarettes, that gives them their "kick," is nicotine, a stimulant. It is habit forming and smokers will work hard to sustain a certain level of nicotine in their bloodstreams. Smoking heightens the risk of cancer, cardiovascular disorders, lung and respiratory disorders, miscarriage, and - in the offspring of pregnant smokers - premature birth, low birth weight, respiratory ailments, and birth defects.

Cocaine. As a psychoactive substance, cocaine provides feelings of euphoria and bolsters self-confidence. Overdoses can lead to restlessness, insomnia, psychotic reactions, and cardiorespiratory collapse.

Marijuana. Marijuana is a mild hallucinogenic drug that produces heightened and distorted perceptions and feelings of relaxation.

Opioids. The opioids morphine and heroin are depressants that reduce pain, but they are also bought on the street because of the euphoric rush they provide. Opioids lead to physiological dependence.

Sedatives. The sedative barbiturates are depressants used to treat epilepsy, high blood pressure, anxiety, and insomnia. They lead rapidly to physiological dependence.

Amphetamines. Amphetamines are stimulants that produce feelings of euphoria when taken in high doses. High doses may also cause restlessness, insomnia, psychotic symptoms, and a crash upon withdrawal. Amphetamines, and a related stimulant called Ritalin, are commonly used to treat hyperactive children.

LSD and Other Hallucinogenics. Hallucinogenic substances produce hallucinations. They are not known to cause physiological dependence.

Learning Objectives

After studying this chapter you should be able to:

1. Compare and contrast substance abuse and substance dependence. Make sure to explain what tolerance and abstinence syndrome are as part of your discussion.
2. Summarize the various viewpoints regarding the causal factors in substance abuse and dependence.
3. Discuss the effects of alcohol and the problems associated with its abuse.
4. Discuss the effects of nicotine and the health problems associated with smoking, including passive smoking.
5. Discuss the effects of "crack" and cocaine and explain the health problems associated with their use.
6. Discuss the effects of marijuana and describe the problems associated with its use.

7. Identify the various opioids, discuss their effects, and describe the problems associated with their use.

8. Identify the various barbiturates, discuss their effects, and describe the problems associated with their use.

9. Identify some of the amphetamines, discuss their effects, and describe the problems associated with their use.

10. Discuss the effects of marijuana, LSD, and other hallucinogens and describe the problems associated with their use.

11. Describe at least five drug-free alternatives for coping with life's problems.

12. Identify and briefly explain at least five self-control strategies for quitting smoking "cold turkey."

13. Identify and briefly explain at least five self-control strategies for cutting down on smoking gradually.

Key Terms

psychoactive
substance abuse
dependence
tolerance
abstinence syndrome
delirium tremens
disorientation
hallucination
alcohol
alcoholics
binge drinking

cirrhosis of the liver
Wernicke-Korsakoff syndrome
nicotine
hydrocarbons
passive smoking
cocaine
"crack"
marijuana
psychedelic
hallucenogenic
hashish

opioids
narcotics
analgesia
morphine
heroin
methadone
barbiturates
methaqualone
amphetamines
LSD
PCP

Key Terms Review

Define each of the following terms:

1. Substance Abuse: ____

____

2. Dependence: ____

____

3. Tolerance: ____

____

4. Abstinence Syndrome: ____________________

____

5. Delirium Tremens: ____________________

____

6. Disorientation: ____________________

____

7. Alcohol: ____________________

____

8. Binge Drinking: ____________________

____

9. Cirrhosis of the Liver: ____________________

____

10. Wernicke-Korsakoff Syndrome: ____________________

____

11. Nicotine: ____________________

____

12. Hydrocarbons: ____________________

____

13. Passive Smoking: ____________________

____

14. Cocaine: ____________________

____

15. Marijuana: ____

____

16. Psychedelic: ____

____

17. Opioids: ____

____

18. Analgesia: ____

____

19. Barbiturates: ____

____

20. Amphetamines: ____

____

Chapter Review

1. **Matching:** Match the terms on the left with the appropriate descriptors or definitions on the right.

_______ a. Substance abuse

_______ b. Substance dependence

_______ c. Tolerance

_______ d. Abstinence syndrome

_______ e. Psychoactive

_______ f. Intoxication

_______ g. Disorientation

_______ h. Delirium tremens

1. having psychological effects
2. a condition characterized by sweating, restlessness, and hallucinations
3. continued use of a drug despite knowledge that it is linked to social, occupational, physical, or psychological problems
4. gross confusion
5. increasingly higher doses of a drug are needed to achieve similar effects
6. symptoms resulting from the sudden decrease in the usage of an addictive drug
7. persistent use of a drug despite efforts to cut down, marked tolerance, and withdrawal symptoms
8. a state of distorted senses and cognitions, like drunkenness

2. There is some evidence that some people may be born with a genetic __________ toward physiological dependence on certain substances, such as alcohol.

3. __________ is a tranquilizer you can buy without a prescription.

4. Men mainly metabolize alcohol in the __________, and women mainly metabolize alcohol in the __________.

5. __________ Americans and __________ Americans have the highest rates of alcoholism in the United States.

6. As a food, alcohol is __________, yet chronic drinkers are often __________.

7. Chronic drinking can lead to a number of disorders such as __________ of the liver, which has been linked to a protein deficiency, and __________-__________ syndrome, which has been linked to vitamin B deficiency.

Harcourt Brace & Company

8. The stimulant in cigarettes is __________.

9. Each cigarette smoked steals about __________ minutes from the smoker's life.

10. It is apparently the __________ in cigarette smoke that lead(s) to lung cancer.

11. __________ smoking is connected with respiratory illnesses, asthma, and other health problems and accounts for more than 50,000 deaths per year.

12. One of the prominent advocates of cocaine, at least initially, was __________.

13. Cocaine relieves __________, enhances __________, heightens __________, and bolsters __________.

14. "Crack" and "bazooka" are inexpensive because they are __________, and produce a prompt and potent __________ that wears off in a few minutes.

15. Cocaine __________ blood vessels in the brain, which can lead to problems in __________ and __________, and may eventually cause __________.

16. Marijuana helps some people relax and can __________ mood, but it can sometimes produce mild __________, and strong intoxication can induce negative symptoms such as__________, __________, and __________.

17. Marijuana impairs __________ __________ and __________ functions used in driving and the operation of other machines.

18. Opioids are a group of __________ that include __________, __________, __________, and __________.

19. Heroin was developed in Germany as a cure for physiological dependence on __________.

20. Methadone is a synthetic __________, used to treat physical dependence on __________.

21. Barbiturates include __________, __________, __________, and __________.

22. Barbiturates have been used to treat tension and __________, pain, __________, high __________ __________, and __________.

23. High doses of methaqualone can cause internal __________, __________, and __________.

24. Amphetamines stimulate areas of the brain that govern __________-__________ and exercise control over more __________ centers of the brain in hyperactive children.

25. Amphetamines include __________, __________, and a related stimulant called __________.

26. Inner-city youth are especially likely to become involved in substance abuse because of __________ usage and the effort to escape a __________ __________.

27. Many problem drinkers have lower-than-normal levels of __________.

28. The two major methods for treating children with ADHD are __________ medication and __________ __________ therapy.

29. Hallucinogenic drugs include __________, __________, __________, and __________.

30. Regular use of hallucinogenic drugs may lead to __________ and __________ dependence, but probably not __________ dependence.

31. **Matching:** Match the drug, or class of drugs, on the left with the appropriate descriptor on the right.

_______ a. Opiates

_______ b. Nicotine

_______ c. Methadone

_______ d. Barbiturate

_______ e. Methaqualone

_______ f. Cocaine

_______ g. Hallucinogenic

_______ h. Marijuana

_______ i. LSD

_______ j. Amphetamines

1. an addictive sedative used to relieve anxiety or induce sleep
2. a class of stimulants used to produce a rush or euphoria in high doses and often used to stay awake or to lose weight
3. a class of drugs that produce hallucinations and sometimes relaxation or euphoria
4. a drug that produces vivid hallucinations and claims to "expand awareness"
5. a group of addictive drugs that provide a euphoric rush but depress the nervous system and are used medicinally for the control of pain
6. an addictive depressant often referred to as "ludes"
7. a substance that helps people relax, can elevate mood, can produce mild hallucinations, and has been linked to amotivational syndrome
8. a stimulant that causes the release of adrenaline resulting in a mental "kick" but is excreted rapidly in stressful periods requiring larger doses to maintain its effects
9. an artificial drug used to allow heroin addicts to abstain from heroin without experiencing withdrawal
10. a powerful stimulant that provides feelings of euphoria and bolsters self-confidence

32. Five suggestions for quitting cigarette smoking "cold turkey" are:

a. ______________________________

b. ______________________________

c. ______________________________

d. ______________________________

e. ______________________________

33. Five suggestions for successfully cutting down gradually on your cigarette smoking are:

a. ______________________________

b. ______________________________

c. ______________________________

d. ______________________________

e. ______________________________

Sample Test

Multiple-Choice Questions

1. According to the table in your text, the number of college students reporting drug usage "during the last 30 days" has ______.
   a. declined fairly steadily since the mid-1980s
   b. remained at about the same rate since the early 1980s
   c. increased steadily since the mid-1980s
   d. decreased until 1988, when it began a steady increase into the 1990s

2. Elrod finds that he has to take more and more cocaine at a time to get the "rush" he so badly craves. The reason for this is most likely that he has developed ______.
   a. intoxication
   b. abstinence syndrome
   c. potentiation
   d. tolerance

3. Delirium tremens is an example of ______.
   a. abstinence syndrome
   b. potentiation
   c. tolerance
   d. intoxication

4. The psychodynamic explanation of substance abuse is that ______.
   a. people commonly try drugs based on the recommendation or obervation of others
   b. drug use is often linked to people's expectancies about the effects of a drug
   c. some people are born with a genetic predisposition toward physiological dependence on various drugs such as alcohol or nicotine
   d. drugs help people control or express unconscious needs and impulses

5. College students with alcoholic parents exhibit ______ muscular control when they drink and feel ______ intoxicated when they drink than do other students.
   a. less, less
   b. greater, less
   c. less, more
   d. greater, more

6. According to your text, ______ million Americans are alcoholics.
   a. 1-10
   b. 10-20
   c. 30-40
   d. 40-50

7. Currently the "big drug on campus" at American colleges is ______.
   a. cocaine
   b. nicotine
   c. marijuana
   d. alcohol

8. Nicotine appears to ______ the appetite and ______ metabolic rate.
   a. stimulate, raise
   b. depress, raise
   c. stimulate, lower
   d. depress, lower

9. About ______ Americans die from smoking-related illnesses each year.
   a. 400,000
   b. 600,000
   c. 800,000
   d. 1,000,000

10. Which of the following people is least likely to smoke cigarettes?
    a. a poor, 26-year-old Native-American male who did not finish high school
    b. a wealthy, 45-year-old Asian-American female with a master's degree
    c. a middle-class Hispanic-American female with a high school diploma
    d. a middle-class, 18-year-old white American male with some college education

11. The use of cocaine is associated with each of the following **EXCEPT** ______.
    a. grand mal seizures
    b. strokes
    c. cancer
    d. malnutrition

12. Marijuana use among college students ______.
    a. is greater now than at any previous time
    b. peaked in the 1980s and early 1990s
    c. peaked in the 1960s and 1970s
    d. peaked in the 1940s and 1950s

13. Which of the following is **NOT** true of marijuana's medicinal uses?
    a. It is known to reduce nausea and vomiting among cancer patients receiving chemotherapy.
    b. It appears to relieve fluid pressure in the eyes of glaucoma sufferers.
    c. It may offer some relief to asthma sufferers.
    d. It appears to reduce bronchial tube irritation from cigarette smoking.

14. "Soldier's disease" was the common name for physiological dependence on ______.
    a. opium
    b. heroin
    c. cocaine
    d. morphine

15. If a drug's name ends with "tal," as in phenobarbital, the drug is probably a(n) ______.
    a. analgesic
    b. barbiturate
    c. stimulant
    d. hallucinogen

16. Barbiturates are technically ______.
    a. stimulants
    b. hallucinogens
    c. opioids
    d. depressants

17. Amphetamine psychosis results in symptoms that mimic the symptoms of ______.
    a. paranoid schizophrenia
    b. conversion hysteria
    c. catatonic schizophrenia
    d. schizoid personality disorder

18. Research has found that in attempting to quit smoking, ______.
    a. neither quitting "cold turkey" nor cutting down gradually are effective
    b. quitting "cold turkey" is much more effective than cutting down gradually
    c. cutting down gradually is much more effective than quitting "cold turkey"
    d. both quitting "cold turkey" and cutting down gradually can be effective

19. Nicotine may actually aid in the treatment of each of the following disorders **EXCEPT** ______.
    a. Alzheimer's disease
    b. Huntington's disease
    c. Parkinson's disease
    d. schizophrenia

20. The most widely used program to treat alcoholism is ______.
    a. incarceration followed by drug abuse counseling
    b. commitment to in-patient drug rehabilitation facilities
    c. Alcoholics Anonymous
    d. prescription of disulfiram, which makes people physically ill when they drink alcohol

True-False Questions

21. Substance abuse is more severe than substance dependence. ______

22. Men are much more likely than women to become alcoholics. ______

23. People with schizophrenia rarely smoke. ______

24. Some people have had psychotic reactions to marijuana. ______

25. Regular use of hallucinogens can lead to physiological dependence. ______

Essay Question

26. Summarize the various viewpoints regarding the causal factors in substance abuse and dependence.

Student Activities

Name ______________________________ **Date** ____________

8.1 Personal Attitudes Toward Some Drug-Related Issues

While considering the drug-related problems discussed in the text, which of the following do you think would cause the most difficult psychological and physical health problems? What would be next, and so forth? Rank from 1 to 5, the worst to the least troubling:

1. Alcoholism ________
2. Addiction to nicotine ________
3. Addiction to heroin ________
4. Chronic marijuana use ________
5. Addiction to crack or cocaine ________

Follow-Up Questions:

1. Why do you consider your "1" choice to be the most troubling and your "5" choice to be the least troubling?

2. Considering these problems, which person is likely to be the object of the most ridicule? What defense could be offered for these people?

3. Which of the problems do you think is the most difficult to correct? Why?

8.2 Questioning Ourselves, Part I

Name ________________________________ **Date** ______________

1. If drugs were to become available that could improve life in some ways but cause life to be shorter, what choices would you make regarding your use of such drugs? How many years of your life, if any, would you give up to experience a 25 percent improvement in:

   a. Intelligence ______ years

   b. Attractiveness ______ years

   c. Physical strength ______ years

   d. Sexual enjoyment ______ years

   e. Popularity ______ years

Which, if any, were you willing to give up the most years of life for? Why?

Which, if any, were you least willing to give up any years for? Why?

What if there were a "magic" potion that could give you unlimited political power, military control, social status, or knowledge of how the universe works? Would you be willing to shorten your life for any of these? Why or why not?

8.3 Questioning Ourselves, Part II

Name ______________________________ **Date** ____________

1. Two Seattle cocktail waiters were fired because they did not want to serve a strawberry daiquiri to a pregnant woman (***Newsweek,*** 1991). It raises an issue that could quickly divide opinions. Would you favor laws that would prevent or restrict pregnant women from smoking, drinking alcohol, or abusing drugs? What would be your most important argument for such laws? On the other hand, what would be the most powerful argument against such laws?

   For:

   Against:

2. If you were throwing a party, would you serve alcohol to a pregnant woman? Justify your response.

3. When do you say when? How many alcoholic beverages at the **most** would you want to see the following people consume in one evening?

   a. Your date ____

   b. Your designated driver ____

Activity continued on the back

c. Your best friend ______

d. Your minister ______

e. The president of the United States ______

f. Your boss ______

g. Your grandparent(s) grandma ______ grandpa ______

h. Your parent(s) mother ______ father ______

i. Your sibling brother ______ sister ______

j. Yourself ______

5. Except for the designated driver, who should not drink any alcohol? How do you explain any differences in your answers? Are any sexist or ageist attitudes or stereotypes influencing your judgments?

6. What answers would you expect other people to give to these questions?

For an interesting variation of this exercise, answer these questions again as if they referred to smoking, using marijuana, or using some other illegal drug. How are your answers different this time than they were before? Why?

Name ________________________________ Date ____________

8.4 Social Approval of Alcohol Abuse

At some point in our lives we decide what our approach to alcohol should be. One influence we can document is peer pressure. If friends and roommates frequently voice approval of "getting wasted," "getting bombed," or "getting ripped," etc., it would be hard to avoid the conclusion that alcohol should be used as a drug, rather than a beverage. Try this exercise for one week:

1. How many times does someone speak of intoxication as if it is desirable or acceptable and how often is it spoken of in disapproving ways?

2. What words or phrases are used as synonyms for intoxication?

3. How many times did you catch yourself speaking of alcohol the same way?

4. How do you react to the desirable as opposed to the undesirable references? Is there a difference? Why or why not?

5. Where do you draw the line between use and abuse of alcohol? How did you decide upon where to draw the line? In other words, what are your reasons for drawing the line where you drew it?

Name ______________________________ **Date** __________

8.5 Binge Drinking

A major concern in recent years for college, and high school, administrators is "binge drinking." Each year several adolescents and young adults die, hundreds more are hospita;ized, and countless numbers made sick from bouts of binge drinking.

1. How many of your friends binge drink occassionally? Regularly? Constantly?

2. What have been the immediate and long-term effects, if any, of this drinking on their health and behavior?

3. What reason can you give for your friends binge drinking?

4. How many times, if any, have you been pressured by your friends to binge drink with them?

5. How did you feel about it and how have you reacted to this pressure?

6. If you have engaged in binge drinking, or have been tempted to binge drink, what factors were key in your drinking or in your being tempted to drink?

7. If you have never engaged in binge drinking, or have been tempted to binge drink and refused to do it, what factors were key in your decision not to do it?

Name ______________________________ **Date** __________

8.6 Does Smoking and Secondary Smoke Affect Heart Rate?

People who are allergic to or bothered by secondary cigarette smoke may not want to participate in this activity except at a distance. If you smoke or know someone who smokes, you may be able to see one of the physiological effects of nicotine first-hand. You would want to be tactful in requesting the cooperation of someone so the request is not interpreted as a challenge.

1. Take a base rate of the smoker's heart rate after a typical amount of time has passed since the last cigarette - at least an hour or so. The pulse can be monitored at the wrist or neck for one minute.

   Record here __________

2. Now, if you intend to remain close enough to be affected by the secondary smoke of the smoker, take your own heart rate before asking the smoker to light up.

   Record your heart rate here __________

3. Allow the smoker to smoke one cigarette and monitor the heart rate at the end of five minutes, even if he or she is still smoking.

   Record the smoker's second heart rate here __________

4. Record your second heart rate here __________

5. What have you been able to demonstrate?

6. Please explain your feelings, pro or con, about smokers' rights.

7. Now you may wish to compare your notes with your classmates.

Name ______________________________ Date ____________

8.7 Should Marijuana Be Legalized?

Ever since the 1960s, a national debate has continued as to whether or not marijuana should be legalized. What do you think?

Reasons for legalization: Give at least three reasons why you think marijuana should be legalized.

a.

b.

c.

Reasons to keep it illegal: Give at least three reasons why you think marijuana should not be legalized.

a.

b.

c.

Consequences (good or bad) of legalization of marijuana: List at least three positive or negative consequences you believe would result from the legalization of marijuana.

a.

b.

c.

9

Psychological Disorders

Chapter Outline

I. What Are Psychological Disorders?

II. Classifying Psychological Disorders

1. Box: Adjustment in the New Millenium: Will Your Problems Be Diagnosed by Computer?

III. Adjustment Disorders

1. Box: Adjustment in a World of Diversity: Psychological Disorders Among Native Americans - Loss of a Special Relationship With Nature?

IV. Anxiety Disorders

A. Types of Anxiety Disorders
B. Theoretical Views

V. Dissociative Disorders

A. Types of Dissociative Disorders
B. Theoretical Views

VI. Somatoform Disorders

A. Types of Somatoform Disorders

VII. Mood Disorders

A. Types of Mood Disorders
B. Theoretical Views
   1. Box: Adjustment in a World of Diversity: The Case of Women and Depression
   2. Box: Self-Assessment: Do Your Own Thoughts Put You Down in the Dumps?

VIII. Schizophrenic Disorders

A. Types of Schizophrenic Disorders
B. Theoretical Views

IX. Personality Disorders

A. Types of Personality Disorders

X. Adjustment and Modern Life

A. Suicide

1. Box: What Do You Say Now? How to Help Prevent Suicide

Chapter Overview

Psychological Disorders. Behavior is likely to be labeled disordered when it is unusual, socially unacceptable, involves faulty perception of reality, is personally distressful, dangerous, or self-defeating.

Classification of Disorders. The most commonly used system for classifying psychological disorders is the Diagnostic and Statistical Manual (DSM) of the American Psychiatric Association. The current edition of the DSM - the DSM-IV - has a multiaxial system with five axes: axes that assess clinical syndromes, personality disorders, general medical conditions, psychosocial and environmental problems, and global assessment of functioning.

Adjustment Disorders. Adjustment disorders are maladaptive reactions to one or more identified stressors that occur shortly after exposure to the stressor(s) and cause impaired functioning and signs of distress beyond that which would normally be expected. Adjustment disorders are usually resolved when the stressor is removed or the person learns to cope with it.

Anxiety Disorders. Anxiety disorders are characterized by motor tension, feelings of dread, and autonomic overarousal. Anxiety disorders include irrational, excessive fears, or phobias, panic disorder, which is characterized by sudden attacks in which people typically fear that they may be losing control or going crazy, generalized, or "free-floating" anxiety, obsessive-compulsive disorders, in which people are troubled by intrusive thoughts or impulses to repeat some activity, and the stress disorders (post-traumatic stress disorder and acute stress disorder), in which stressful events are followed by persistent fears and intrusive thoughts about them.

Dissociative Disorders. Dissociative disorders are characterized by a sudden temporary change in consciousness or self-identity. They include dissociative amnesia, or "motivated forgetting" of personal information, dissociative fugue, which involves forgetting plus fleeing and adopting a new identity, dissociative identity disorder, in which a person behaves as if distinct personalities occupy the body, and depersonalization, which is characterized by feelings that one is not real, or that one is standing outside one's body and observing one's own thought processes.

Somatoform Disorders. In somatoform disorders, people complain of physical problems, although no evidence of a medical abnormality can be found. The somatoform disorders include conversion disorder and hypochondriasis. In a conversion disorder, there is loss of a body function with no organic basis. Hypochondriacs insist that they are suffering from illnesses, although there are no medical findings to support their claims.

Mood Disorders. Mood disorders are characterized by disturbances in expressed emotions. Major depression is characterized by persistent feelings of sadness, loss of interest, feelings of worthlessness or guilt, inability to concentrate, and physical features that may include disturbances in the regulation of eating and sleeping, Feelings of unworthiness and guilt may be so excessive that they are considered delusional. In bipolar disorder there are mood swings from elation to depression and back. Manic people tend to show high energy levels, boundless optimism, pressured speech, and rapid flight of ideas.

Schizophrenia. Schizophrenia is characterized by disturbances of thought and language, such as loosening of associations and delusions, disturbances in perceptions and attention, as found in hallucinations, disturbances in motor activity, as shown by a stupor or by excited behavior, mood disturbances, as in flat or inappropriate emotional responses, and by withdrawal and autism. There are three major types of schizophrenia: disorganized, catatonic, and paranoid. Disorganized schizophrenia is characterized by disorganized delusions and vivid, abundant hallucinations. Catatonic schizophrenia is characterized by impaired motor activity. Paranoid schizophrenia is characterized by paranoid delusions.

Personality Disorders. Personality disorders are inflexible, maladaptive behavior patterns that impair personal or social functioning and are a source of distress to the individual or others. Persons with antisocial personality disorders persistently violate the rights of others and encounter conflict with the law. They show little or no guilt or shame over their misdeeds and are largely undeterred by punishment.

Learning Objectives

After studying this chapter you should be able to:

1. Explain what psychological disorders are and identify the various criteria used to decide if someone should be labeled as "disordered."
2. Explain what the DSM is, what it is used for, and what each of its axes does.
3. Explain what adjustment disorders are and identify and describe the various adjustment disorders.
4. Explain what anxiety disorders are and identify and describe the various anxiety disorders.
5. Summarize the various theoretical perspectives on anxiety disorders.
6. Explain what dissociative disorders are and identify and describe the various dissociative disorders.
7. Summarize the various theoretical perspectives on dissociative disorders.
8. Explain what somatoform disorders are and identify and describe the various somatoform disorders.
9. Explain what mood disorders are and identify and describe the various mood disorders.
10. Summarize the various theoretical perspectives on mood disorders.
11. Explain what schizophrenia is and identify and describe the three major subtypes of schizophrenia.
12. Summarize the various theoretical perspectives on schizophrenia.
13. Explain what personality disorders are and identify and describe the various types of personality disorders.
14. Summarize the various theoretical views on personality disorders.
15. Identify at least five myths about suicide and explain why each one of them is incorrect.

Key Terms

dissociative identity disorder
multiple personality disorder
insanity
schizophrenia
hallucination
ideas of persecution
DSM-IV
neuroses
CASPER
adjustment disorder
anxiety disorders
specific phobias
social phobias
claustrophobia
acrophobia
agoraphobia
panic disorder
generalized anxiety disorder
obsession
compulsion
posttraumatic stress disorder
acute stress disorder
GABA
benzodiazepines
dissociative disorders
dissociative amnesia
dissociative fugue
depersonalization
somatoform disorders
conversion disorders
la belle indifference
hypochondriasis
mood disorders
major depression
hypochondriasis
psychomotor retardation
bipolar disorder
rapid flight of ideas
learned helplessness
attributional styles
neuroticism
lithium
schizophrenia
delusions
stupor
disorganized schizophrenia
catatonic schizophrenia
waxy flexibility
mutism
paranoid schizophrenia
the dopamine theory
personality disorders
paranoid personality disorder
schizotypal personality disorder
schizoid personality disorder
antisocial personality disorder

Key Terms Review

Define each of the following terms:

1. Dissociative Identity Disorder: ______________________________

____

2. Insanity: ____

____

3. Hallucination: ____

____

4. Ideas of Persecution: ______________________________________

____

5. DSM-IV: ____

____

6. Neurosis: ____

____

7. CASPER: ____

____

8. Validity: ____

____

9. Neuroticism: ____

____

10. Compulsion: ____

____

11. La Belle Indifference: ____________________________________

____

12. Psychomotor Retardation: __________________________________

____

13. Rapid Flight of Ideas: ____________________________________

____

14. Learned Helplessness: ____________________________________

____

15. Attributional Style: ______________________________________

____

16. Autism: ____

____

17. Delusions: ____

____

18. Stupor: ____

____

19. Waxy Flexibility: ____

____

20. Mutism: ____

____

Chapter Review

1. Six criteria for determining whether somone has a psychological disorder are:

   a. ____

   b. ____

   c. ____

   d. ____

   e. ____

   f. ____

2. **Matching:** Match the Axis from the DSM on the left with its appropriate descriptor on the right.

_______ a. Axis I	1. Psychosocial and environmental problems
_______ b. Axis II	2. Global assessment of functioning
_______ c. Axis III	3. General medical conditions
_______ d. Axis IV	4. Clinical syndromes
_______ e. Axis V	5. Personality disorders

3. The DSM-IV groups disorders on the basis of __________ features or __________.

4. According to the psychodynamic model, all __________ were caused by unconscious conflict.

5. Three advantages that computer diagnostic programs offer when compared to traditional human interviewers are:

   a. ____

   ____

   b. ____

   ____

   c. ____

   ____

6. __________ disorders are maladaptive reactions to identified stressors, and are considered to be among the __________ psychological disorders.

7. Six types of anxiety disorders are:

   a. ____

   b. ____

   c. ____

   d. ____

   e. ____

   f. ____

8. Phobias can be broken down into three major types: __________ phobias, which involve excessive fears of specific objects or situations; __________ phobias, which involve persistent fears of scrutiny by others; and __________, which involves fears of being in open spaces or places from which it might be difficult to escape.

9. An __________ is a recurring thought or image that seems irrational or beyond control, whereas a __________ is a seemingly irresistible urge to engage in an act.

10. **Matching:** Match the psychological disorder on the left with its appropriate description on the right.

_______ a. Dissociative amnesia

_______ b. Dissociative fugue

_______ c. Dissociative identity disorder

_______ d. Depersonalization disorder

_______ e. Phobia

_______ f. Panic disorder

_______ g. Generalized anxiety disorder

_______ h. Obsessive-compulsive disorder

_______ i. Post-traumatic stress disorder

_______ j. Acute stress disorder

1. persistent or recurrent feelings that one is not real or is detached from one's own experience or body
2. recurring irrational and uncontrollable thoughts that lead to irresistible urges to engage in ritualistic behaviors
3. a person experiences amnesia and flees to a new location and establishes a new lifestyle
4. recurrent attacks of extreme anxiety in the absence of any known or obvious source
5. a disorder which follows an emotionally distressing event characterized by intense fear, avoidance of stimuli associated with the event, and reliving of the event
6. loss of memory or self-identity
7. two or more identities, each with distinct traits and memories, exist simultaneously within the same person
8. irrational fear of specific objects, people or situations
9. feelings of dread and foreboding and sympathetic arousal of at least one month's duration
10. symptoms involving reliving of an event, and intense fear and anxiety develop within four weeks of the event but do not persist for more than four weeks

11. In panic disorder, faulty regulation of the neurotransmitters __________ and __________ may be involved, whereas in other anxiety disorders, the brain may not be sensitive enough to ________, a neurotransmitter that may help calm anxiety reactions.

12. Four major dissociative disorders are:

a. ______________________________

b. ______________________________

c. ______________________________

d. ______________________________

13. Two types of somatoform disorders are __________ disorder, in which unconscious conflicts are turned into physical symptoms, and __________, which is marked by the persistent belief that one has a medical disorder despite the lack of medical findings.

14. Lack of concern over their severe symptoms shown by people suffering from conversion disorder is called __________ __________ __________.

15. Two types of mood disorders are __________ __________ and __________ __________.

16. Learning researchers have found links between depression and __________ __________.

17. Seligman notes that depressed people are likely to attribute their failures to __________, __________, and __________ factors.

18. Depression is often associated with the trait of __________, which is heritable.

19. Genetic research has linked susceptibility to depression with imbalances of the neurotransmitters __________ and __________.

20. __________ has been referred to as the worst disorder affecting human beings.

21. Three types of delusions are delusions of __________, delusions of __________, and delusions of __________.

22. Three types of schizophrenia are the __________ type, which is characterized by disorganized delusions and vivid hallucinations, the __________ type, which is characterized by striking impairment in motor activity, and the __________ type, which is characterized by delusions, usually of persecution, and by vivid hallucinations.

23. According to psychodynamic theory, schizophrenia occurs because the __________ is overwhelmed by impulses from the __________, leading to regression to an early phase of the __________ stage.

24. Schizophrenic persons constitute about __________ percent of the general population, but children with one schizophrenic parent have about a __________ percent chance of developing schizophrenia, and children with two schizophrenic parents have about a __________ percent chance of developing the disorder.

25. Most investigators today favor a __________ model for the causes of schizophrenia.

26. __________ disorders are characterized by enduring patterns of inflexible and maladaptive behaviors that impair personal and social functioning.

27. **Matching:** Match the personality disorder on the left with the appropriate description on the right.

_______ a. Paranoid personality disorder

_______ b. Schizotypal personality disorder

_______ c. Schizoid personality disorder

_______ d. Antisocial personality disorder

1. characterized by social withdrawal and indifference
2. characterized by persistent suspiciousness
3. characterized by oddities of thought, perception, and behavior
4. characterized by frequent conflict with society undeterred by punishment and with little or no guilt, remorse, or anxiety

28. People with antisocial personality disorder often show lower-than-normal levels of __________.

Harcourt Brace & Company

29. Compared to females, males are more likely to choose __________-acting and __________-lethal means to attempt suicide.

30. Suicide attempts are more frequent following __________ life events, especially events that involve loss of __________ __________.

31. Four common, but untrue, myths about suicide are:

a. ____________________

b. ____________________

c. ____________________

d. ____________________

32. Five things you can do to help someone who has threatened suicide while talking to you are:

a. ____________________

b. ____________________

c. ____________________

d. ____________________

e. ____________________

Sample Test

Multiple-Choice Questions

1. The **LEGAL**, not psychological, term meaning incapable of rational judgment or recognizing right from wrong is ______.
   a. mental illness
   b. psychosis
   c. schizophrenia
   d. insanity

2. Collecting yarn and rolling it into a 12-foot ball in your backyard, walking backward everywhere you go, or becoming the only person on your street to paint your house "Day-Glo" orange are examples of ______.
   a. self-defeating behavior
   b. unusual behavior
   c. socially unacceptable behavior
   d. faulty perception of reality

3. The current edition of the DSM is the ______.
   a. DSM-II
   b. DSM-III
   c. DSM-IV
   d. DSM-V

4. Deeply ingrained maladaptive ways of perceiving others and notable problem personality traits are described under _______ of the DSM-IV.
   a. Axis I
   b. Axis II
   c. Axis III
   d. Axis IV

5. Psychiatrist Thomas Szasz believes that disorders described in the DSM are ______.
   a. not really disorders at all
   b. biologically caused and should be treated with chemotherapy
   c. learned in early childhood and should be treated with behavioral methods
   d. caused by a failure to self-actualize and require spiritual growth and exploration to "cure" them

6. Nancy broke up with her boyfriend about three months ago. She has felt depressed and has been unable to keep up with her schoolwork since. She just mopes around thinking of her lost love. She is best diagnosed as having _______ disorder.
   a. a personality
   b. a conversion
   c. an adjustment
   d. posttraumatic stress

7. Shelly has an irrational fear of leaving her home or being in crowds where it might be difficult to escape. Her fears are best described as ______.
   a. agoraphobia
   b. claustrophobia
   c. acrophobia
   d. hydrophobia

8. A recurring thought, which appears irrational, such as powerful and persistent doubts that you have locked your doors and windows even after you have checked them, is called ______.
   a. an obsession
   b. a delusion
   c. a phobia
   d. a compulsion

9. Disorders characterized by disturbances in normal functions of identity, memory, or consciousness that distort our ability to feel whole are called ______ disorders.
   a. anxiety
   b. somatoform
   c. dissociative
   d. personality

10. Social-cognitive theorists generally regard dissociative disorders as being maintained by ______.
    a. punishment
    b. repression
    c. negative reinforcement
    d. positive reinforcement

11. "La belle indifference" is a characteristic symptom of ______.
   a. schizoid personality
   b. dissociative fugue
   c. hypochondriasis
   d. conversion disorder

12. The so-called "common cold" of psychological problems is ______.
   a. depression
   b. hypochondriasis
   c. phobia
   d. generalized anxiety

13. Which of the following sets of attributions is most closely linked to depression and helplessness and is most difficult to change?
   a. external, stable, and specific
   b. external, stable, and global
   c. internal, unstable, and specific
   d. internal, stable, and global

14. Deficiencies of ______ may be linked with depression.
   a. serotonin alone
   b. serotonin combined with deficiencies of dopamine
   c. serotonin combined with deficiencies of noradrenaline
   d. serotonin combined with excess noradrenaline

15. George believes he is Napoleon. Joyce believes she is Madonna. These people are both experiencing ______.
   a. hallucinations
   b. delusions of reference
   c. delusions of persecution
   d. delusions of grandeur

16. Ned's behavior is characterized by vivid delusions and hallucinations that often involve sexual or religious themes, as well as giddiness, nonsensical speech, and lack of hygiene. He is most likely suffering from ______.
   a. conversion schizophrenia
   b. disorganized schizophrenia
   c. paranoid schizophrenia
   d. catatonic schizophrenia

17. Twin studies have found about a ______ percent concordance rate for the occurrence of schizophrenia among pairs of monozygotic (identical) twins.
   a. 20-30
   b. 40-50
   c. 60-70
   d. 80-90

18. Elwood's behavior is marked by an absence of psychotic behavior, but the presence of excessive fantasy and suspicion, odd word usages, and feelings of being unreal. He is most likely suffering from ______.
   a. schizotypal personality
   b. disorganized schizophrenia
   c. schizoid personality
   d. antisocial personality

19. Which of the following people is most likely to commit suicide?
   a. a teenage male
   b. a teenage female
   c. an elderly male
   d. an elderly female

20. Native Americans attribute their psychological problems to ______
   a. loss of their traditional culture
   b. spiritual weakness
   c. lack of a competitive ethic
   d. flaws in their traditional culture

True-False Questions

21. Disorders are grouped by the DSM on the basis of theoretical speculation about their origins. _____

22. Adjustment disorders are among the most severe psychological disorders. _____

23. Agoraphobia is rare among adults. _____

24. Women are more likely than men to be diagnosed with major depression. _____

25. Men are more likely than women to exhibit antisocial personality disorder. _____

Essay Question

26. Explain what anxiety disorders are and identify and describe the various anxiety disorders.

Student Activities

Name ________________________________ Date ____________

9.1 What Is Abnormal?

When legal cases such as John Hinckley's and Billy Milligan's involve pleas of "not guilty by reason of insanity," it is common to read that the defense was able to find expert witnesses who testified the defendant was "insane," while the prosecution was also able to call expert witnesses who testified the defendant was "sane." Who is right? Much of the problem is created by the difficulty of defining insanity. The same problem occurs when we try to define abnormal. It is easy to recognize the extreme cases, but often difficult to decide the cases in between, which are the majority. Consider the text's criteria of psychological disorder and think of a case that satisfies the definition, yet would not be likely to be called abnormal. For example, wearing bow ties or beehive hair styles may be unusual, which is the first criterion, but will not cause a diagnosis of "psychological disorder."

1. Identify an **unusual behavior** that is not an example of a psychological disorder. Why is it not a disorder?

2. Identify an **unacceptable behavior** that is not an example of a psychological disorder. Why is it not a disorder?

3. What **faulty perception of reality** is not an example of a psychological disorder? Why is it not a disorder?

4. When might **severe personal distress** fail to be considered an example of a psychological disorder? Why is it not a disorder?

5. Name a **self-defeating behavior** that would not be an example of a psychological disorder. Why is it not a disorder?

Activity continued on the back

6. Name a behavior that is **dangerous** but not considered an example of a psychological disorder. Why is it not a disorder?

7. For a real challenge, identify a behavior that is all of the above, or as much of the above as possible, but is not regarded as a psychological disorder.

8. Now write an alternative definition of psychological disorder. (If you can manage this, you might become famous!)

9. Which theoretical model of psychological disorders would your definition best fit? Why?

Name ______________________________ **Date** ____________

9.2 Checking Our Attitudes Toward People With Psychological Disorders

Suppose the government leased the apartments or home next door to your residence and converted them into use for the following people. Which types of handicaps or disorders, if any, would create the most discomfort for you? Rank each from 1 to 4, with 1 representing the most alarming, and 4 representing the least alarming.

_____ Mentally retarded

_____ Psychologically disordered

_____ Recovering alcoholics

_____ Returning convicted criminals

1. What would be your worst fears in each case above?

   1.

   2.

   3.

   4.

2. Ask others the same questions and record their responses here:

   1.

   2.

   3.

   4.

Activity continued on the back

3. Have you any evidence that prejudices exist against the people who are labeled psychologically disordered? If so, what is it?

4. Why do you believe that prejudices exist against people who are labeled as being psychologically disordered?

5. What are three things you believe can be done to help alleviate prejudices against the psychologically disordered?

6. What ill effects could prejudices cause the psychologically handicapped?

Name ______________________________ **Date** ____________

9.3 You Make the Diagnosis

Diagnosis is not always as easy as it looks, and diagnosticians can disagree about a label easily if certain features of a person's problems are more prominent at some times and not at other times, or if behaviors associated with one disorder can be associated with a different disorder as well. For instance, people can cry when they are sad, but people can also cry when they are happy. Take another look at the case of "Bonnie" in Chapter 9 and answer these questions:

1. Which of her behaviors could lead to a diagnosis of **phobia**? Why?

2. Which of her behaviors could lead to a diagnosis of **depression**? Why?

Name________________________________ **Date** ________________

9.4 A Second Look at Bonnie's Case

Good diagnosticians want to look for a phenomenon known as **secondary gain**. Secondary gain occurs when the disorder results in rewards. An example in the text described the inability to fly missions when some bomber pilots developed a type of conversion disorder, including night blindness. You may remember that memory failures in dissociative disorders were linked to avoidance of painful thoughts, and thus can also illustrate secondary gain.

1. Can you detect any possible secondary gain for Bonnie? If so, what is it?

2. In your opinion, what is the merit in hypothesizing that secondary gain plays any role in the problems Bonnie is experiencing?

3. How could you test to see whether secondary gain is involved or not?

4. Is it necessary to assume that secondary gain is the only principle that is needed to explain Bonnie's difficulties? Why or why not?

Name ______________________________ Date __________

9.5 Finding Help for Someone Considering Suicide

After reading the discussion of suicide, you probably found the suggestions for helping someone who is contemplating suicide quite valuable. In a real crisis it might be difficult to comply quickly with some of the recommendations, including finding professional help. Answer these questions and you can be steps ahead in a real crisis.

1. What is the phone number of a "hotline" (other than 911) you can call?

2. How long did it take you to answer question number one? What problems did you run into? If you gathered the results for your class, the emergency service that administers the hotline might appreciate learning your results.

3. Does your school have a counseling center or any service that can respond to emergencies, including potential suicide? Does this service have data on the frequency of emergency phone calls? Is it a 24-hour service? How would someone in crisis typically access this service?

Harcourt Brace & Company

10

Therapies: Ways of Helping

Chapter Outline

I. What Is Therapy?

II. Psychoanalysis

A. Traditional Psychoanalysis: Where Id Was, There Shall Ego Be
B. Modern Psychoanalysis

III. Phenomenological Therapies

A. Client-Centered Therapy: Removing Roadblocks to Self-Actualization
C. Gestalt Therapy: Getting It Together

IV. Behavior Therapy: Adjustment Is What You Do

A. Fear-Reduction Methods
B. Aversive Conditioning
C. Operant Conditioning Techniques
D. Self-Control Techniques

V. Cognitive Therapies

A. Cognitive Therapy: Correcting Cognitive Errors
B. Rational-Emotive Therapy: Shutting Ten Doorways to Distress
    1. Box: Self-Assessment: Are You Making Yourself Miserable? The Irrational Beliefs Questionnaire

VI. Group Therapy

A. Encounter Groups
B. Family Therapy

VII. Does Psychotherapy Work?

1. Box: Adjustment in a World of Diversity: Should We Match Clients and Therapists According to Ethnicity?

Harcourt Brace & Company

VIII. Biological Therapies

A. Drug Therapy
   1. Box: Adjustment in the New Millennium: Looking Ahead to "Designer Drugs"
B. Electroconvulsive Therapy
C. Psychosurgery

IX. Adjustment and Modern Life

A. Psychotherapy and Human Diversity

Chapter Overview

Psychotherapy. Psychotherapy is a systematic interaction between a therapist and a client that brings psychological principles to bear in helping the client overcome psychological disorders or to adjust problems in living.

Psychoanalysis. Psychoanalysis is the treatment approach originally developed by Sigmund Freud. Its goals are to provide self-insight, allow the spilling forth (catharsis) of psychic energy, and replace defensive behavior with coping behavior. It uses the methods of free association and dream analysis. Modern psychoanalytic approaches are briefer and more directive than Freud's approach, and the therapist and client usually sit face to face.

Client-Centered Therapy. Client-centered therapy was developed by Carl Rogers. It uses nondirective methods to help clients overcome obstacles to self-actualization. Therapists show unconditional positive regard, empathic understanding, and genuineness.

Behavior Therapy Methods for Fear Reduction. These include flooding, systematic desensitization, and modeling. Systematic desensitization counterconditions fears by gradually exposing clients to fear-evoking stimuli while they remain deeply relaxed.

Aversive Conditioning. This is a behavior-therapy method for discouraging undesirable behavior by repeatedly pairing the goals (for example, alcohol, cigarette smoke, deviant sex objects) with aversive stimuli so that the goals become aversive rather than tempting.

Operant Conditioning. This is a behavior therapy method that fosters adaptive behavior through principles of reinforcement. Examples include extinction of maladaptive behavior, successive approximations, social skills training, and biofeedback training.

Self-Control Methods. These are behavior therapy methods for adopting desirable behavior patterns and breaking bad habits. They focus on modifying the antecedents of behavior, the behavior itself, and reinforcers.

Cognitive Therapy. Cognitive therapies aim to provide clients with insight into irrational beliefs (such as excessive needs for approval and perfectionism) and cognitive distortions, and to replace these cognitive errors with rational beliefs and accurate perceptions. Beck reports that clients may become depressed because of minimizing accomplishments, catastrophizing failures, and general pessimism.

Group Therapy. Group therapy is more economical than individual therapy. Moreover, group members profit from one another's social support and experiences.

Does Psychotherapy Work? Apparently it does. People receiving most forms of psychotherapy fare better than people left untreated. Psychoanalytic and person-centered approaches are particularly helpful with highly verbal and motivated individuals. Cognitive and behavior therapies are probably most effective, and behavior therapy also helps in the management of retarded and severely disturbed populations.

Practicing Psychotherapy With Clients from Ethnic Minority Groups. Various cultural and ethnic factors are related to therapeutic process with African Americans, Asian Americans, Hispanic Americans, and Native Americans. For example, clinicians must avoid stereotypes and be sensitive to the values, languages, and cultural beliefs of members of minority groups.

Drug Therapy. Antipsychotic drugs often help schizophrenic individuals, apparently by blocking the action of dopamine. Antidepressants often help severely depressed people, apparently by raising the levels of noradrenaline and serotonin. Lithium often helps persons with bipolar disorder, apparently by moderating levels of noradrenaline.

Electroconvulsive Therapy (ECT). ECT passes an electrical current through the temples, inducing a seizure and frequently relieving major depression.

Psychosurgery. Psychosurgery is an extremely controversial method for alleviating severe agitation by severing nerve pathways in the brain.

Learning Objectives

After studying this chapter you should be able to:

1. Explain what psychotherapy is, describing its essential features.
2. Describe the goals and methods of psychoanalysis, and explain how modern psychodynamic approaches differ from traditional psychoanalysis.
3. Explain what client-centered therapy is, what its methods are, and discuss the qualities of a client-centered therapist.
4. Explain what Gestalt therapy is, describing its essential features and techniques.
5. Describe the goals and methods of behavior therapy, and briefly describe at least three behavior therapy methods for reducing fears.
6. Compare and contrast aversive conditioning and operant conditioning, identifying several specific types of operant conditioning in your discussion.
7. Identify several self-control methods, explaining their focus and how they work.
8. Describe the goals and methods of Beck's cognitive therapy.
9. Describe the philosophy, goals, and methods of Ellis's rational emotive behavior therapy.
10. Compare and contrast individual therapy with group therapy, and briefly describe at least two types of group therapy.

Harcourt Brace & Company

11. Summarize the research on the efficacy of psychotherapy, and explain the problems associated with conducting this type of research.

12. Identify three biological approaches to therapy, explaining how they work and any problems associated with them.

13. Discuss the issues involved in the practice of psychotherapy with clients from ethnic minority groups.

Key Terms

psychotherapy
psychoanalysis
insight
catharsis
free association
compulsion to utter
resistance
interpretation
wish fulfillment
manifest content
latent content
phallic symbol
ego analyst
phenomenological therapy
client-centered therapy
unconditional positive regard
empathic understanding
frames of reference
genuineness
Gestalt therapy
dialogue
behavior therapy
systematic desensitization
hierarchy
modeling
aversive conditioning
rapid smoking
token economy
successive approximations
social-skills training
biofeedback training
functional analysis
cognitive therapies
Beck's cognitive therapy
cognitive triad
overgeneralize
magnify
absolutist thinking
rational-emotive therapy
catastrophize
irrational beliefs
group therapy
encounter groups
family therapy
nonspecific factors
meta-analysis
biological therapies
drug therapy
minor tranquilizers
rebound anxiety
major tranquilizers
antidepressant drugs
lithium
electroconvulsive therapy (ECT)
psychosurgery
acculturation
Cuento therapy
feminist psychotherapy

Key Terms Review

Define each of the following terms:

1. Insight: ______________________________

____

2. Catharsis: ______________________________

____

3. Free Association: ______________________________

____

4. Compulsion to Utter: ______________________________

____

5. Resistance: ______________________________

____

6. Ego Analyst: ______________________________

____

7. Unconditional Positive Regard: ______________________________

____

8. Frames of Reference: ______________________________

____

9. Dialogue: ______________________________

____

10. Systematic Desensitization: ______________________________

____

11. Catastrophize: ______________________________

____

12. Token Economy: ______________________________

____

13. Successive Approximations: ______________________________

____

14. Modeling: ______________________________

____

15. Functional Analysis: ____

____

16. Encounter Group: ____

____

17. Rebound Anxiety: ____

____

18. Major Tranquilizer: ____

____

19. Electroconvulsive Therapy: ____

____

20. Psychosurgery: ____

____

Chapter Review

1. Four essential elements of psychotherapy are:

   a. ____

   b. ____

   c. ____

   d. ____

2. __________ is the clinical method devised by Sigmund Freud which seeks to allow clients to express repressed __________ and __________, and provide __________ into the conflicts at the root of the clients' problems.

3. For Freud, clients' compulsions to the process of __________ __________, the uncensored expression of all thoughts that come to mind, was crucial to achieve the phenomenon of __________, in which the client felt relief from the expression of previously repressed feelings and impulses.

4. For Freud, unconscious urges tend to be expressed in dreams as a form of __________ __________.

5. In psychodynamic theory, dreams contain both __________, or shown, content and __________, or hidden, content.

6. Modern psychoanalysts put more emphasis on the __________ than did Freud.

7. Phenomenological therapists focus on clients' __________, __________ experiences, and focus on the __________.

8. Three qualities shown by the person-centered therapist are:

   a. ____

   b. ____

   c. ____

9. Gestalt therapy aims to help people ______________________________

   ____

10. A Gestalt therapy technique in which people verbalize conflicting parts of their personality is called __________.

11. Behavior therapists rely heavily on principles of __________ and __________ learning.

12. Three methods behavior therapists use for reducing fears are __________, __________ __________, and __________.

13. Systematic desensitization assumes that maladaptive behaviors are __________ and, therefore, can be eliminated through __________.

14. The use of rapid smoking to cure cigarette smoking is a form of __________ conditioning.

15. Four operant conditioning methods for managing behavior problems are:

a. ______________________________

b. ______________________________

c. ______________________________

d. ______________________________

16. Three behavioral self-control strategies aimed at stimuli that trigger unwanted behavior are:

a. ______________________________

b. ______________________________

c. ______________________________

17. Three behavioral self-control strategies aimed directly at unwanted behavior are:

a. ______________________________

b. ______________________________

c. ______________________________

18. Five behavioral self-control strategies aimed at reinforcements of behavior are:

a. ______________________________

b. ______________________________

c. ______________________________

d. ______________________________

e. ______________________________

19. According to Beck's "cognitive triad," depressed people expect the worst of __________, the __________ at large, and their __________.

20. Four basic types of cognitive errors noted by Aaron Beck are:

a. ______________________________

b. ______________________________

c. ______________________________

d. ______________________________

21. Albert Ellis believed in an "ABC" approach to psychological problems in which __________ events lead to __________ which result in __________. Ellis believed that many people hold __________ beliefs that lead to __________.

22. Five commonly held irrational beliefs described by Ellis are:

a. ______________________________

b. ______________________________

c. ______________________________

d. ______________________________

e. ______________________________

23. Six advantages to group therapy include:

a. ______________________________

b. ______________________________

c. ______________________________

d. ______________________________

e. ______________________________

f. ______________________________

24. Encounter groups are not appropriate for treating __________ __________ problems; rather, they are meant to promote __________ __________.

25. Family therapists usually assume that the identified patient is a __________ for other problems within and among family members.

26. Two types of problems in evaluating methods of psychotherapy include:

    a. ____

    b. ____

27. Research on the effectiveness of therapy has relied heavily on a technique termed __________-__________.

28. Most psychotherapists in the United States are __________ Americans whose primary language is __________.

29. Three types of biological therapies are __________, __________ __________, and __________.

30. Four classes of drugs used in chemotherapy for psychological disorders are:

    a. ____

    b. ____

    c. ____

    d. ____

31. Electroconvulsive therapy is used mainly for people with severe __________.

32. African Americans and Asian Americans tend to __________ people with psychological disorders.

33. Many Asians experience psychological complaints as __________ __________.

34. Three measures that can be adapted by therapists to bridge the gap between psychotherapists and Hispanic-American clients are:

    a. ____

    b. ____

    c. ____

35. Efforts to help Native Americans should focus on strengthening their cultural __________, __________, and __________, in addition to helping them regain a sense of __________ over their world.

36. Feminist therapy developed as a response to __________ __________ of health professions and institutions.

37. The great majority of gay males and lesbians are __________ with their sexual orientation and seek therapy because of conflicts that arise from __________ __________ and __________.

Sample Test

Multiple-Choice Questions

1. Which of the following is **NOT** one of the three types of clients commonly seen by psychologists, according to your text?
   a. people who are sent to therapy as an alternative to going to jail
   b. people who have been diagnosed with psychological disorders
   c. people who seek help in adjusting to problems
   d. people who wish to develop as individuals

2. A client, when asked to discuss a threatening issue, claims that she can't remember or that her mind has gone blank. The client's reaction was labeled ______ by Freud.
   a. catharsis
   b. regression
   c. sublimation
   d. resistance

3. A man dreams that he is flying. According to Freud, flying represents erection and sexual potency. In this case, sexual potency is the ______ content of the dream.
   a. primary
   b. secondary
   c. manifest
   d. latent

4. Newer methods of psychoanalysis differ from Freud's approach in that they focus more on the _____ and less on the ______.
   a. id, superego
   b. ego, superego
   c. superego, id
   d. ego, id

5. Phenomenological therapies focus on ______.
   a. internal conflicts and unconscious processes
   b. the quality of clients' subjective, conscious, experience
   c. biological roots to psychological problems
   d. the role of environmental factors in shaping human behavior

6. Elwood goes to his therapist to get treatment for his severe depression. His therapist is directive, focusing on the here and now in an effort to heighten Elwood's awareness of current feelings and behaviors. Elwood's therapist is practicing ______.
   a. person-centered therapy
   b. psychoanalysis
   c. Gestalt therapy
   d. transactional analysis

7. Techniques such as systematic desensitization, flooding, and modeling are essential to ______ therapy.
   a. client-centered
   b. Gestalt
   c. cognitive
   d. behavior

8. Elwood goes to his therapist to try and get help in quitting smoking. His therapist makes him engage in rapid smoking in which he must inhale every 6 seconds, while cigarette smoke is being blown in his face by a hair dryer positioned in back of 10 other cigarettes. This technique is called ______.
   a. operant conditioning
   b. systematic desensitization
   c. aversive conditioning
   d. participant modeling

9. Elwood goes to his therapist to get help quitting smoking. His therapist tells him to set up a "smoking chair" in the basement of his home. He can smoke as much as he wants, but **ONLY** in that chair. The therapist is using ______.
   a. stimulus control
   b. restriction of the stimulus field
   c. stimuli avoidance
   d. chain breaking

10. Overgeneralizing, magnifying, selective perception, and absolutist thinking are important parts of ______.

a. rational-emotive behavior therapy
b. person-centered therapy
c. Beck's cognitive therapy
d. Skinner's behavior therapy

11. The originator of rational-emotive behavior therapy is ______.

a. Aaron Beck
b. Spencer Rathus
c. Albert Ellis
d. Albert Bandura

12. Groups that encourage personal growth in individuals by heightening their awareness of their needs, the needs of others, and the ways in which they relate to others; where growth is sought and the focus of the group is on the "here and now" are called ______ groups.

a. marathon
b. encounter
c. sensitivity training
d. psychodrama

13. A technique that combines and averages the results of numerous individual studies is called a(n) ______.

a. analysis of variance
b. factor analysis
c. reciprocal analysis
d. meta-analysis

14. ______ therapies are effective with psychotic disorders.

a. Neither psychodynamic nor person-centered
b. Psychodynamic but not person-centered
c. Person-centered but not psychodynamic
d. Psychodynamic and person-centered

15. Librium, Serax, and Xanax are all ______.

a. antianxiety drugs
b. antipsychotic drugs
c. antidepressant drugs
d. stimulants

16. ______ is frequently used to treat major depression among patients who have not responded to antidepressant drugs.

a. Psychosurgery
b. Major tranquilization
c. Hallucinogenic drug therapy
d. Electroconvulsive shock therapy

17. The most controversial and well-known psychosurgical technique is the ______.

a. prefrontal lobotomy
b. split-brain operation
c. brain transplant
d. spinal tap

18. Each of the following statements is true **EXCEPT** _______.

a. Mental health problems carry a severe social stigma among Asian Americans.
b. Asian Americans prefer an unstructured, open-ended, ambiguous style of therapy to structured, highly directive approaches.
c. Asian Americans may have little understanding of, or faith in, Western psychotherapeutic approaches.
d. Asian Americans often use somatic terms to convey emotional distress.

19. The American Psychological Association ______.

a. has never considered homosexuality to be a psychological disorder
b. considered homosexuality to be a psychological disorder until 1973
c. did not consider homosexuality to be a psychological disorder until 1973
d. has always considered, and still considers, homosexuality to be a psychological disorder

20. There are about ______ different kinds of receptors in the brain for dopamine.
    a. 5
    b. 10
    c. 15
    d. 20

True-False Questions

21. Traditional psychoanalysis teaches people to repress self-destructive impulsive urges. ______

22. Modern psychoanalysis is nondirective. ______

23. Aaron Beck's therapy methods help clients detect self-defeating thoughts. ______

24. Encounter groups can be damaging when they urge overly rapid disclosure of intimate matters. ______

25. Antidepressant drugs are called minor tranquilizers. ______

Essay Question

26. Identify three biological approaches to therapy, explaining how they work and any problems associated with them.

Student Activities

Name ________________________________ Date ____________

10.1 Asking Ourselves

After reading this chapter on therapies, you probably will have some opinions about psychotherapies. If you have not read the chapter yet, look at the first question and keep it in mind as you read.

1. If you or someone you know were looking for a psychotherapist, which system or type of therapy would you choose or recommend and why?

2. Now consult the yellow pages of your local phone directory under the two headings "psychologists" and "psychiatrists" (the latter are often listed under physicians). Which schools of psychotherapy are represented, and is your choice included?

3. Without asking, write down how you believe your adjustment instructor would answer question number 1 above. Why do you believe this to be true? Even if your instructor has no preference, he or she might be interested in knowing what kind of impression you have.

Name ______________________________ **Date** ____________

10.2 As Simple as ABC

Based on the discussion of Albert Ellis's Rational Emotive Therapy, try to interpret the following situation and offer some hypothetical assistance. A student-acquaintance informs you that he or she has failed an important exam in a required math class and is depressed and considers the situation in that class hopeless.

1. What is "A," the activating event?

2. What seems to be the "C," or consequences in this case?

3. Which irrational belief(s), or "B," could be applicable in this example?

4. What arguments would you propose to dispute these irrational beliefs?

5. What was the last event that upset you?

6. What feelings and thoughts did that event cause?

7. Which irrational belief or beliefs could account for your responses?

8. How would Albert Ellis challenge the ABC's in your example?

Name ______________________________ Date ____________

10.3 Constructing the Anxiety Item Hierarchy

To conduct systematic desensitization, clients help their therapists to arrange disturbing stimuli in an order of increasing challenge known as an anxiety item hierarchy. For this exercise, choose a topic, behavior, or situation you associate with fear or anxiety. It does not need to be something that results in feelings of phobic proportions. For example, it could be competing in a race, telling the boss she or he made a mistake, looking over the edge of "Lover's Leap," or taking lessons in scuba. Some people find that the construction of the hierarchy alone can reduce some of their apprehension.

1. Identify one item for a hierarchy that could be the first and least disturbing item. For example, related to the challenges discussed above, first items could be registering one week before the race, telling the boss the mail has arrived, standing 100 feet from the edge of Lover's Leap, or calling the scuba school to inquire about the cost of lessons.

2. Now identify the most distressing situation you can imagine for the challenge you have chosen. Again, for example: a competitor says "You don't belong in the race," the boss yells "You're fired," you lean over the edge of the cliff, or you find no air coming to the mouthpiece.

3. Now for your challenge, arrange eight to eighteen stimuli inbetween the two you have chosen, trying your best to make the perceived difference between each item about equal. If you have chosen a complex situation to cope with, it may take more than 20 items in your hierarchy, so don't hesitate to write more.

Name ________________________________ Date ____________

10.4 Identifying Caffeine Consumption

Among the self-control techniques outlined in this chapter is the functional analysis of behavior. By recording information about problem behaviors, including the stimuli that encourage the behavior, and the situation in which the behavior occurs, we may see change occur in reaction to functional analysis, or at least gain ideas about the steps that could lead to successful intervention. For our project we can focus on consumption of caffeine. Prepare a note card so you can record caffeine consumption, including all caffeinated beverages and over-the-counter medications you use, the time, location, and rewards for use. Remember the colas, Dr Pepper, Mountain Dew, chocolate, some analgesics, and some cold preparations are likely candidates for inclusion. You may find possible rewards include stimulation, socialization, prevention of headaches, or you may chalk it up to simple "habit." Can you record any adverse consequences you experience caused by caffeine, such as sleeplessness, nervousness, headaches, stomach complaints, and so on?

Follow-Up Questions:

1. What situations prompt you to use caffeine?

2. What effects, if any, have you noticed if you fail to get your average daily dosage of caffeine? How have you dealt with those effects?

3. What is the average number of doses of caffeine taken per day? How does this compare to numbers reported by classmates?

4. What self-control strategies could help reduce your caffeine consumption based on your functional analysis?

Harcourt Brace & Company

11

Methods of Coping: Ways of Helping Ourselves

Chapter Outline

I. Stress Management
- A. Defensive Coping
- B. Active Coping

II. Controlling Stressful Cognitions
- A. Controlling Irrational and Catastrophizing Thoughts

III. Coping with the Type A Behavior Pattern
- A. Alleviating Your Sense of Time Urgency
- B. Alleviating Your Hostility

IV. Enhancing Psychological Hardiness
- A. Situational Reconstruction: "It's Not So Bad, But How Can You Make It Better?"
- B. Focusing: "What's Really Bothering You?"
- C. Compensatory Self-Improvement: "If Love Eludes You, Take Up Skiing?"

V. Coping with Emotional Responses to Stress
- A. Coping With Fears and Phobias
  1. Box: Adjustment in the New Millennium: Reaching New Heights with Virtual Reality
- B. Coping With Anger

VI. Adjustment and Modern Life
- A. Relaxing (Chilling, That Is)
- B. Coping With Test Anxiety
  1. Box: Self-Assessment: Do You Choke up During Tests? The Suinn Test Anxiety Behavior Scale (STABS)
- C. Alleviating Depression (Getting Out of the Dumps)
  1. Box: Self-Assessment: Are You Blue? The Self-Rating Depression Scale
  2. Box: Self-Assessment: What Turns You On? The Pleasant Events Schedule

Chapter Overview

Coping With Stress. Psychologists usually speak of defensive and active methods for coping with stress. Defensive coping methods blunt the immediate impact of stressors, but there is usually a personal or social cost - as in socially inappropriate behavior, withdrawal, or self-deception. Direct or active coping methods manipulate the environment to reduce or remove sources of stress. They also involve changing our responses to unavoidable stressors so that their harmfulness is abated.

Meichenbaum's Methods for Controlling Irrational and Catastrophizing Thoughts. Meichenbaum suggests pinpointing irrational thoughts, replacing them with rational thoughts, and rewarding ourselves for doing so.

Meditation. Meditation lowers arousal by reducing awareness of the surrounding world and the problems of the day.

Progressive Relaxation. Progressive relaxation reverses muscle tension associated with arousal and may also help us through its suggestions of warm and heavy limbs.

Alleviating Type A Behavior. Using the various methods suggested by Friedman and Ulmer can alleviate our sense of time urgency and hostility.

Enhancing Psychological Hardiness. Maddi and Kobasa suggest techniques that enhance our sense of commitment, challenge, and control over our situations, including situational reconstruction, focusing, and compensatory self-improvement.

Coping Directly With Fears and Phobias. We can use gradual approach and systematic desensitization to cope with fears and phobias. Each approach allows us to reappraise fear-evoking stimuli.

Coping Directly With Anger. We can begin by analyzing the ways in which social provocations can trigger irrational beliefs. Then we can challenge the beliefs, lower our arousal, and replace aggressive behavior with assertive behavior.

Learning Objectives

After studying this chapter you should be able to:

1. Identify both active and defensive methods for coping with stress and compare and contrast the effectiveness of defensive versus active coping methods.

2. Explain the role of irrational thoughts in people's reactions to stress and describe Meichenbaum's methods of controlling irrational and catastrophizing thoughts.

3. Explain what Type A behavior is and describe the methods proposed by Friedman and Ulmer for alleviating our sense of time urgency and hostility.

4. Explain what psychological hardiness is and describe the methods proposed by Maddi and Kobasa for enhancing it.

5. Compare and contrast the gradual approach technique and systematic desensitization. Explain how each helps us cope with stress.

6. Construct a program for helping someone cope directly with anger based upon the ideas presented in your text.

7. Explain what meditation is and describe how it lowers arousal and help people cope with stress.

8. Describe how progressive relaxation works and explain the progressive relaxation procedure.

9. Construct a program for helping someone cope directly with test anxiety, based upon the ideas presented in your text.

10. Construct a program for helping someone cope directly with depression based upon the ideas presented in your text.

Key Terms

stress management
defensive coping
aggression
withdrawal
fantasy
defense mechanisms
repression
regression
rationalization
displacement
projection
reaction formation
denial
sublimation
active coping
situational reconstruction
focusing
compensatory self-improvement
gradual approach
systematic desensitization
assertive behavior
meditation
progressive relaxation
cognitive restructuring

Key Terms Review

Define each of the following terms:

1. Stress Management: ______________________________

____

2. Defensive Coping: ______________________________

____

3. Aggression: ______________________________

____

4. Withdrawal: ______________________________

____

Harcourt Brace & Company

5. Defense Mechanisms: ____

____

6. Repression: ____

____

7. Regression: ____

____

8. Displacement: ____

____

9. Projection: ____

____

10. Reaction Formation: ____

____

11. Active Coping: ____

____

12. Situational Reconstruction: ____

____

13. Focusing: ____

____

14. Compensatory Self-Improvement: ____

____

15. Gradual Approach: ____

____

16. Systematic Desensitization: ____

____

17. Assertive Behavior: ____

____

18. Meditation: ____

____

19. Progressive Relaxation: ____

____

20. Cognitive Restructuring: ____

____

Chapter Review

1. Two methods of coping with stress include __________ coping, which reduces the immediate impact of the stressor but does not permanently remove the stressor or its effects, and __________ coping, which changes the environment to modify or remove the stressor permanently or buffer its harmfulness.

2. Five types of defensive coping mechanisms for dealing with stress are:

   a. ____

   b. ____

   c. ____

   d. ____

   e. ____

Harcourt Brace & Company

3. **Matching:** Match the defense mechanism on the left with its correct definition on the right.

_______ a. Repression

_______ b. Regression

_______ c. Denial

_______ d. Rationalization

_______ e. Projection

_______ f. Displacement

_______ g. Reaction formation

_______ h. Sublimation

1. unacceptable ideas or impulses are attributed to others
2. threatening events are perceived to be harmless
3. finding justifications for unacceptable ideas, impulses, or behaviors
4. unacceptable ideas and impulses are kept unconscious through exaggerated public expression of opposite feelings or behaviors
5. return, under stress, to a form of behavior characteristic of an earlier stage of development
6. primitive impulses, usually sexual or aggressive, are channeled into positive, constructive activity
7. ideas or impulses are transferred from a threatening or unsuitable object to a suitable or nonthreatening object
8. unconsciously placing threatening or stressful events or ideas out of awareness

4. Meichenbaum's three steps for controlling catastrophizing thoughts are:

a. ____

b. ____

c. ____

5. Two methods of coping with the Type A behavior pattern are:

a. ____

b. ____

6. Three methods for enhancing one's psychological hardiness are:

a. ____

b. ____

c. ____

7. Two methods of coping with fears and phobias are:

   a. ____

   b. ____

8. Many automatic thoughts are __________ and reflect ongoing sources of

   __________.

9. Four methods of coping with anger are:

   a. ____

   b. ____

   c. ____

   d. ____

10. Two methods of lowering arousal are:

   a. ____

   b. ____

11. Transcendental meditation produces a __________ __________ in many people which is typified by a lowered rate of __________.

12. Edmund Jacobson noted that people __________ __________ __________ when they are under stress so he developed the technique of __________ __________ to help them relax.

13. Three methods of coping with test anxiety are:

   a. ____

   b. ____

   c. ____

14. Four steps to restructuring your own cognitions concerning test taking (to cope with test anxiety) are:

a. ______________________________

b. ______________________________

c. ______________________________

d. ______________________________

15. Four methods of coping with depression are:

a. ______________________________

b. ______________________________

c. ______________________________

d. ______________________________

Sample Test

Multiple-Choice Questions

1. Which of the following is **NOT** an active method for coping with stress?
   a. using defense mechanisms
   b. manipulating the environment to change or eliminate sources of stress
   c. directly modifying cognitive responses so that the impact of stressors is reduced
   d. directly modifying physiological responses so that the impact of stressors is reduced

2. Which of the following responses may be the most appropriate when you are faced with a situation in which there is no successful way to cope with stress?
   a. alcoholism
   b. aggression
   c. fantasy
   d. withdrawal

3. The unconscious thrusting out of awareness of unacceptable ideas or urges is called ______.
   a. denial
   b. repression
   c. regression
   d. suppression

4. A man explains his cheating on his income taxes by saying, "Everyone does it! I just got caught!" This is an example of ______.
   a. projection
   b. denial
   c. a reaction formation
   d. rationalization

5. A woman who is frustrated at work comes home and kills her family. This is an example of ______.
   a. a reaction formation
   b. displacement
   c. sublimation
   d. projection

6. A conservative woman who cannot accept her sexual desires goes on a holy crusade to ban pornography. This is an example of ______.
   a. a reaction formation
   b. rationalization
   c. projection
   d. sublimation

7. According to Ellis, the way to change catastrophizing thoughts is to ______.
   a. change them
   b. engage in behaviors that are incompatible with your thoughts
   c. use negative reinforcement
   d. keep a diary

8. According to your text, the first step in controlling your sense of time urgency is ______.
   a. recognizing and controlling hidden life-change units
   b. confronting the values and beliefs that support it
   c. changing your behavior to Type B behavior
   d. using progressive relaxation

9. Getting a pet, making new friends, looking for the beauty in things, and playing to lose (once in a while) are methods for alleviating ______.
   a. your sense of time urgency
   b. your hostility
   c. self-destructive tendencies
   d. introspective tendencies

10. The technique which seeks to place stressful situations in a broad perspective by alerting people to their frequently irrational assumptions about those situations is called ______.
    a. situational reconstruction
    b. focusing
    c. compensatory self-improvement
    d. stimulus control

11. The method of treating fears and phobias which is based on the concept that you cannot experience fear or anxiety and deep muscle relaxation at the same time is called ______.
   a. gradual approach
   b. systematic desensitization
   c. participant modeling
   d. rational restructuring

12. Which of the following is **NOT** true of anger?
   a. It is a common emotional response to frustration and social provocations such as insults and threats.
   b. It can be troublesome when it leads to excessive arousal or self-defeating aggression.
   c. It can be adaptive in some situations.
   d. It is nearly always an inappropriate response to a situation.

13. Activating events, beliefs, and consequences are three steps theorized in the ______ approach to controlling anger.
   a. psychoanalytic
   b. classical conditioning
   c. rational-emotive
   d. Gestalt

14. According to your text, the method to use when coping with frustrations which cannot be avoided or eliminated is ______.
   a. count slowly from one to ten
   b. progressive relaxation
   c. stimulus control
   d. rational alternatives

15. Alan is trying to lower his bodily arousal by focusing on relaxing, repetitive stimuli, and thereby narrowing his consciousness so that the outside world seems to "fade away." This technique is called ______.
   a. meditation
   b. withdrawal
   c. biofeedback
   d. progressive relaxation

16. Research on meditators has found that in comparisons of heart rate, blood pressure, and sweaty palms ______.
   a. meditators have healthier levels than novice "resters"
   b. there are no differences between meditators and novice "resters"
   c. novice "resters" have healthier levels than experienced meditators
   d. nonmeditators have healthier levels than both meditators and novice "resters"

17. The proper sequential order of the steps involved in the cognitive restructuring method is ______.
   a. pinpoint, construct, practice, reward
   b. construct, practice, pinpoint, reward
   c. practice, pinpoint, construct, reward
   d. construct, practice, pinpoint, reward

18. The case of Bill, discussed in your text, describes him as being depressed due to ______.
   a. the death of his father
   b. failing an entrance examination
   c. losing his job
   d. the breakup of a romance

19. According to Henry David Thoreau, what is typically the **REAL** tyrant that determines one's fate?
   a. public opinion
   b. the opinion of one's spouse
   c. one's own private opinion
   d. the political and religious systems under which one lives

20. According to your text, virtual reality headsets have been successfully used to treat ______.
    a. depression
    b. paranoia
    c. phobias
    d. hyperactivity

True-False Questions

21. Defensive coping grants us time to marshal our resources. _______

22. Defense mechanisms are used only by abnormal people. _______

23. Assertive and aggressive behavior are essentially the same. _______

24. Many people are born with test anxiety. _______

25. Depressed people tend to have excessive needs for social approval. _______

Essay Question

26. Identify both active and defensive methods for coping with stress and compare and contrast the effectiveness of defensive versus active coping methods.

Student Activities

Name ______________________________ **Date** ____________

11.1 Challenging Irrational Thoughts

In the previous chapter we read about irrational beliefs, and we identified an occasion of some personal distress to analyze by applying Albert Ellis's ABC approach. The current chapter on ways of helping ourselves is described as a do-it-yourself chapter and asks us to take on some very valuable challenges. We can begin by practicing some of the recommendations with hypothetical cases before addressing our own situations. For each example of catastrophizing, write an incompatible, and rational rebuttal, and/or alternative as illustrated in Chapter 11.

1. "If I flunk this test I'll just die!"

2. "I'll feel stupid if the teacher calls on me today."

3. "I'm too embarrassed to exercise in public."

4. "My parents never gave me a chance to develop any self-esteem."

5. "That @#%^&* driver had no right pulling out in front of me!"

6. "There will never be another love like the one I just lost."

Harcourt Brace & Company

Name ______________________________ **Date** ____________

11.2 Controlling Our Own Disturbing Thoughts

We should be ready to take the steps recommended in Meichenbaum's three-step procedure. For this week, keep a diary of any occasions when you feel any discomfort, including fear, anger, frustration, pessimism, anxiety, and so forth. For some of us, a day of experience could keep us busy writing for a week, but a full week is a better representation of our experience. Note cards or slips of paper will serve, as long as we record each step for each occurrence. We will not provide all of the space you might need for a diary, but answer the following questions in the spaces below.

1. How many events during this week were recorded as distressing?

2. Choose six that appear to involve the use of unnecessary, catastrophizing thoughts. For each case, compose more appropriate thoughts as practiced in the above exercise.

   a.

   b.

   c.

   d.

   e.

   f.

Name ______________________________ **Date** ____________

11.3 Monitoring Arousal and Relaxation

It is hard to imagine a more positive step we can take in gaining control of our lives than deciding to control stress by learning to lower arousal. Chapter 10 details two very effective and well-researched techniques - meditation and progressive relaxation. Monitoring the effects of these techniques can be interesting and rewarding. The easiest way to verify the arousal-lowering potential of meditation or progressive relaxation is to take one-minute heart rates before and after practice. However, not everyone will detect a change in heart rate. For some people, improvements from relaxation are experienced as slower breathing, less muscle tension, or blood chemistry changes. To see if your heart rate is indicative of changes in your level of arousal, take your pulse for one minute, then engage in one of the recommended techniques detailed in the text, and finish by taking your pulse again for one minute.

1. Your resting pulse prior to meditation or relaxation:

   ____

2. Your pulse immediately after the chosen technique:

   ____

3. For comparison purposes, see how you respond to music. Record your heart's BPM before listening here:

   ____

4. What happens if you vary the musical choices between rowdy and relaxing?

5. If possible, compare yourself with others in your class and record your observations:

Name ________________________________ **Date** ____________

11.4 Monitoring Progress in Lowering Arousal

You have read that lowering arousal is worthwhile and will lead to possible improvements in health and performance, so it would be rewarding to verify our progress as we practice meditation and relaxation over days and weeks. One thing that has worked well is to keep a simple arousal diary that records how strong muscle tension is when you first notice it and how strong it remains as you attempt to lower it. Make a note every time you become aware of muscle tension, such as hunching your shoulders during class, or clutching your steering wheel with white knuckles, or wrinkling your forehead while you study or work. Rank your tension on a 10-point scale with 10 equal to the most severe strain possible and 1 equal to a total lack of any tension. Next, try to relax as well as possible and judge the new level of muscle tension on the same 10-point scale. What is commonly reported is 1) to notice more and more unnecessary cases of muscle tension, and 2) to include less severe examples as you become more sensitive to signals about your level of arousal, and 3) to record improvement in the ability to reduce tension to lower levels. Keep a note card or slip of paper in your pocket, purse, or wallet so you can record the two numbers on each occasion. Keep the days separate and at the end of the week answer these questions:

1. Record the total number of times you noticed tension each day.

2. For each day, record the average level of tension which you first noticed.

3. For each day, record the average amount of improvement when you tried to relax.

4. At the end of the project, can you find any changes or improvement in:

   a. Increased recognition of occasions of tension?

   b. Greater sensitivity to even lower levels of unnecessary tension?

   c. Greater reductions in tension after attempting to relax?

5. Explain how this information might be useful to you in helpig you cope with stress.

Harcourt Brace & Company

Name ______________________________ Date ____________

11.5 Handling Hostility and Frustration

In Chapter 11, the text summarizes the rational restructuring procedures described by Albert Ellis. Putting yourself in the shoes of other people and imagining the reasons they may have for their behavior can help you control hostility and frustration when their behavior interferes with your efforts to achieve your own goals. These procedures work! Try this exercise to practice empathizing with others, in order to manage the ill feelings that are sometimes created by their actions.

1. Think of a reasonable justification another driver would possibly give you for pulling out in front of your car from a side street, in a way which would cause you to have to brake quickly to avoid hitting him or her.

2. Think of the reasonable justifications an instructor could have for asking students not to call his or her house the night before tests to confirm information about the assigned reading.

3. Consider the last time someone, whom you were not able to talk to, did something that made you angry. For example, it might have been the way one of your least favorite politicians voted on a bill or measure. Now try to put yourself in their shoes to imagine the justification they would offer for the situation.

4. How can this information be useful to you in future coping with situations like those described above.

12

Gender Roles and Gender Differences

Chapter Outline

I. Gender Roles and Stereotypes

1. Box: Adjustment in a World of Diversity: Machismo/Marianismo Stereotypes in Culture

II. Gender Differences: Vive la Différence or Vive la Similarité?

A. Cognitive Abilities
B. Social Behavior

III. On Becoming a Man or a Woman: Theoretical Views

A. Biological Influences
B. Psychodynamic Theory
C. Social-Cognitive Theory
D. Gender-Schema Theory: "If That's What I Am, What Do I Do?"

IV. Adjustment and Psychological Androgyny: The More Traits the Merrier?

1. Box: Self-Assessment: Are You a "Chesty" Male or a "Fluffy" Female? The ANDRO Scale
2. Box: Adjustment in a World of Diversity: Name That Baby! Thoughts on Macho, Wimpy, "Feminissima," and Androgynous Names

V. Adjustment and Modern Life

A. Costs of Gender-Role Stereotyping
   1. Box: Adjustment in a World of Diversity: School Days, School Days - Dear Old Sexist School Days?
   2. Box: What Do You Say Now? Handling a Sexist Remark

Harcourt Brace & Company

Chapter Overview

Gender-Role Stereotypes. A stereotype is a fixed conventional idea about a group, and a gender role is a cluster of stereotypes attributed to one of the genders. The masculine gender-role stereotype includes aggressiveness, independence, logic, and competence in the business world or the realm of objects. The feminine gender-role stereotype includes nurturance, passivity, and dependence.

Sexism. Sexism is the prejudgment that a person, because of gender, will possess negative traits. Sexism is usually directed against women, but increasingly, men are also the targets of sexism.

Cognitive Gender Differences. Girls generally excel in verbal abilities, while boys excel in math and spatial-relations abilities. Girls excel in computational ability in elementary school, but boys excel in mathematical problem-solving in high school and college.

Gender Differences in Sexuality. Men are more likely than women to masturbate and to hold permissive attitudes toward casual sex.

Gender Differences in Aggression. Boys are more aggressive than girls under most circumstances. Aggressiveness in girls may be inhibited by social anxiety (caused by aggression's inconsistency with the feminine gender-role stereotype) and by empathy with the victim.

Gender Differences in Personality and Behavior. Men talk more and interrupt more often than women do. Males are more likely to make demands and curse. Females require less personal space and they prefer to sit next to companions, while males prefer to sit across from them. Greater brain lateralization in boys might be associated with differences in cognitive abilities. Prenatal influences of male sex hormones may increase activity level and masculine gender-typed preferences.

The Psychodynamic View of Gender Typing. According to psychodynamic theory, gender typing stems from resolution of the conflicts of the phallic stage. However, children assume gender roles at much earlier ages than the theory would suggest.

The Social-Cognitive View of Gender Typing. Social-cognitive theory explains gender-typing in terms of observational learning, identification, and socialization. Observational learning may largely account for children's knowledge of "gender-appropriate" preferences and behavior patterns. Children generally identify with adults of the same gender and attempt to broadly imitate their behavior, but only when it is perceived as gender-appropriate. Children are also guided into stereotypical gender-role behaviors by early socialization messages and reinforcement.

The Gender-Schema View of Gender Typing. Gender-schema theory proposes that children use the gender schema of their society to organize their perceptions, and that children attempt to blend their self-concepts with the gender schema. Evidence in support of gender-schema theory shows that children process information according to their gender schema.

Psychological Androgyny. Psychological androgyny apparently fosters adjustment and personal development. Psychologically androgynous people show high "identity" and "intimacy" - using the concepts of Erik Erikson. They show both independence and nurturance, depending on the situation. They have higher self-esteem and greater ability to bounce back from failure. Wives of psychologically androgynous husbands are happier than wives of husbands who adhere to a strict stereotypical masculine gender role.

Learning Objectives

After studying this chapter you should be able to:

1. Explain what gender roles and gender-role stereotypes are, and describe the characteristics typical of the traditional masculine and feminine gender roles in the United States.
2. Discuss the various gender-based differences in cognitive functioning and explain why these differences need to be viewed cautiously.
3. Identify and describe the various gender differences in sexuality, aggression, and communication.
4. Identify and explain the various gender differences in personality and behavior and discuss the biological influences that contribute to these differences.
5. Compare and contrast the psychodynamic, social-cognitive, and gender-schema views of gender typing.
6. Explain what psychological androgyny is and how it is different from other personality styles.
7. Discuss how androgyny contributes to healthy adjustment and personal development.
8. Define sexism and discuss the various personal and job-related costs of gender-role stereotyping.

Key Terms

stereotype
physical androgyny
psychological androgyny
gender roles
machismo
marianismo
acculturation
identification
socialization
gender norm
gender-schema theory
ego identity
sexism
aptitude
dyslexia
role overload

Key Terms Review

Define each of the following terms:

1. Stereotype: ______________________________

____

2. Physical Androgyny: ______________________________

____

3. Psychological Androgyny: ____________________

____

4. Gender Roles: ____________________

____

5. Machismo: ____________________

____

6. Marianismo: ____________________

____

7. Acculturation: ____________________

____

8. Identification: ____________________

____

9. Socialization: ____________________

____

10. Gender Norm: ____________________

____

11. Gender-Schema Theory: ____________________

____

12. Ego Identity: ____________________

____

13. Sexism: ____________________

____

14. Aptitude: ____

____

15. Dyslexia: ____

____

16. Role Overload: ____

____

Chapter Review

1. Complex clusters of ways in which men and women are expected to behave within a culture are called __________ __________.

2. Three beliefs about women and men that have prevailed throughout the history of Western culture are:

   a. ____

   b. ____

   c. ____

3. Gender polarization in the United States is linked to the traditional view of men as __________ and women as __________.

4. __________ is a cultural stereotype that defines masculinity in terms of being strong, virile, and dominant, while __________ is a cultural stereotype that defines femininity in terms of the virtuous woman who "suffers in silence."

5. It is now believed that males' greater knowledge of world affairs and skill in science and industry is largely due to:

   ____.

6. It appears that girls are somewhat superior to boys in __________ ability, whereas boys seem to be somewhat superior in __________-__________ abilities.

7. In math, male-female differences at all ages are __________ and seem to be __________.

8. Males spend __________ time talking than women. They are __________ likely to introduce new topics and __________ likely to interrupt.

9. Women interact at __________ distances than men do, and seek to keep __________ space between themselves and strangers of the other gender than men do.

10. In our culture, __________ are more interested in casual sex and having more than one sex partner, and __________ are more interested in combining sex with a romantic relationship.

11. Researchers have found four basic circumstances that affect how aggressively females will act. These are:

    a. ____

    b. ____

    c. ____

    d. ____

12. __________ hormones may "masculinize" or "feminize" the brain by creating predispositions that are consistent with some gender-role stereotypes.

13. Language skills seem to depend on __________ hemisphere functioning in the brain while spatial-relations skills appear to depend on __________ hemisphere functioning.

14. According to psychodynamic theory, gender roles are acquired through a process of __________.

15. Freud believed that gender identity remains flexible until the resolution of the ____ at the age of 5 or 6.

16. According to social-cognitive theory, __________ learning, __________, and __________ all play a role in the acquisition of gender roles and gender-role stereotypes.

17. Girls frequently learn to respond to social provocations by feeling __________. Boys, however, are often encouraged to __________ when necessary.

18. __________-__________ theory holds that children use gender as one way of organizing their perceptions of the world.

19. Research has found that boys show better memory for __________ toys and objects, and girls show better memory for __________ objects and toys.

20. __________ hormones may contribute to some gender-typed behavior. Yet, the effects of __________ __________ may be strong enough to counter most biological predispositions.

21. People who show high levels of independence, aggressiveness, and dominance are seen as __________. Those who show high levels of warmth, nurturance, and expressiveness are seen as __________. Those who show high levels of both dominance and nurturance are said to be __________, while those who show low levels of both are said to be __________.

22. In terms of Erikson's concepts of ego identity and intimacy, __________ college students are most likely to show "high identity" and "high intimacy."

23. Antill's study of marital happiness found that husbands' levels of happiness were linked to their wives' __________, and wives' levels of happiness were linked to their husbands' __________.

24. In adolescence, __________ and __________ are associated with popularity and higher self-esteem in both boys and girls.

25. Sandra Bem found that __________ percent of students adhered to traditional gender-role stereotypes, while about __________ percent adhered to traits stereotypic of the opposite sex, and about __________ percent were androgynous.

26. __________ is the prejudgment that a person, because of gender, will possess negative traits.

27. __________ dominate classroom discussions in grade school, but teachers reprimand __________ more for talking in class.

28. Far more American __________ than __________ have reading problems, in part because reading is considered a __________ activity in the United States.

29. Spatial ability is linked to the number of __________ courses taken.

30. By high school, students perceive math as part of the __________ domain. Boys are more likely to have __________ feelings about math, where girls are more likely to have __________ about math.

31. Many women are prevented from reaching the top echelons of management because of "__________ ceilings," and if they have openly discussed having children they are often placed in "__________ tracks."

32. Women who work are more likely to feel role __________ and being pulled in different directions from the dual roles of ________ and ________.

Sample Test

Multiple-Choice Questions

1. The belief that **ALL** women are emotional is a ______.
   a. sex norm
   b. stereotype
   c. archetype
   d. role norm

2. About ______ out of every 10 new jobs in the United States are held by women.
   a. 2
   b. 4
   c. 6
   d. 8

3. In math, females tend to ______.
   a. be outperformed by males in grade school, high school, and college
   b. outperform males in grade school and high school, but are outperformed by males in college
   c. outperform males in grade school, but are outperformed by males in high school and college
   d. outperform males in grade school, high school, and college

4. According to your text, the small differences which exist between males and females in cognitive functioning may represent ______.
   a. genetic differences
   b. brain size and capacity differences
   c. flawed methodology in the research
   d. cultural expectations and environmental influences

5. Which of the following is true of communication style differences between men and women?
   a. Women are more likely to introduce new topics in a conversation.
   b. Men are more likely to reveal their personal experiences in a conversation.
   c. Men are more likely to interrupt others.
   d. Women are more likely to curse.

6. Men are more likely to feel "invaded" by strangers who sit ______, and women are more likely to feel invaded by strangers who sit ______ them.
   a. next to, next to
   b. across from, next to
   c. next to, across from
   d. across from, across from

7. Your text suggests that sex hormones in utero ______.
   a. only influence the development of male and female sex organs
   b. appear to have no measurable effect on the developing fetus
   c. influence the development of male and female sex organs and may masculinize or feminize the brain
   d. may cause the child to begin sexual activity earlier than normal

8. Left-brain functioning appears to control ______.
   a. aesthetic responses
   b. visual-spatial skills
   c. language skills
   d. emotional responses

9. Of the following, who is most likely to show spatial-relations deficits?
   a. a male with right-brain damage
   b. a female with right-brain damage
   c. a female with left-brain damage
   d. a male with left-brain damage

10. According to Freud, identification takes place ______.
   a. during the resolution of the Oedipus and Electra complexes
   b. during the resolution of the oral stage
   c. during the resolution of the anal stage
   d. during the resolution of the genital stage

11. Perry & Bussey's study on how children learn masculine or feminine behaviors suggests that much of the learning ______.
   a. occurs by observational learning
   b. occurs as a result of consistent and harsh punishment
   c. appears to be instinctive
   d. occurs only when children are bribed with "goodies" like candy or cookies

12. In the Richardson study of females and aggression, what determined the level of electric shock a woman would give to a male participant in the experiment?
   a. how much electric shock male subjects gave females
   b. social approval or disapproval
   c. the amount of money received for giving the shock
   d. the attractiveness of the male receiving the shock

13. ______ holds that children use gender as one way of organizing their perceptions of the world.
   a. Social learning theory
   b. Gender-schema theory
   c. Social-cognitive theory
   d. Field theory

14. People who are low in both stereotypical masculine and feminine traits are ______.
   a. undifferentiated
   b. androgynous
   c. traditional
   d. opposite

15. The Antil study of marital happiness found that which of the following people would be the happiest?
   a. husbands whose wives had low levels of femininity
   b. husbands whose wives were undifferentiated
   c. wives whose husbands had only high levels of masculinity
   d. wives whose husbands were androgynous

16. Bem's research found that ______ percent of students adhered to traditional gender-role stereotypes.
   a. 15
   b. 35
   c. 50
   d. 65

17. According to Bem, throughout Western history, "naturalness" has been viewed as ______.
   a. nontechnological
   b. whatever males decided it was
   c. God's scheme of things
   d. whatever females decided it was

18. According to your text, women are more frequently ______ than men.
   a. protective
   b. aroused
   c. talkative
   d. depressed

19. Which of the following is **NOT** true as to why more American boys than girls take math?
   a. Boys are more likely than girls to have math anxiety.
   b. Math is likely to be seen as a "male" subject by high school.
   c. By high school, boys are more likely than girls to have positive feelings about math.
   d. Advanced math courses are more likely to be taught by men.

20. The Hispanic concept of marianismo refers to ______.
   a. a childhood version of machismo for little boys
   b. women who have become acculturated into American culture and abandoned traditional Hispanic values
   c. women who have reached the age of 30 and are still not married
   d. an idealized notion of femininity

True-False Questions

21. Girls have greater computational ability than boys in elementary school. _______

22. Females are more likely than males to empathize with a victim in a situation where aggressive behavior might be called for. _______

23. Boys are more likely than girls to imitate film-mediated aggressive models. _______

24. Statistically, most college students are psychologically androgynous. _______

25. Teachers show higher expectations for boys in math classes. _______

Essay Question

26. Compare and contrast the psychodynamic, social-cognitive, and gender-schema views of gender typing.

Student Activities

Name ________________________________ **Date** ____________

12.1 Riddles

These riddles have been around for quite a while, but they may still be useful for our purposes.

1. A man and his son are in a serious car accident. Both are rushed to the nearest hospital while unconscious. The boy needs emergency surgery, but the emergency room surgeon says, "I can't operate on him, he's my son." How is this possible?

2. If you enjoy sports, you might get this one. How can two softball teams play a complete softball game, and the score ends 1 to nothing, even though not one man for either team has crossed home plate?

3. I really doubt the riddles fooled you, given they are old and given the subject for this chapter. However, you may find they will work on a friend or acquaintance. Try them one at a time, separate them by a day or so, and see if your subject learns anything from the first to the second riddle, assuming you told him or her the answer to the first. What happens and what hypotheses might be generated from this information?

4. Do you think that people today would be more likely to answer the riddles correctly than people 40 years ago? Why or why not?

Name ________________________________ Date ____________

12.2 Reversal of Roles

It is not uncommon to read about or be entertained by people's real or imagined experience with role reversal. What kinds of answers do you come up with to the following questions?

1. Movies I can think of that have featured the theme of role reversal go backl to such Hollywood classics as "Some Like It Hot," and include more recent films such as *Mr. Mom*, *Mrs. Doubtfire*, *Tootsie*, *Three Men and a Baby*, the *Alien* trilogy, and *Three Men and a Little Lady*. What movies can you add to this list? How have such films affected your views, if at all, of men's and women's roles in society?

2. Our nation's experience in the Persian Gulf War brought home the reality of women in combat missions. Do you believe that women should be serving in combat roles in the military? Why or why not? What limits, if any, would you recommend for women serving in the armed services when it comes to combat missions, and/or the draft?

3. Ask someone else the same question found in 2 above. What is her or his opinion? Why do you think he or she is right or wrong?

Harcourt Brace & Company

Name ________________________________ Date ______________

12.3 Dear Old Sexist School Days

In the text, Rathus and Nevid detail how gender roles are reinforced in the education system. Researchers have found that sex bias continues beyond primary and secondary education right into the lecture halls and laboratories of American universities and colleges. For example, a University of Illinois study found that while high school valedictorians, salutatorians, and honor students were attending the University of Illinois, self-concepts remained steady for males, but dropped dramatically for females. Upon graduating from high school, 23 percent of the males and 21 percent of the females rated themselves as "far above average" in intelligence. By the time they were seniors in college, the numbers for the males and females were respectively, 25 percent and **zero**.

Are college instructors biased in the ways research suggests, such as calling on male students more, making better eye contact with males, supporting male students more, and coaching males more? To assess such possibilities at your school, select one class other than this adjustment class, and record for one week the following information.

1. Did the instructor favor one gender by disproportionately calling on, helping, encouraging, or agreeing with either the men or the women in that class? How can you accurately record this data? Can anyone else in the class you have chosen also record the same data, so you could check for agreement (which we call reliability)?

2. In addition to your effort to carefully look at one selected class, where else in your school have you run into gender bias? How did it affect you? I have been utterly astonished at the stories of blatant as well as less obvious sexism that are still reported on college campuses, where people are supposed to be "enlightened" enough to know better. If you cannot think of any examples from your own experience, ask your friends if they have had such experiences. What have you learned?

Activity continued on the Back

3. What hypotheses could you create to systematically test and document the effects of gender bias in higher education?

4. What other explanations might account for the University of Illinois findings?

5. What are at least four things people can do to effectively respond to biased and discriminatory behavior?

Name ________________________________ Date ______________

12.4 Thinking Makes It So

Shakespeare wrote: "Nothing is either good or bad, but thinking makes it so." What may be meat for one person may be poison for another. It's in the eye of the beholder. And so forth and so forth. By the same token, we can substitute an attractive synonym for something much less attractive, or we can turn things around the other way and make something wonderful or grand sound ugly or base. Word games like these can be used to create or maintain sexual bias. For each of the words below, think of two synonyms that can be substituted for the word - one positive and one negative. For example, we can substitute both "rational" and "unfeeling" for "stable," or "childish" and "creative" for "spontaneous."

	POSITIVE	NEGATIVE
consistent	__________	__________
warm	__________	__________
generous	__________	__________
stubborn	__________	__________
self-righteous	__________	__________
different	__________	__________
ambitious	__________	__________
serious	__________	__________
jaded	__________	__________
assertive	__________	__________
meticulous	__________	__________
sensitive	__________	__________
focused	__________	__________
intelligent	__________	__________
principled	__________	__________

Name ______________________________ Date ____________

12.5 Interviewing Others

Since we can learn so much from others, consider one or both of these possible interviews. One could be a child and the other an adult engaged in a career not typical for that person's gender, such as a male nurse, or a female firefighter.

1. With parental permission, question a child about issues raised in this chapter about early appearance of gender-role stereotyping. What questions can you think of and what are the child's answers?

2. Interview the adult with some questions prepared in advance, but also with flexibility to pursue some unanticipated but promising leads. What can you share from your conversations?

3. What did you learn from your questioning of these people? How did it change your thinking, if at all, on this matter?

13

Interpersonal Attraction: Of Friendship, Love, and Loneliness

Chapter Outline

I. Attraction

A. Physical Attractiveness: How Important Is Looking Good?
   1. Box: Adjustment in a World of Diversity: "Your Daddy's Rich and Your Ma is Good Looking": Gender Differences in the Importance of Physical Attractiveness
   2. Box: Adjustment in the New Millennium: Who Are the Ideal Men for the New Millennium?
   3. Box: Adjustment in a World of Diversity: "Let's Make a Deal": On Gender and Lonely Hearts Ads

B. Attraction and Similarity: Birds of a Feather Flock Together

C. Reciprocity: If You Like Me, You Must Have Excellent Judgment

D. Sexual Orientation
   1. Box: Adjustment in the New Millennium: http://www.planetout.com

II. Friendship

A. Qualities of Good Friends

B. On Friendship and Love

C. Fraternities and Sororities: Are They for You?

III. Love

A. Styles of Love

B. Romantic Love in Contemporary Western Culture

C. The Love Triangle - That Is, the Triangular Model of Love
   1. Box: Self-Assessment: Has Cupid Shot His Arrow into Your Heart? Sternberg's Triangular Love Scale

D. Romantic versus Companionate Love: Is Romantic Love Any Basis for Marriage?

IV. Adjustment and Modern Life

A. Coping With Loneliness

Harcourt Brace & Company

Chapter Overview

Attraction. Attraction is an attitude of liking or disliking. Attraction involves good or bad affective responses, approach or avoidance behavior, and positive or negative evaluations. In our society, slenderness is found attractive in both genders. Tallness is found attractive in men, but not in women. When we meet new people of the opposite gender, our first impressions focus on their clothing, figure, and face, although men give the figure more priority than women do. Smiling enhances attractiveness.

Stereotypes About Attractive People. One assumption commonly made is that good things come in pretty packages. Physically attractive people are assumed to be more successful and well-adjusted, but they are also perceived as more vain, self-centered, and given to extramarital affairs. Attractive people are less likely to be judged guilty of crimes. Attractive people have greater social skills. Research suggests that we expect attractive people to show greater social skills and we elicit skillful behavior from them. Attractive men have more social interactions with women, but fewer with men than their less attractive peers. Attractive men and women are more likely to date and to attend parties than less attractive peers and more likely to find these activities satisfying.

Attitudinal Similarity and Attraction. Experimental "coke dates" reveal that we are most attracted to those people we find physically attractive and who share attitudes similar to our own.

The Matching Hypothesis. This is the tendency to ask out and marry people who are similar in attractiveness to ourselves - largely because of fear of rejection. Examination of lonely hearts ads suggests that people are frequently willing to swap good looks for financial security. Traditional men and nontraditional women are most likely to be attracted to dates who hold similar attitudes.

Sexual Orientation. Gay male and lesbian sexual orientations are ones in which people are erotically interested in, and desirous of forming romantic relationships with, people of their own gender. Psychodynamic theory connects sexual orientation with resolution of the Oedipus complex. Learning theorists explain sexual orientation in terms of reinforcement of early sexual preferences. Evidence of a genetic contribution to sexual orientation is accumulating, and prenatal sex hormones may play a role in determining sexual orientation.

The Role of Friends. Friends play important roles in our lives. We share activities, interests, and confidences with friends. We seek loyalty, social support, and generally positive traits, such as frankness and intelligence, from our friends.

Styles of Love. The styles of love include: passionate (eros), storgic (affectionate), ludic (game-playing), pragmatic (practical), manic (possessive), and agapic (selfless) styles.

Romantic Love. Romantic love is a positive, intense emotion that develops in a culture that idealizes the concept. It involves arousal, the presence of a person who is attractive to us, and some reason to label the arousal as "love." We think of ourselves as being in love when we experience physical arousal in the presence (actual or fantasized) of another person and have some reason to label that arousal love. Experiments support the view that feelings of attraction are enhanced when we experience higher levels of physiological arousal and can attribute them to the presence of an attractive person.

Loneliness. There are many factors that contribute to loneliness, such as lack of social skills, fear of social rejection, cynicism about human nature, and general pessimism. In order to combat loneliness we need to challenge our pessimism and our beliefs about other people. We can also develop social skills. In addition, we can join groups, express our ideas, become good listeners, and when necessary, fight fair.

Learning Objectives

After studying this chapter you should be able to:

1. Define attraction, describe the various traits that contribute to physical attractiveness in our culture, and discuss the accuracy of the various stereotypes about attractive people.
2. Explain what the matching hypothesis is and how it influences who we choose as potential partners.
3. Explain the role of attitudinal similarity in interpersonal attraction and discuss the specific areas where similar attitudes are most likely to affect a developing relationship.
4. Explain what sexual orientation is and how it is different from sexual preference, and summarize research findings in regard to the origins of sexual orientation, and the psychological adjustment of gay males and lesbians.
5. Describe the role played by friends in our lives and identify the various qualities we seek in friends throughout childhood and into adulthood.
6. Identify at least five advantages and five disadvantages to joining a sorority or a fraternity.
7. Identify and briefly describe each of the six styles of love discussed in the text.
8. Explain Sternberg's "love triangle" and identify at least five possible kinds of love that can emerge from this model.
9. Compare and contrast romantic love with companionate love.
10. Explain what loneliness is, describe the factors that contribute to it, and identify various measures that can be taken to cope with it.

Key Terms

attraction
matching hypothesis
reciprocity
sexual orientation
heterosexual
homosexual
gay male
lesbian
bisexual
sexual preference
organizing effects
activating effects
testosterone
clique
crowd
love
eros
ludus
storge
pragma
mania
agape
romantic love
triangular model of love
intimacy
passion
commitment
infatuation
empty love
companionate love
fatuous love
consumate love
loneliness

Key Terms Review

Define each of the following terms:

1. Attraction: ______________________________

   ____

2. Matching Hypothesis: ______________________________

   ____

3. Reciprocity: ______________________________

   ____

4. Sexual Orientation: ______________________________

   ____

5. Organizing Effects: ______________________________

   ____

6. Activating Effects: ______________________________

   ____

7. Clique: ______________________________

   ____

8. Crowd: ______________________________

   ____

9. Romantic Love: ______________________________

   ____

10. Eros: ______________________________

    ____

Harcourt Brace & Company

11. Ludus: ____

____

12. Storge: ____

____

13. Pragma: ____

____

14. Mania: ____

____

15. Agape: ____

____

16. Triangular Model of Love: ____

____

17. Commitment: ____

____

18. Infatuation: ____

____

19. Companionate Love: ____

____

20. Loneliness: ____

____

Chapter Review

1. Two positive outcomes of interpersonal attraction are __________ and __________.
2. In our society, tallness is a(n) __________ for men, and tall women tend to be viewed __________ attractively.
3. Men prefer women to be __________ than they expect, and women prefer men to be __________ than they expect.
4. The __________-chested look was the ideal for women in the 1920s, but in more recent years, men seem to desire women with __________-size breasts and see __________-busted women as less intelligent, moral, and less modest than other women.
5. Women viewing videotapes of prospective dates preferred men who acted __________ and self-__________. Men responded __________ to women who acted similarly.
6. When involved in a long-term relationship, men are more swayed by __________ characteristics, while women are more swayed by qualities such as __________, __________, __________, and __________ orientation. Both genders claimed that the single most important quality in a partner is __________.
7. According to the "parental investment model," a woman's appeal is more strongly connected to __________ and __________, whereas a man's appeal is more closely linked to __________ standing and __________.
8. By and large, we rate beautiful people as __________ people.
9. Attractive people are less likely to develop psychobiological __________ and the disorders of unattractive people are __________ severe.

10. The major motive for asking out "matches" in physical attractiveness appears to be ____.

11. In "lonely hearts" ads, women are more likely to advertise themselves as __________ __________, while men are more likely to tout __________ __________ as a come-on.

12. We tend to be attracted to people who have __________ attitudes. We also tend to assume that those we find attractive have __________ similar to our own.

13. In computer matched dates at the University of Nevada, men were more influenced by __________ attitudes, while women were influenced by __________ attitudes.

14. Reciprocity is a __________ determinant of attraction.

15. __________ males and __________ are sexually attracted to, and interested in forming romantic relationships with, members of their own gender.

16. Surveys in the United States and Europe find that about __________ percent of men identify themselves as gay and about __________ percent of American women surveyed say they have a lesbian sexual orientation.

17. Genes connected with sexual orientation may be found on the __________ chromosome and may be transmitted from __________ to child.

18. Sexual behavior among many lower animals is almost completely governed by __________.

19. Lee Ellis theorizes that sexual orientation is hormonally determined prior to birth and is affected by __________ factors, synthetic __________ sex hormones, and maternal __________.

20. The origins of sexual orientation are __________ and __________.

Harcourt Brace & Company

21. Gay males and lesbians are __________ adjusted as heterosexuals.

22. For primary schoolers, friendship is based mostly on ____________________________

____,

whereas for middle schoolers it is based more on __________ __________.

23. By puberty, people want friends with whom they can share __________ __________.

24. In high school and college, we tend to belong to __________ or __________.

25. The quality deemed most important in friends is ______________________________

____

26. Five advantages conferred by joining fraternities or sororities are:

a. ____

b. ____

c. ____

d. ____

e. ____

27. Five drawbacks to joining fraternities or sororities are:

a. ____

b. ____

c. ____

d. ____

e. ____

28. **Matching:** Match the term on the left with its appropriate description on the right.

_______ a. Storge

_______ b. Agape

_______ c. Eros

_______ d. Ludus

_______ e. Pragma

_______ f. Mania

_______ g. Companionate love

_______ h. Romantic love

1. characterized by intense, idealized passion and the belief that one is "in love"
2. similar to attachment and affection, also friendship love
3. similar to liking and respect
4. based on sharing, mutual respect, and willingness to sacrifice
5. based on sexual attraction or lust
6. selfless love, similar to generosity
7. game-playing love
8. practical, logical love
9. possessive, excited love

29. According to Sternberg, love involves __________, __________, and __________.

30. __________ love assails us in a flash and then dissipates when our involvement with the loved one grows. The relationship must develop __________ love if it is to last.

31. Loneliness tends to peak during __________, when most of us begin to replace close links to our parents with __________ relationships.

32. Loneliness is linked to feelings of __________. Also, lonely people are more likely to get __________.

33. Five causes of loneliness are:

a. ____

b. ____

c. ____

d. ____

e. ____

34. Seven steps to making friends and combating loneliness are:

a. ______________________________

b. ______________________________

c. ______________________________

d. ______________________________

e. ______________________________

f. ______________________________

g. ______________________________

Sample Test

Multiple-Choice Questions

1. According to the story in your text, Candy's religious beliefs ______.
   a. prevent her from marrying Stretch because he's Jewish
   b. prevent her from using contraception
   c. prevent her from having an abortion
   d. prevent her from divorcing Stretch

2. In Western society, women prefer men with ______.
   a. a V-taper
   b. a "beer" belly
   c. a "Mr. Universe" build
   d. a sumo-wrestler build

3. Women prefer men to be ______.
   a. more muscular than most men can realistically become
   b. heavier than most men expect
   c. about the same as most men expect
   d. thinner than most men expect

4. College men and women are more concerned about their dating partner's physical attractiveness when the relationship is primarily ______.
   a. platonic
   b. companionate
   c. professional
   d. sexual

5. Which of the following is **NOT** true of attractive people?
   a. They are less likely to be found guilty of some crimes.
   b. If found guilty of a crime, they are more likely to receive a lighter or less severe sentence.
   c. They are more likely to be vain or self-centered than unattractive people.
   d. They are less likely to develop psychological disorders than unattractive people.

6. The idea that we tend to ask out, or go out with, people who are similar to ourselves in attractiveness is a central part of ______.
   a. propinquity
   b. reciprocity
   c. the matching hypothesis
   d. complementarity

7. According to one study, women who were asked to choose between two male dates on the basis of physical attractiveness (from photographs) were likely to choose ______.
   a. an extremely unattractive male
   b. a moderately unattractive male
   c. a moderately attractive male
   d. an extremely attractive male

8. According to a study of University of Nevada women, they were ______.
   a. not affected by either the sexual or religious attitudes of their partners
   b. more affected by the sexual than by the religious attitudes of their partners
   c. more affected by the religious than by the sexual attitudes of their partners
   d. equally affected by both the sexual and religious attitudes of their partners

9. Studies of gay males and lesbians have found that ______.
   a. they show higher levels of anxiety than heterosexuals
   b. they are more likely to complain of psychosomatic ailments such as headaches and ulcers
   c. they are more likely to be depressed than heterosexuals
   d. they are about as well-adjusted as heterosexuals

10. Becky is 10 years old. Which of the following is **MOST** likely to characterize how she feels about friendship?
   a. Friends are people who keep confidences.
   b. Friends are people who are similar to you and share interests with you.
   c. Friends are those with whom you do things and have fun.
   d. Friends are those with whom you can share intimate feelings.

11. Jeff is 16 years old. Which of the following is **MOST** likely to characterize how he feels about friendship?
   a. Friends are people who keep confidences.
   b. Friends are people who are similar to you and share interests with you.
   c. Friends are those with whom you do things and have fun.
   d. Friends are those with whom you can share intimate feelings.

12. A small group of friends at a party who share their innermost feelings about other people at the party is called a ______.
   a. gang
   b. clique
   c. crowd
   d. club

13. The Hendricks' scale suggests ______ styles of love.
   a. 2
   b. 4
   c. 6
   d. 8

14. Joshua's attitude about love is summed up by the statement "The best love grows out of an enduring friendship!" His style of love is called ______.
   a. ludus
   b. agape
   c. pragma
   d. storge

15. Female college students are significantly more likely than male college students to feel each of the following styles of love **EXCEPT** ______.
   a. storge
   b. pragma
   c. mania
   d. agape

16. According to Sternberg, ______ is the emotional component of romantic love.
   a. intimacy
   b. trust
   c. passion
   d. commitment

17. Berscheid and Walter suggest that ______ may allow people to maintain their relationships once the romance has begun to fade.
   a. companionate love
   b. infatuation
   c. eros
   d. storge

18. Loneliness peaks during ______.
   a. childhood
   b. adolescence
   c. early adulthood
   d. late adulthood

19. In initial attraction, women place greater emphasis than men on each of the following **EXCEPT** ______.
   a. thrift
   b. dependability
   c. kindness
   d. fondness for children

20. Which of the following was **NOT** one of the five traits most frequently listed by women in a recent ***Psychology Today*** poll when discussing what makes a man ideal.
   a. a doer/takes charge
   b. receptive/responsive to others
   c. expresses feelings of sadness
   d. pays attention to diet/exercise

True-False Questions

21. Plumpness is valued in many cultures. ______

22. Men who viewed videotapes of women showing dominance rated them as very attractive. ______

23. Beautiful people are perceived as less intelligent and talented. ______

24. Sexual orientation has been solidly linked to adult levels of male and female sex hormones. ______

25. Psychologists find that love is a simple concept, based primarily on physiological attraction. ______

Essay Question:

26. Identify and briefly describe each of the six styles of love discussed in the text.

Student Activities

Name ________________________________ **Date** ____________

13.1 What Kind of Face Could Launch a Thousand Ships?

As our text says, it may not seem intelligent and sophisticated, but physical appearance is given a lot of importance in interpersonal attraction. Homer claimed that it was the face of Helen of Troy that precipitated the Trojan War. Certainly the Greeks knew how to appreciate physical appearance, and they left a classical, idealized legacy for Western civilization to admire, ponder, and replicate. They are often given credit for defining the ideal characteristics of faces still followed by plastic surgeons today. While most of us might not know much about art, or faces, we know what we like. However, before we examine this fascinating information, seriously try to draw an idealized face in the space below.

Many of you may not have a clue as to how to begin, so here are some rules for shaping the face at least basically.

1. Construct a rectangle so that the height is approximately 25 percent taller than the width (for example, four inches wide by five inches tall). Now divide the height by two horizontal lines so the rectangle is divided into equal thirds (for example, one line 1 and 2/3 inches from the top, and one line 1 and 2/3 inches from the bottom of the original rectangle).

2. Next, divide the length of the rectangle into equal fifths. In our example, this requires four vertical lines spaced 0.80 inches apart from each other and the sides of the original rectangle.

3. Now do what you do when you doodle, and doodle the ears between the middle horizontal lines.

4. Place the nose in the middle section, neatly fitting on the bottom line and between the two sides.

5. Place the eyebrows at the tops of the two sections to the sides of the nose section.

Activity continued on the back

6. Place the eyes under the eyebrows and fully between the side lines of this section.

7. In the section immediately below the nose place the lips, one third of the way down the section and fully extending to and slightly past the sides of the section.

8. Find a magazine photo of the most attractive face you can and report how well the face conforms to the specifications above.

9. Collect five photos of faces you find attractive, and identify any additional specifications for attractiveness that were omitted above. Believe me, there are many more.

Name ______________________________ Date ___________

13.2 Is Your Love Like a Red, Red Rose?

Clearly the word "love" gets overused when it can be applied to the most important person in our life and broccoli. Rathus and Nevid recognize this and make some suggestions about a more exact language of love, especially the different styles of love. The discussion suggests most people in love experience a combination of several different styles.

Think about the "ideal" you have of love, and see if you can assign some percentage from 0 to 100 percent to each of the styles. Beside each style enter your ideal percentage.

1. __________ Eros or romantic love
2. __________ Ludus or game-playing love
3. __________ Storge or friendship love
4. __________ Pragma or pragmatic, logical love
5. __________ Mania or possessive, excited love
6. __________ Agape or selfless love

Follow-Up Questions:

1. Would the relationship you describe above best be described as romantic love, companionate love, or some other love described in the text? How is it similar?

2. Looking back on a relationship in your past which ended, what percentages would you have assigned in that case?

Activity continued on the back

4. How is the relationship described in question 2 (above) similar to or different from the ideal relationship you described in question 1 (above)? Is there any lesson in that?

5. If you are involved in a relationship, have your partner write down the percentages for his or her vision of ideal love. How does this compare with your ideal? Is it similar to or different from what you expected?

6. Try comparing your ideal love with a relationship portrayed in a novel, on a television show, or in a movie. What percentages could you use to describe the couple's relationship?

7. Think about an influential couple you knew while growing up - perhaps your parents, grandparents, or close family friends. What percentages would you assign to their love? Would you want a relationship like theirs? If so, why? If not, how would you want it to be different?

Name ______________________________ **Date** ____________

13.3 Coffee Shop Observations

Next time you are in the student union, coffee shop, cafeteria, or any place where people sit at a table together, observe some of the nonverbal communication and answer these questions:

1. What body language do people use to convey they are "in love" with the other person?

2. What body mannerisms suggest to you that two people are not romantically interested in each other, even though they are talking?

3. Looking at still another conversation, what can be deduced about the relationship being experienced by the two people at that table, and why?

Harcourt Brace & Company

Name ______________________________ **Date** ____________

13.4 Is Love Insane?

George Bernard Shaw is quoted as saying love is "the most violent, most insane, most delusive, and most transient of emotions."

1. What arguments or examples from experience, could you use to **support** his characterization of love?

2. What rebuttals could be used to refute his contentions?

3. Based on your arguments (above), what reasons can you provide to argue that lifetime marriage should be based on love?

4. What reasons can you provide to argue that lifetime marriage should not be based on love?

14

Relationships and Communication: Getting From Here to There

Chapter Outline

I. Stages in Relationships

A. Attraction
B. Building
   1. Box: What Do You Say Now? How to Improve Date-Seeking Skills
C. Continuation
D. Deterioration
E. Ending

II. Marriage

A. To Whom Do We Get Married? Are Marriages Made in Heaven or in the Neighborhood?
   1. Box: Adjustment in the New Millennium: Modem Matchmaking
B. The Marriage Contract: A Way of Clarifying Your Expectations
C. Marital Satisfaction: Is Everybody Happy?
D. Affairs: Who, What, and Truth and Consequences
   1. Box: Self-Assessment: Do You Endorse a Traditional or a Liberal Marital Role?

III. Divorce

   1. Box: Adjustment in the New Millennium: ***Modern Bride*** and ***Parenting***, or ***Divorce***? - Which Will Help You Cope With Relationships in the New Millennium?

IV. Alternative Styles of Life

   1. Box: Adjustment in a World of Diversity: Snug in Their Beds for Christmas Eve - In Japan, December 24th Has Become the Hottest Night of the Year
A. The Singles Scene: Swinging, Lonely, or All of the Above?
B. Cohabitation: "There's Nothing That I Wouldn't Do If You Would Be My POSSLQ"

V. Adjustment and Modern Life

A. Making It Work: Ways of Coping With Conflict in a Relationship
   1. Box: What Do You Say Now? Delivering Criticism
   2. Box: What Do You Say Now? Receiving Criticism

Chapter Overview

Intimate Relationship. In an intimate relationship, people share their innermost thoughts and feelings.

Levinger's Stages in the Development of a Relationship. According to Levinger, relationships undergo a five-stage developmental sequence: attraction, building, continuation, deterioration, and ending. Relationships need not advance beyond any one of these stages.

Small Talk. Small talk is a broad exploration for common ground that permits us to decide whether we wish to advance the relationship beyond surface contact.

Self-Disclosure. Self-disclosure is the revelation of personal information. Self-disclosure invites reciprocity and can foster intimacy. However, premature self-disclosure suggests maladjustment and tends to repel people.

Marriage. Today's marriages are usually based on attraction and love and the desires for emotional and psychological intimacy and security. We tend to marry people similar in race, religion, social class, intelligence, and even eye color. Four factors predict marital satisfaction: affective communication, problem-solving communication, sexual satisfaction, and agreement about finances.

Divorce. About one-half of all marriages end in divorce. Divorced people usually encounter a great deal of stress and show some decline in health.

Remaining Single. Many people remain single because they have not found the right marital partner. Others prefer sexual variety and wish to avoid making a commitment.

Cohabitation. Cohabitation is living together without being married. Most cohabiting college students come from stable families and expect to get married someday, but not necessarily to their current partners. Most cohabiting students do not see their behavior as immoral. They tend to encounter adjustment problems similar to those of young married couples.

Learning Objectives

After studying this chapter you should be able to:

1. Explain what an intimate relationship is and briefly describe Levinger's five stages in the development of a relationship.

2. Identify and discuss the positive and negative factors that affect each of Levinger's five stages in the development of a relationship.

3. Discuss the importance of small talk and self-disclosure in the development of a relationship.

4. Explain why people get married, describe whom they marry, and discuss the factors that affect marital satisfaction.

5. Discuss who has affairs, how many people have them, why they have them, how they affect the primary relationship, and how Americans feel about whether affairs are right or wrong.

6. Discuss the reasons for changes in the divorce rate in recent years and explain the costs and effects of divorce on all of those involved.

7. Discuss the various alternatives to traditional marriage, focusing on why many people remain single, and the reasons for and types of cohabitation.

8. Describe the various methods of coping with marital conflict described in your text.

9. Explain the various methods presented in your text for improving your communications and listening skills, as a means for resolving marital conflict.

10. Explain the methods presented in your text for learning about your partner's needs when trying to improve marital communication.

11. Describe the methods presented in your text for making requests when trying to improve marital communication.

12. Describe the methods presented in your text for delivering and receiving criticism when trying to improve marital communication.

13. Explain the methods presented in your text for coping with impasses when trying to improve marital communications.

Key Terms

intimate relationships
ABCDE model
attraction
need for affiliation
matching hypothesis
surface contact
small talk
self-disclosure
confederates
mutuality
successive approximations
jealousy
equity
self-efficacy expectation
marriage
homogamy
divorce
divorce mediation
eebu
singlehood
open marriage
group marriage
communes
cohabitation
POSSLQ
exchange contracting
active listening
empathy
paraphrasing

Key Terms Review

Define each of the following terms:

1. Intimate Relationships: ______________________________

____

2. ABCDE Model: ______________________________

____

3. Need for Affiliation: ______________________________

____

4. Surface Contact: ______________________________

____

5. Small Talk: ______________________________

____

6. Self-Disclosure: ______________________________

____

7. Confederate: ______________________________

____

8. Mutuality: ______________________________

____

9. Equity: ______________________________

____

10. Jealousy: ______________________________

____

11. Homogamy: ______________________________

____

12. Active Listening: ______________________________

____

13. Empathy: ______________________________

____

14. Paraphrasing: ____

____

15. Eebu: ____

____

16. Divorce Mediation: ____

____

17. Singlehood: ____

____

18. Open Marriage: ____

____

19. Group Marriage: ____

____

20. Cohabitation: ____

____

Chapter Review

1. According to the ABCDE model, the five stages through which relationships develop are:

   a. ____

   b. ____

   c. ____

   d. ____

   e. ____

2. The positive factors during the attraction stage of a relationship are _________, _________ emotions, and need for _________. The negative factors are lack of _________, _________ emotions, and low need for _________.

3. Our impressions of another person are mostly _________ during the stage of initial attraction.

4. The positive factors during the building stage of a relationship are matching _________ attractiveness, _________ similarity, and _________ _________ evaluations. The negative factors in this stage are nonequivalent _________ attractiveness, _________ dissimilarity, and _________ _________ evaluations.

5. Five steps in building a relationship are:

   a. ____

   b. ____

   c. ____

   d. ____

   e. ____

6. Psychologists have found that we can enhance social skills, such as date-seeking skills, through _________ _________.

7. Once a relationship is built, it enters the stage of _________.

8. Highly jealous people are frequently _________, harboring feelings of _________ and concerns of lack of sexual _________.

9. _________ involves feelings that one is getting as much from a relationship as one is giving to the relationship.

10. Deterioration is a stage in relationships that is neither _________ nor _________.

11. Two active responses to a deteriorating relationship are:

a. ______________________________

b. ______________________________

12. Passive responses to a deteriorating relationship are essentially characterized by

__________ or __________ __________.

13. Relationships are likely to come to an end when:

a. ______________________________

b. ______________________________

c. ______________________________

d. ______________________________

14. __________ is our most common lifestyle.

15. The concept of like marrying like is called __________.

16. By and large, we tend to be attracted to and to get married to __________________

____

17. Five items that should be included in a marriage contract are:

a. ______________________________

b. ______________________________

c. ______________________________

d. ______________________________

e. ______________________________

18. Studies show that __________ ability is a prime factor in satisfying relationships.

19. Snyder found four factors that constantly predicted marital satisfaction. They are:

a. ______________________________

b. ______________________________

c. ______________________________

d. ______________________________

20. Men are about __________ as likely as women to admit to affairs, and a __________ of married people admit to having affairs.

21. In explaining why they have affiars, __________ and desire for __________ __________ are cited as more common reasons than marital dissatisfaction.

22. Usually, men are seeking __________ in affairs, and women are seeking __________ __________.

23. Most married couples embrace the value of __________ as the cornerstone of their marital relationship.

24. In 1920, about one marriage in __________ ended in divorce. By 1960, this figure had risen to one in __________. Today about one in __________ marriages end in divorce.

25. The most common reasons given for a divorce today are problems in __________ and a lack of __________. Years ago it was more likely to be lack of __________ __________.

26. Divorce usually has __________ and __________ repercussions.

27. People who are __________ and __________ have the highest rates of mental and physical illness in the population.

28. Christmas Eve in Japan has become the __________ night of the year.

29. Three factors contributing to the rise in the number of single people are:

a. ____

b. ____

c. ____

30. Other alternative lifestyles besides singlehood are __________ marriage, __________ marriage, __________, and __________.

31. __________ was once referred to as "living in sin" but today is more likely to be termed __________ __________.

32. Three styles of cohabitation are:

a. ____

b. ____

c. ____

33. Five methods of coping with marital conflict are:

a. ____

b. ____

c. ____

d. ____

e. ____

34. Two ways to get started in improving communications are to:

a. ____

b. ____

35. Four methods of improving listening skills for more effective communication with your partner are:

a. ____

b. ____

c. ____

d. ____

36. Three methods for learning about your partner's needs are:

a. ____

b. ____

c. ____

37. Three steps in making requests effectively are:

a. ____

b. ____

c. ____

38. Six steps in delivering effective criticism are:

a. ____

b. ____

c. ____

d. ____

e. ____

f. ____

39. Four steps in receiving criticism effectively are:

a. ______________________________

b. ______________________________

c. ______________________________

d. ______________________________

40. Five techniques to help cope with communications impasses are:

a. ______________________________

b. ______________________________

c. ______________________________

d. ______________________________

e. ______________________________

Sample Test

Multiple-Choice Questions

1. Levinger's ABCDE model deals with ______.
   a. development of relationships
   b. coping with marital conflict
   c. coping with divorce
   d. enhancing communication skills

2. After initial attraction comes the stage of ______.
   a. zero contact
   b. building
   c. continuation
   d. deterioration

3. Small talk is most important during the ______ stage.
   a. initial attraction
   b. mutuality
   c. building
   d. continuation

4. Research indicates that very early self-disclosure of personal information may ______.
   a. increase your attractiveness
   b. repel the other person
   c. move you directly from the attraction stage to the continuation stage
   d. have little, if any, effect on the relationship

5. About ______ percent of adults describe themselves as jealous.
   a. 14
   b. 34
   c. 54
   d. 74

6. Which of the following is **NOT** a factor that will contribute to the ending of a relationship?
   a. There is little satisfaction in the relationship.
   b. Alternative partners are available.
   c. Partners are not committed to maintaining the relationship.
   d. The partners argue and disagree frequently.

7. According to the authors of your text, each of the following is a recent addition to the structure of marriage **EXCEPT** ______.
   a. romantic love
   b. equality
   c. males being faithful
   d. females being faithful

8. The concept of like marrying like is called ______.
   a. polyandry
   b. androgyny
   c. homogamy
   d. misogyny

9. According to your text, whom are you **MOST** likely to marry?
   a. the boy or girl next door
   b. a mysterious stranger
   c. someone you were fixed up with on a blind date
   d. someone you met in a "singles" bar or some similar social spot

10. According to Snyder's study, which of the following is **MOST** important to marital satisfaction?
    a. affective communication
    b. sexual satisfaction
    c. agreement about finances
    d. child rearing patterns

11. In recent surveys, ______ of cohabitors report that they have remained loyal to their partners.
    a. only a small minority
    b. a large minority
    c. only a slight majority
    d. a vast majority

12. Today's divorce rate is about ______ percent.
   a. 40
   b. 50
   c. 60
   d. 70

13. Which of the following is **NOT** true of the cost of divorce?
   a. The couple's resources may not extend far enough to maintain the former standard of living for both partners.
   b. The divorced woman who has not pursued a career may find herself competing for jobs with younger, more experienced people.
   c. The divorced man may not be able to manage alimony, child support, and establishing a new home of his own.
   d. Divorce rarely requires extensive waiting and legal conflict in today's world of liberalized divorce laws.

14. The most difficult aspect of divorce is likely to be ______.
   a. the loss of a regular sexual partner
   b. the loss of the financial security a marriage usually offers
   c. the splitting up of the property which has been collected through the course of the marriage
   d. separating psychologically from the personality and influence of the ex-spouse

15. The nation's most common lifestyle for people in their early twenties is ______.
   a. singlehood
   b. traditional marriage
   c. cohabitation
   d. group marriage

16. Many singles decide they would prefer to marry and to perhaps have children when they reach their ______.
   a. late twenties
   b. early thirties
   c. late thirties
   d. early forties

17. Each of the following is a reason people cohabit **EXCEPT** ______.
   a. economic factors
   b. it provides a relationship without the legal entanglements of marriage
   c. a greater commitment toward the relationship than married people feel
   d. to avoid the disapproval of and resistance from relatives

18. Which of the following is a method for getting started when trying to talk about marital communication?
   a. paraphrasing
   b. take responsibility for what happens to you
   c. acknowledge criticism
   d. talk about talking

19. Jim asks a person out on a date in a manner consistent with his behavioral rehearsal. This is most likely to occur during the ______ level.
   a. self-disclosure
   b. target behavior
   c. medium practice
   d. easy practice

20. In Japan, Christmas Eve is referred to as ______ day.
   a. "B"
   b. "D"
   c. "H"
   d. "J"

True-False Questions

21. The majority of adults describe themselves as jealous. ______

22. Historically, marriage has been built on notions of romantic love. ______

23. Most Americans are dissatisfied with their marriages. ______

24. Most single mothers in the U. S. are young and poorly educated. ______

25. Stable and global attributions about one's partner make marital problems somewhat easier to solve. ______

Essay Question

26. Describe the methods presented in your text for making requests when trying to improve marital communication.

Student Activities

Name ______________________________ Date ____________

14.1 Opening Lines

When it comes to winning friends and influencing people, many of us find it all too easy to identify with Allan Felix (from the text). When we spy someone who is appealing and apparently available, we would like to know what to say, and we might rehearse a line or two to break the ice. What do you think is appropriate, and what do you think is shallow and a turn-off? Test your thoughts on this by writing examples of "good," "mediocre," and "shallow" opening lines in the space below. Then tell a friend what you are up to and ask him or her to evaluate the examples you have written.

Follow-Up Questions:

1. How well did you do? Was your friend able to tell correctly what your intentions were? If not, what went wrong? What could you do to fix the problem?

2. Generally, what goals do you recommend people try to achieve with their opening remarks to someone they find attractive?

3. What do people of the opposite sex report are appropriate for opening lines? Ask your classmates or friends for ideas. If you cannot ask others, try to imagine what they would say. Write down what you can and ask your instructor to provide some feedback or class discussion.

Name ________________________________ **Date** ____________

14.2 It May Be in How We Say It

While the suave lines we invent to initiate relationships are important, the nonverbal cues we give may be even more significant. Try to imagine you are a screenwriter working on a movie. You are writing a line for the heroine or hero, whomever you identify with, who is approaching the other star for the first time, and simply says: "Good evening," or alternatively "Hi, my name is ________." Now write the stage direction, referring to vocal tone, eye contact, bodily postures, and movement.

1. First, write this for yourself.

2. Second, write this for someone who is very shy. How is this different from what you wrote for yourself? Is it better or worse? Why?

3. Finally, write this for your favorite actor or actress. Is this different from either or both of the first two you wrote? If so, how? Is it better or worse? Why?

4. Describe how the president says this before a televised talk. How is it different from any of the others you wrote above? Is it better or worse? Why?

Follow-Up Questions:

1. What did you rely on most for creating different nonverbal communication in this exercise?

2. What would you most like to change about your own nonverbal communication and how can you change it?

Name________________________________ **Date** _______________

14.3 It May Be When We Say It

After initial attraction, we are still "on approval," meaning we still want to keep Mr. or Ms. "Right" favorably impressed with us. In our first and early testing opportunities, we can, and likely must, disclose information to each other. Rathus and Nevid point out how we must consider what is safe to disclose and what could be self-damaging and prematurely revealing. Consider the research project discussed in Chapter 14, where researchers had their confederates reveal intimate information early in a ten-minute conversation, or late in the conversation, and as a consequence either come across as immature and phony if they revealed too early, or more attractive when revealing the same information toward the end of the ten minutes.

Write down three items of disclosure you think the researchers could have used in their study to create the effects they found.

1.

2.

3.

You will need some feedback on how well you did, so share your three ideas with your confidant, your class, or your instructor. Be prepared for some criticism because these are judgment calls. Others may have a less than adequate idea of the context you have imagined. Let's hear them out because we are at least being sensitized to some of the relevant points the text is trying to make. How did you do? What could you do differently next time to do it better?

Name ________________________________ **Date** ____________

14.4 A Tall Job

A tall job is what Rathus and Nevid call the preparation of a marriage contract, even an informal one. But to avoid ending up like Donald Trump, let us do it anyway. Consider each of the eleven issues discussed in the questions below, and decide how each would be resolved for you.

1. What name will the wife use after marriage?

2. How will chores be allocated?

3. Will there be children, and if so, how many and when?

4. Will there be contraception, and if so, what kind?

5. How will child care be distributed?

6. Whose career will determine where you live?

7. Who will work and who will make financial decisions?

8. Which relatives will be visited and how often?

9. What leisure activities will be shared and unshared?

10. How will sexual issues be decided, and what will the decisions be?

11. How can changes in this contract be accommodated?

12. Do you agree with some experts who believe marriages should be free of such contractual specifications? Why?

13. What things might you add to this list? Why?

15

Sexual Behavior

Chapter Outline

I. The Biological Basis of Sex

A. Female Sexual Anatomy
   1. Box: Adjustment in a World of Diversity: The Ritual Destruction of Female Sexuality
B. Male Sexual Anatomy
C. The Sexual Response Cycle
   1. Box: Adjustment in the New Millennium: Sex Becomes "Interactive"
C. Effects of Sex Hormones
   1. Box: Adjustment in the New Millennium: Will We Finally Have Love Potions in the New Millennium?

II. Rape

A. Why Do Men Rape Women?
B. Rape Myths: Do You Harbor Beliefs That Encourage Rape?
   1. Box: Self-Assessment: Do You Subscribe to Cultural Myths That Create a Climate That Supports Rape?

III. Sexual Dysfunctions

A. Causes of Sexual Dysfunctions
   1. Box: Adjustment in the New Millennium: Enter the "Brave New World" of Viagra?

IV. AIDS and Other Sexually Transmitted Diseases

A. AIDS
   1. Box: Self-Assessment: The AIDS Awareness Inventory

VI. Contraception

VII. Adjustment and Modern Life

A. Preventing Rape (Shout "Fire!" Not "Rape!")
   1. Box: What Do You Say Now? Resisting Verbal Sexual Pressure
B. Preventing STDs in the Age of AIDS
   1. Box: What Do You Say Now? Making Sex Safe(r) in the Age of AIDS

Harcourt Brace & Company

Chapter Overview

Cultural Differences in Sexual Practices. Sexual practices vary from culture to culture a great deal. For example, sexual behavior is greatly restricted on Inis Baeg, whereas the natives of Mangaia enjoy varied sexual practices from a relatively young age. Societies differ in sexual permissiveness and, to some degree, in the behaviors and stimuli that are deemed sexually arousing.

Biological Features of Sexual Arousal and Behavior. The male and female sex organs respond to sexual stimulation and make reproduction possible. Although the male sex organs are more visible than the female organs, females' organs are complex and, like men's, are oriented toward sexual pleasure.

The Sexual Response Cycle. Masters and Johnson have identified a sexual response cycle that occurs in both males and females and includes four phases: excitement, plateau, orgasm, and resolution.

Sex Hormones. Sex hormones promote biological sexual differentiation, regulate the menstrual cycle, and have organizing and activating effects on sexual behavior. In lower animals, sex is controlled largely by hormones and pheromones.

Reason for Rape. Rape appears to be motivated more by anger and desire to exercise power over women than by sexual needs. Our culture may socialize men to be aggressive toward women and in some cases to become rapists.

Sexual Dysfunctions. Sexual dysfunctions are problems in becoming sexually aroused or reaching orgasm. Sexual dysfunctions now and then reflect physical factors, such as disease, alcohol, or fatigue, but most reflect psychosocial factors such as negative attitudes toward sex, psychosexual trauma, troubled relationships, lack of sexual skills, and irrational beliefs. Any of these may lead to performance anxiety, which compounds sexual problems.

Sexually Transmitted Diseases (STDs). STDs are diseases that can be transmitted by sexual contact. STDs are caused by a variety of pathogens. For example, gonorrhea and syphilis are caused by bacteria, while herpes and AIDS are caused by viruses. Most STDs can be cured. Gonorrhea and syphilis are cured by antibiotics. Unfortunately, there are no cures for herpes and AIDS.

AIDS. Acquired immune deficiency syndrome (AIDS) is caused by a virus that kills white blood cells in the immune system, leaving the body prey to opportunistic diseases. AIDS is transmitted by sexual intercourse, by sharing contaminated hypodermic needles, by transfusions, and by childbirth. AIDS appears to be invariably fatal to those who develop full-blown cases of the disease. Although recently developed methods of treatment have prolonged the lives of people with HIV infection and AIDS, they are not considered a cure. The best thing to do about AIDS is to prevent it by avoiding risky behavior patterns - for example, casual sex, unprotected sex, sharing needles. And to help educate others about AIDS.

Contraception. Contraception is the prevention of pregnancy. Many safe, effective methods of contraception are available, as described in the chapter. Male condoms, for example, are highly reliable when used carefully and have virtually no side effects. "The pill" is effective and safe for most women. Sterilization is inappropriate for people who may decide to have children later on.

Learning Objectives

After studying this chapter you should be able to:

1. Discuss the reasons why sexual practices vary so much from culture to culture and describe some of the differences that exist in these cultures.

2. Describe the male and female sex organs and explain the functions of the various components of these organs.

3. Identify the four stages of the sexual response cycle and briefly explain what happens during each stage of the cycle.

4. Identify the hormones involved in human sexual response and explain what role they play in human sexual arousal and behavior.

5. Describe the prevalence of rape in the United States, discuss the reasons for this prevalence, and identify at least three myths about rape.

6. Identify the various sexual dysfunctions and briefly explain the causes for each of them as well as for sexual dysfunctions in general.

7. Explain what STDs are and identify the various causes of five of the most prevalent STDs. Also, briefly discuss which STDs can and cannot be treated or cured.

8. Compare and contrast at least five major methods of contraception in terms of their effectiveness, how they prevent pregnancy, and drawbacks associated with them.

9. Explain the possible strategies for reducing the risk of being raped by a stranger.

10. Explain the possible strategies for reducing the risk of date rape.

11. Identify lines used to put pressure on someone to have sex, and describe possible responses to those lines that will help successfully resist sexual pressure.

12. Identify and briefly explain various measures you can take to protect yourself from AIDS and other STDs.

Key Terms

vulva
pudendum
urethra
mons veneris
clitoris
glans
major lips
minor lips
cervix
fallopian tubes
clitoridectomy
semen
testes
scrotum
the sexual response cycle
vasocongestion
myotonia
excitement phase
plateau phase
orgasmic phase
resolution phase
refractory period
estrogen
progesterone
menstruation
endometrium
ovulation
organizing effect
activating events
testosterone
estrus
menopause
pheromones
vomeronasal organ
rape
date rape
hypoactive sexual desire disorder
female sexual arousal disorder
male erectile disorder
orgasmic disorder
premature ejaculation
dyspareunia
vaginismus
performance anxiety
sex therapy
HIV
AIDS
Viagra
opportunistic diseases
bacterial vaginosis
candidiasis
chlamydia
nongonococcal urethritis
genital herpes
genital warts
gonorrhea
public lice
syphilis
trichomoniasis
CD4 lymphocytes
B lymphocytes
contraception
contraceptive pills
Norplant
Depo-Provera
morning-after pill
IUD
diaphragm
cervical cap
male condom
female condom
coitus interruptus
rhythm method
douching
sterilization

Key Terms Review (Due to the number and complexity of the terms in this chapter, there are two review sections. The first deals with sexual anatomy. The second deals with sexual disorders, sexual diseases, and contraception.)

Key Terms Review #1

Define each of the following terms:

1. Vulva: ______________________________

____

2. Pudendum: ______________________________

____

3. Urethra: ______________________________

____

4. Mons Veneris: ______________________________

____

5. Clitoris: ______________________________

____

6. Glans: ______________________________

____

7. Major Lips: ______________________________

____

8. Minor Lips: ______________________________

____

9. Cervix: ______________________________

____

10. Clitoridectomy: ______________________________

____

11. Testes: ______________________________

____

12. Scrotum: ______________________________

____

13. Menstruation: ______________________________

____

14. Endometrium: ______________________________

____

15. Ovulation: ______________________________

____

16. Organizing Effects: ______________________________

____

17. Activating Effects: ______________________________

____

18. Estrus: ______________________________

____

19. Menopause: ______________________________

____

20. Concordance: ______________________________

____

Key Terms Review # 2

Define each of the following terms:

1. Heterosexual: ______________________________

____

2. Gay Male: ______________________________

____

3. Lesbian: ______________________________

____

4. Sexual Orientation: ______________________________

____

5. Hypoactive Sexual Desire Disorder: ______________________________

____

6. Female Sexual Arousal Disorder: ______________________________

____

7. Male Erectile Disorder: ______________________________

____

8. Orgasmic Disorder: ______________________________

____

9. Premature Ejaculation: ______________________________

____

10. Dyspareunia: ______________________________

____

11. Vaginismus: ______________________________

____

12. Performance Anxiety: ______________________________

____

13. Sex Therapy: ______________________________

____

14. AIDS: ______________________________

____

15. Genital Herpes: ______________________________

____

16. Gonorrhea: ____

____

17. Syphilis: ____

____

18. Contraception: ____

____

19. Coitus Interruptus: ____

____

20. Rhythm Method: ____

____

Chapter Review

1. The residents of Inis Beag don't believe that women experience __________, and men believe that sex saps their __________.
2. From an early age, Mangaian children are encouraged to get in touch with their sexuality through __________.
3. Nearly every society has an __________ taboo.
4. Among the Aleut people of Alaska, it is considered good manners for a man to offer his __________ to a houseguest.
5. Perhaps no other natural function has been influenced so strongly by religious and moral beliefs, cultural tradition, folklore, and superstition, as __________ has been.

6. **Matching:** Match the term on the left with its appropriate description on the right.

_______ a. Vulva	1. the tubelike organ that contains the penis during sexual intercourse
_______ b. Mons veneris	2. a tube that conducts urine from the body
_______ c. Clitoris	3. the female external genital organs
_______ d. Glans	4. the folds of the skin that enclose the urethral and vaginal openings
_______ e. Major lips	5. the lower part of the uterus that opens into the vagina
_______ f. Minor lips	6. the tip or head
_______ g. Cervix	7. the female sex organ whose only known function is the transmission and reception of sensations of sexual pleasure
_______ h. Urethra	8. the large folds of skin that run along the sides of the vulva
_______ i. Vagina	9. the pad of fatty tissue that covers the joint of the pubic bones and cushions the female during intercourse
_______ j. Ovaries	10. the female sexual organs that produce ova and the hormones estrogen and progesterone
_______ k. Fallopian tube	11. the tubelike organ that connects the ovaries to the uterus

7. Some cultures in Africa and the Middle East practice __________ as a means of ensuring chastity.

8. The Greeks held their __________ when offering testimony.

9. The __________ produce sperm and the male sex hormone __________.

10. The __________ allows the testes to hang away from the body.

11. The male urethra transports __________ as well as __________.

12. The penis consists mainly of __________ __________ tissue.

13. The four phases of the sexual response cycle are the __________ phase, the __________ phase, the __________ phase, and the __________ phase.

14. Unlike women, men enter a __________ period after orgasm in which they cannot experience another __________ or __________.

15. The ovaries produce __________ and __________.

16. Sex hormones have __________ and __________ effects on sexual behavior.

17. The hormones __________ and __________ regulate the menstrual cycle in females, while the hormone __________ affects sexual desire and drive in males.

18. While sex hormones affect sexual behavior, __________ factors also play a role.

19. Scientists believe that natural "love potients" exist in the form of chemical secretions known as __________, which are detected by humans through the __________ organ.

20. The great majority of rapes are committed by __________.

21. Many rapists appear to be using rape as a means of expressing __________ toward, or __________ over, women, rather than for sexual satisfaction.

22. Social scientists contend that our society socializes men into becoming __________ and women into becoming __________.

23. Five myths about rape are:

a. ____

b. ____

c. ____

d. ____

e. ____

24. **Matching:** Match the term on the left with its appropriate description on the right.

_______ a. Hypoactive sexual desire	1. lack of interest in sexual activity
_______ b. Female sexual arousal disorder	2. painful coitus
_______ c. Male erectile disorder	3. difficulty becoming sexually aroused as defined by vaginal lubrication
_______ d. Orgasmic disorder	4. involuntary contraction of the muscles surrounding the vagina, making entry difficult or impossible
_______ e. Premature ejaculation	5. difficulty in becoming aroused as defined by achieving erection
_______ f. Dyspareunia	6. difficulty achieving orgasm despite adequate sexual arousal
_______ g. Vaginismus	7. fear concerning whether one will be able to perform adequately
_______ h. Performance anxiety	8. ejaculation that occurs prior to the couple's desires

25. Fewer than __________ million Americans are thought to be infected with HIV, whereas __________ million are infected with other STD-causing viruses.

26. AIDS is a fatal condition in which the person's __________ system is so weakened that he or she falls prey to __________ diseases.

27. HIV is transmitted by infected __________, __________, __________ and __________ secretions, and __________ __________.

28. HIV kills __________ cells.

29. ____ accounts for the majority of the cases of HIV infection in the world today, although __________ __________ and __________ __________ have been hardest hit by the epidemic.

30. Infection by HIV is generally diagnosed by means of __________, __________, or __________ tests.

31. The standard treatment for AIDS patients today is __________ therapy.

32. **Matching:** Match the sexually transmitted disease on the left with its appropriate symptoms and cause on the right

________ a. Gonorrhea

________ b. Syphilis

________ c. Herpes

________ d. AIDS

________ e. Moniliasis

________ f. Trichomoniasis

________ g. Chlamydia

________ h. "Crabs"

1. caused by a bacterium; symptoms include penile discharge about three to five days after infection that turns yellow-green and becomes puslike; urination accompanied by a burning sensation; can lead to PID in females

2. caused by a bacterium; four stages of development: formation of painless chancre; chancre disappears and skin rash develops along with "flu-like" symptoms; latency period; large ulcers and damage to cardiovascular and central nervous systems

3. caused by a virus; reddish painful bumps that turn to pus-filled blisters and rupture; blisters heal about 10-16 days later; recurrent episodes, no cure

4. caused by a fungus; vaginal irritation and white cheesy discharge; cured by vaginal creams or suppositories

5. caused by a bacterium; in men - burning urination and discharge; testes feel heavy and scrotum sore; in women -- PID; disrupted menstrual periods; treated with antibiotics

6. body lice; can cause itching; can be seen with naked eye

7. caused by a protozoan; irritation of the vulva, white or yellow vaginal discharge and an unpleasant odor

8. caused by a virus; destroys immune system by killing white blood cells; fatal; no cure

33. The most widely used contraceptive method by unmarried women between the ages of 15 and 44 is the __________.

34. **Matching:** Match the birth control technique on the left with its appropriate description on the right.

________ a. Birth control pill

________ b. Norplant

________ c. The "morning after" pill

________ d. IUDs

________ e. Diaphragms

________ f. Contraceptive sponges

________ g. Cervical cap

________ h. Male condoms

________ i. Female condoms

________ j. Coitus interruptus

________ k. Rhythm method

1. shallow cups with flexible rims made of thin rubber, used with a spermicide and inserted against the cervix within six hours before intercourse
2. tracking the ovulation cycle and avoiding intercourse for 3 days prior to ovulation and 2 days afterward
3. prescription medications that prevent pregnancy by using hormones to fool the brain into thinking a pregnancy exists and preventing implantation
4. a plastic sheath inserted into the vagina and held in place by plastic rings fitted over the vaginal opening and against the cervix
5. a device, often made of copper, that is inserted into the uterus by a physician
6. silicon tubes containing progestin that are surgically implanted under the skin of a woman's upper arm
7. removal of the penis from the vagina prior to ejaculation
8. disposable nonprescription device that is inserted into the vagina and does not need to be fitted. Holds spermicide and can be inserted up to 18 hours before intercourse
9. prescription medication taken within 72 hours of intercourse that prevents implantation of a fertilized egg
10. device made of rubber or plastic that is fitted over the cervix and kept in place for several weeks at a time
11. rubberized plastic sheath placed over the penis

35. The most common birth control method used by married people is __________.

36. Five techniques for lowering the risk of rape by a stranger are:

a. ____________________

b. ____________________

c. ____________________

d. ____________________

e. ____________________

37. Five techniques for lowering the risk of date rape are:

a. ____________________

b. ____________________

c. ____________________

d. ____________________

e. ____________________

38. Five steps to reduce your risk of contracting a sexually transmitted disease are:

a. ____________________

b. ____________________

c. ____________________

d. ____________________

e. ____________________

Sample Test

Multiple-Choice Questions

1. Mangaian women are expected to ______.
   a. climax, or reach orgasm, several times before their partners do
   b. fight off their husbands' sexual advances until they have "protected their dignity"
   c. engage in sexual activity only during ovulation, so they can conceive children
   d. satisfy their husbands' "animal cravings" at the expense of their own pleasure

2. The ______ is (are) also known as the pudendum.
   a. glans c. minor lips
   b. mons veneris d. vulva

3. According to research, ______.
   a. the entire vagina is relatively insensitive to touch
   b. only the inner two-thirds of the vagina is sensitive to touch
   c. the outer third of the vagina is very sensitive to touch
   d. the entire length of the vagina is very sensitive to touch

4. Conception normally takes place in the ______.
   a. vagina c. fallopian tube
   b. uterus d. cervix

5. Erections in males result from ______.
   a. engorgement of penile tissue with blood
   b. expansion of the penile muscle
   c. hardening of the bone tissue inside the penis
   d. engorgement of the penile tissue with semen

6. The phase of the sexual response cycle characterized by increases in heart rate and blood pressure, development of erection and increase in the size of the testes in males, and vaginal lubrication, vasocongestion in the clitoris and vaginal lips, expansion of the inner part of the vagina, and breast enlargement and nipple erection in females is the ______ stage.
   a. plateau c. orgasm
   b. excitement d. resolution

7. When estrogen reaches peak blood levels, ______ occurs.
   a. menstruation c. ovulation
   b. PMS d. nothing

8. Androgens influence ______ sexual response.
   a. neither male nor female c. female but not male
   b. male but not female d. both male and female

9. It is believed that between _______ women in the United States have been raped.
   a. one in two and one in four c. one in seven and one in ten
   b. one in four and one in seven b. one in ten and one in twelve

10. Marge has normal sexual desires but has difficulty in achieving vaginal lubrication or remaining sexually excited long enough to engage in satisfying sexual relations. She is suffering from _____
    a. hypoactive sexual desire disorder c. dyspareunia
    b. female sexual arousal disorder d. vaginismus

Harcourt Brace & Company

11. When Mort has sexual intercourse, he feels recurrent pain in his genitals. This sexual dysfunction is called ______.
    a. male erectile disorder
    b. vaginismus
    c. dyspareunia
    d. a hernia

12. Mort suffers from diabetes and heart disease. Which sexual dysfunction is most likely to be associated with his physical problems?
    a. hypoactive sexual desire
    b. premature ejaculation
    c. male erectile disorder
    d. inhibited orgasm

13. HPV is linked to the development of ______.
    a. AIDS
    b. SIDS
    c. breast cancer
    d. cervical cancer

14. A few days after having sexual intercourse, Irving develops a rash of reddish, painful bumps, or papules, in the genital region. These papules turn to painful blisters that become pus-filled and rupture. At this time he also develops headaches, muscle aches, swollen lymph nodes, fever, and burning urination. About 10 to 16 days later, the blister crusts over and heal. About 2 weeks later he develops the same symptoms again. He appears to have contracted ______.
    a. syphilis
    b. gonorrhea
    c. chlamydia
    d. herpes

15. The AIDS virus attacks and kills ______.
    a. bone marrow
    b. red blood cells
    c. blood plasma
    d. white blood cells

16. The majority of users of birth control pills do not become high risk for most disorders related to their use until they reach the age of ______.
    a. 35
    b. 45
    c. 55
    d. 65

17. Morning-after pills consist of ______.
    a. androgens
    b. estrogens but not progestins
    c. progestins but not estrogens
    d. both estrogens and progestins

18. Sterilization operations such as tubal ligations and vasectomies are ______.
    a. never reversible
    b. sometimes reversible
    c. usually reversible
    d. always reversible

19. The practice of clitoridectomy is often performed ______.
    a. at birth
    b. during childhood
    c. as a puberty ritual
    d. after menopause

20. Each of the following is a side effect of Viagra **EXCEPT** ______.
    a. headaches
    b. diarrhea
    c. depression
    d. distorted color vision

True-False Questions

21. Some cultures feel that the female armpit is highly erotic. ______

22. Clitoridectomies are the female equivalent of males being circumcised. ______

23. Menstruation occurs about halfway through the menstrual cycle. ______

24. Most men commit rapes to fulfill their sexual needs. ______

25. HIV has infected more Americans than most other STDs. ______

Essay Question

26. Describe the prevalence of rape in the United States and discuss the reasons for this prevalence.

Student Activities

Name ______________________________ **Date** ____________

15.1 The Perfect Sex Questionnaire

In this chapter we learn how reliant we are on information from surveys and questionnaires to understand sexual behavior. We also learn that many questionnaires are open to some methodological flaws, or are dated, or just didn't ask the "right" people. There is only one way to find the "perfect sex questionnaire." You will have to write it. Try writing five relevant questions about sexual behavior that would answer questions that are important to you. They may reflect a concern, or an issue related to your interests.

1.

2.

3.

4.

5.

Your instructor may wish to follow up this exercise with class discussion.

Name ______________________________ **Date** ____________

15.2 Sex and Entertainment

The last movie or television show you saw that included sexual intimacy will serve as our target for this exercise. The answers may tell us much about the attitudes and behaviors being encouraged today.

1. Did the script suggest that safe sex was being practiced? If so, how?

2. What kind of relationship was the couple involved in? Was it a long-term relationship, such as a marriage or cohabitation, or a brief fling, or what?

3. What was the state of the relationship at the end of the movie? Was there an implication of any type of long-term committment that would extend after the end of the movie? If so, what was it?

4. Do you think there are different standards of sexual behavior for yourself, for others, or for entertainment? If so, what are those standards and how are they different from yours?

Name ______________________________ **Date** ____________

15.3 What Are Your State's Laws?

The laws governing sexual behavior differ from state to state. Occasionally we read about obviously outdated laws that are still on the books, but not enforced. Missouri once had a law forbidding a woman from refusing her husband's sexual advances.

What does your state say about the following sexual issues? Answer a) what you believe the law says, and then b) find a good source for the law to check yourself.

1. What is your state's age for statutory rape?

   a)

   b)

2. Is homosexuality legal in your state?

   a)

   b)

3. What is your state's age for legally being allowed to get married?

   a)

   b)

4. Does your state allow cohabitation or recognize common law marriage? If so, under what conditions?

   a)

   b)

Activity continued on the back

5. Does your state require a blood test for a marriage license, and if it does, is AIDS included in the screening? What other diseases are screened for, if any?

   a)

   b)

6. Which of the laws are not enforceable? Why not?

7. Would you like to see any of these laws changed? Why?

Name ________________________________ Date ____________

15.4 Critical Thinking

Researchers have found evidence that rape victims tend to be less dominant and less self-assertive than nonvictims. The results suggested that women who appear to be vulnerable are more likely to be attacked. If we look critically at this research, we will see that it is a bit premature to conclude that women have been socialized into the role of victims who are "asking for it."

1. What other explanations could account for research findings such as this?

2. What kind of study could more successfully test the hypothesis that being less dominant and self-assertive could increase the risk of being a rape victim? Explain how you would design such a study.

Name ___________________________________ Date ____________

15.5 Sexual Expectations

Historically, adolescents in this country have faced numerous stereotypic expectations regarding their sexual behavior. At one extreme, males were supposed to be ready, willing, and eager at every sexual opportunity no matter who the partner or what kind of commitment they have to someone else. Females were divided into "nice girls" who saved themseleves until marriage, and "bad girls" who were sexually promiscuous. Males encouraged each other to have sex with the "bad girls," but them labeled them "sluts," and gave them "reputations" that were unappealing at best. The males on the other hand were labeled "studs" and looked up to by other males. Males would then marry the "nice girls," while the "bad girls" were left to mend their own reputations and fend for themselves.

1. How are these stereotypic expectations different today, if at all, from years past?

2. Who have they changed more for, men or women? Why do you believe this is so?

3. Do you see the changes as for the better or the worse? Why?

4. Have you ever found yourself under pressure to behave sexually in a way you did not want to? What happened, how did you handle it, and how did it affect you afterwards?

5. What do you think can be done to lower the amount of sexual pressure on adolescents today?

Harcourt Brace & Company

16

Adult Development: Going Through Changes

Chapter Outline

I. Introduction

1. Box: Self-Assessment: How Long Will You Live? The Life-Expectancy Scale

II. Young Adulthood

A. Physical Development
B. Cognitive Development
C. Personality Development and Adjustment

III. Middle Adulthood

A. Physical Development
   1. Box: Adjustment in a World of Diversity: Is There a *Man*opause?
B. Cognitive Development
   1. Box: Adjustment in the New Millennium: Two Views of Parenting in the New Millennium: Childfree by Choice, and *What* Biological Clock?
C. Personality Development and Adjustment
   1. Box: Self-Assessment: What Are Your Attitudes Toward Aging?

IV. Late Adulthood

A. Physical Development
   1. Box: Adjustment in the New Millennium: Will We Discover a Real Fountain of Youth?
B. Cognitive Development
C. Personality Development and Adjustment

V. On Death and Dying

1. Box: Self-Assessment: How Concerned Are You About Death?

A. Theoretical Perspectives

VI. Adjustment and Modern Life

A. Dying With Dignity

Harcourt Brace & Company

Chapter Overview

Stages of Adulthood. Most researchers divide adulthood into young adulthood (ages 20 to 40), middle adulthood (ages 40 to 65), and late adulthood (age 65 and above).

Major Theorists of Adult Personality Development. These include Erik Erikson, who theorized eight stages of psychosocial development, Robert Havighurst, who cataloged developmental tasks at different stages of adult development, Daniel Levinson, who described "seasons" of men's lives, and Gail Sheehy, who proposed various "passages" we go through. Psychologists such as Judith Barwick and Carol Gilligan have focused on the development of women.

Young Adulthood. Erikson sees the central task of young adulthood as the establishment of intimate relationships. Other theorists focus on striving to advance in the career world. Many suggest some sort of reassessment at about age 30, and Levinson proposes that we settle into our roles at about age 35. Men's development during this period seems to be characterized by a transition from restriction to control, and women's development, according to Gilligan, is characterized by a transition from being cared for to caring for others. Many women are conflicted about success in the career world because of a career's impact on family life.

Middle Adulthood. A slight and gradual decline occurs in overall cognitive abilities and in physical functioning. Because of declining estrogen production, women usually encounter the climacteric in the 40s and menopause in the late 40s or early 50s.

Menopause. Menopause is a normal process with mild symptoms for most women. Menopause is cessation of menstruation, and it can have complex and powerful meanings for women. Despite stereotypes of middle-aged women as irritable and depressed, women are frequently peppier and more assertive following menopause.

The Midlife Transition. The midlife transition is characterized by a psychological shift in focus from how many years we have lived to how many years we have left. In men it usually arrives at about age 40 and is triggered by a marker event, such as the death of a parent or peer. According to Sheehy, women undergo a midlife transition about five years earlier than men do, and it is triggered by the awareness of the approach of the end of the childbearing years.

The Midlife Crisis. The midlife crisis is a period of major reassessment during which we evaluate the discrepancies between our achievements and our youthful dreams. It is here that we come to recognize our limits, including our mortality.

The Empty-Nest Syndrome. This refers to feelings of depression and loss of purpose that are theorized to affect parents, especially mothers, when the last child leaves home. Although an "empty nest" requires adjustment and the ability to let go, many parents enjoy their new-found freedom.

The Freestyle 50s. Sheehy refers to the 50s as the "freestyle 50s" because many of us reach our peaks of productivity, a measure of financial freedom, and are also "over the hump" in child-rearing.

Late Adulthood. Several physical and cognitive changes take place during late adulthood. The elderly show less sensory acuity, and reaction time increases. Some presumed cognitive deficits may actually reflect declining motivation or psychological problems such as depression. Decline continues in strength, stamina, and the immune system, increasing vulnerability to disease. The tasks of late adulthood include adjusting to retirement and maintaining one's ego in the face of physical decline.

Aging. Heredity plays a role in longevity. We do not know exactly why people age, although one possibility is that cells lose the ability to maintain themselves and reproduce adequately. But environmental factors such as exercise, proper diet, and the maintenance of responsibility can apparently slow down or delay aging.

Psychological Adjustment in the Elderly. Most elderly people rate their life satisfaction and their health as generally good. Retirement can be a positive step, so long as it is voluntary. Having adequate financial resources is a major contributor to satisfaction among the elderly.

Death and Dying. Kubler-Ross identifies five stages of dying among the terminally ill: denial, anger, bargaining, depression, and final acceptance. However, research by other investigators shows that psychological reactions to approaching death are varied and related to the person's personality and philosophy of life.

The Funeral. The funeral provides rituals that relieve the bereaved of the need to plan and take charge during the crisis of death. The rituals help the bereaved accept the finality of death and point to a return to communal life.

Learning Objectives

After studying this chapter you should be able to:

1. Identify the major theorists of adult personality development discussed in your text and briefly explain how each of them characterized adult development.

2. Describe the major events of young adulthood, according to the major theorists, and explain the "age 30 transition," why it is important, and why it affects women differently than men.

3. Describe the gender-based differences in the development of personality during young adulthood.

4. Describe the physical and cognitive changes that take place during middle adulthood, focusing on the midlife transition and midlife crisis, and why they are important.

5. Describe what menopause and the climacteric are and discuss how they affect women in middle adulthood.

6. Explain what empty-nest syndrome is and discuss what evidence there is to support or refute this concept.

7. Discuss adult development during the 50s and explain why your text call the 50s "freestyle."

8. Describe the physical and cognitive changes that take place in late adulthood and the effects they have on elderly people.

9. Identify and explain various theories of aging discussed in your text.

10. Summarize the research on the prevalence, causes, and effects of Alzheimer's disease, and explain what can be done to treat and cope with Alzheimer's disease.

11. Discuss adjustment and life satisfaction among the elderly and describe the relationship between most elderly people and their children and grandchildren.

12. Discuss the impact of retirement on older persons and present the reasons for the differences between happily retired persons and retired persons who deteriorate and are unhappy in their retirement.

13. Identify Elisabeth Kubler-Ross's stages of death and dying and discuss what evidence there is in support or rebuke to her theory.

14. Explain how funerals affect the adjustment of survivors and describe what bereavement is and how it helps people recover from the loss of a loved one.

Key Terms

young adulthood
intimacy versus isolation
ego identity
dream
trying 20s
individuation
age 30 transition
catch 30s
middle adulthood
menopause
the climacteric
*man*opause
crystallized intelligence

fluid intelligence
generativity versus stagnation
midlife transition
midlife crisis
middlescence
empty-nest syndrome
freestyle 50s
late adulthood
reaction time
melatonin
DHEA
human growth hormone

telomerase
longevity
programmed senescence
wear-and-tear theory
Alzheimer's disease
acetylcholine
ego integrity versus despair
hospice
euthanasia
living will
the funeral
bereavement

Key Terms Review

Define each of the following terms:

1. The Dream: ______________________________

____

2. Individuation: ______________________________

____

3. Ego Identity: ______________________________

____

4. Age 30 Transition: ______________________________

____

5. Menopause: ____

6. Manopause: ____

7. Midlife Transition: ____

8. Crystallized Intelligence: ____

9. Fluid Intelligence: ____

10. Empty-Nest Syndrome: ____

11. Reaction Time: ____

12. Longevity: ____

13. Programmed Senescence: ____

14. Wear-and-Tear Theory: ____

15. Alzheimer's Disease: ____

16. Acetylcholine: ____

____

17. Hospice: ____

____

18. Euthanasia: ____

____

19. Living Will: ____

____

20. Bereavement: ____

____

Chapter Review

1. Most of us reach our physical and cognitive peaks during our __________.

2. According to Erikson, young adulthood is the stage of __________ versus __________ and we are not capable of committing ourselves to others in a meaningful way until we have achieved __________ __________.

3. Men who develop a strong sense of ego identity by young adulthood get married __________ than men who do not, and women with well-developed senses of identity __________ more stable marriages.

4. Havighurst's eight developmental tasks for young adulthood are:

   a. ______________________________

   b. ______________________________

   c. ______________________________

   d. ______________________________

   e. ______________________________

   f. ______________________________

   g. ______________________________

   h. ______________________________

5. In young adulthood, men's development seems to be guided mainly by needs for __________ and __________, while for women the establishment and maintenance of __________ __________ is of primary importance.

6. According to Levinson, the ages of 28 to 33 are characterized by the __________ ____________ transition, followed by a period of __________ __________ during the ages of 33 to 40.

7. For men and women, the late 20s and early 30s are characterized by self-__________.

8. The years between 40 and 60 are reasonably __________. There is __________ physical decline, but it is __________.

9. __________ is the final stage of a broader female experience called the __________, in which __________ and reproductive capacity draw to an end.

10. Five myths about menopause are:

a. ______________________________

b. ______________________________

c. ______________________________

d. ______________________________

e. ______________________________

11. During middle age, a diet rich in __________ and vitamin __________ can help ward off bone loss in both women and men.

12. Although testosterone replacement appears to boost __________, __________, and the __________ drive, it is connected with increased risks of __________ cancer and __________ disease.

13. People tend to retain their __________ skills into advanced old age. It is their performance on tasks that require __________ and __________ skills that tends to fall off as they age.

14. Five factors that contribute to intellectual functioning across the lifespan are:

a. ______________________________

b. ______________________________

c. ______________________________

d. ______________________________

e. ______________________________

15. Erikson labels the life crisis of the middle years as that of __________ versus __________.

16. Havighurst's seven tasks for middle adulthood are:

   a. ____

   b. ____

   c. ____

   d. ____

   e. ____

   f. ____

   g. ____

17. The midlife transition may trigger a crisis called the __________ __________.

18. Until midlife, the men studied by the Levinson group were largely under the influence of their __________.

19. Women enter midlife at about age __________, whereas men enter it at about age __________.

20. Older men tend to be __________ involved, __________ nurturing, and __________ flexible as fathers.

21. Despite years of emphasis on the so-called __________ __________ syndrome, studies indicate that most middle-aged women show increased __________, self-__________, and __________ after the children have left home.

22. Late adulthood begins at age __________.

23. Women in the United States outlive men by __________ years, and their prospects for a happy and healthy old age are __________.

24. Members of ethnic minority groups are __________ likely to be poor, and tend to eat __________ nutritious diets, encounter __________ stress, and have __________ access to health care.

25. A major reason for the increase in life expectancy during this century is the lowered mortality rate for __________ and __________.

26. Six possibilities currently being explored for extending the average lifespan are:

    a. ____

    b. ____

    c. ____

    d. ____

    e. ____

    f. ____

27. Our bodies continually produce unhealthful chemicals called __________-__________, that can be disarmed by chemicals called __________, found in foods containing vitamins __________, __________ and beta ___________.

28. Three naturally occurring hormones whose levels decline as we age, and whose loss may be involved in the aging process are __________, __________, and __________ __________ hormone.

29. An enzyme that has the effect of helping cells continue to divide is __________.

30. Elderly people show better health and psychological well-being when they _________ ____.

31. The __________ __________ theory sees aging as determined by a biological clock.

Harcourt Brace & Company

32. The __________-__________-__________ theory suggests that the DNA within cells suffers damage from external factors, like ultraviolet light and random internal changes.

33. Alzheimer's disease is associated with degeneration of the cells in the area of the brain called the __________ that normally produce __________.

34. According to Erikson, late adulthood is the stage of __________ __________ versus __________ with adjustment requiring the wisdom to be able to __________ __________.

35. Peck's six psychological shifts that aid us in adjusting to aging are:

a. ______________________________

b. ______________________________

c. ______________________________

d. ______________________________

e. ______________________________

f. ______________________________

36. Havighurst's seven developmental tasks for late adulthood are:

a. ______________________________

b. ______________________________

c. ______________________________

d. ______________________________

e. ______________________________

f. ______________________________

g. ______________________________

37. Adjustment among older people, as among younger people, is related to __________ __________ and __________.

38. Three components of successful aging are:

a. ______________________________

b. ______________________________

c. ______________________________

39. Atchley's six phases of retirement are:

a. ______________________________

b. ______________________________

c. ______________________________

d. ______________________________

e. ______________________________

f. ______________________________

40. Kubler-Ross's five stages of death and dying are __________, __________, __________, __________, and __________.

41. A __________ is a homelike environment in which the terminally ill can face death with dignity.

42. __________ is also referred to as "mercy killing."

43. A document through which people request that they not be kept "alive" by artificial support systems is a __________ __________.

44. Funerals tend to have five common phases. They are:

a. ______________________________

b. ______________________________

c. ______________________________

d. ______________________________

e. ______________________________

Sample Test

Multiple-Choice Questions

1. Once most people leave school and enter their chosen fields, their knowledge tends to ______.
   a. become deeper in certain areas of specialization, but become superficial in other areas
   b. become broader and more in depth as they begin to apply what they learned in school to "real-life" situations
   c. remain about the same until the natural declines of old age
   d. begin a slow, but steady decline, even in their areas of expertise

2. Chuck is 25 years old. According to Erikson's theory, with which of the following is he **MOST** likely to be struggling?
   a. identity versus role diffusion
   b. intimacy versus isolation
   c. ego integrity versus despair
   d. generativity versus stagnation

3. Research on men, women, and ego identity indicates that ______.
   a. men who develop strong senses of ego identity get married earlier than men who do not
   b. men who develop strong senses of ego identity get married later than men who do not
   c. men who develop strong senses of ego identity maintain more stable marriages than men who do not
   d. men who develop strong senses of ego identity fail to maintain stable marriages as well as men who do not

4. Which of the following is **NOT** one of Havighurst's developmental tasks of young adulthood?
   a. resolving "the dream"
   b. assuming some civic responsibilities
   c. establishing a social network
   d. assuming the responsibilities of managing a home

5. Moane's study found which of the following to be true of college women between the ages of 21 and 27?
   a. They fail to develop individuation and autonomy and they become more introspective and vulnerable.
   b. They fail to develop individuation and autonomy and they become less introspective and vulnerable.
   c. They develop individuation and autonomy and they become more introspective and vulnerable.
   d. They develop individuation and autonomy and they become less introspective and vulnerable.

6. Middle adulthood is characterized by ______.
   a. dramatic physical decline
   b. gradual physical decline
   c. no loss of physical ability
   d. increased physical ability

7. Which of the following women is likely to find menopause **MOST** stressful?
   a. one who equates menopause with loss of her femininity
   b. one who equates menopause with no further worries about an unwanted pregnancy
   c. one who equates menopause with becoming a more "mature" individual
   d. one who equates menopause with her grown children leaving home

8. According to Levinson, the "turning point" where men realize they are not kids anymore and start to adjust to the specter of old age and death occurs in their ______.
   a. late 20s
   b. mid 30s
   c. early 40s
   d. early 50s

9. By the year 2020, about one American in _____ will be over age 65.
   a. 5
   b. 10
   c. 15
   d. 20

10. B.F. Skinner argues that much of the fall-off in the cognitive performance of elderly people is due to ______.
   a. irreversible physical declines in the sensory organs
   b. an "aging environment" that fails to adequately reward old people
   c. impairment of cognitive functioning
   d. declines in the brain's ability to process new environmental stimuli

11. Alzheimer's disease attacks the areas of the brain responsible for ______.
   a. the storage and transmission of old memories
   b. balance and fine-muscle coordination
   c. perceptual continuity
   d. the formation of new memories

12. Which of the following is **NOT** a developmental task of late adulthood as proposed by Havighurst?
   a. assuming important social and civic responsibilities
   b. adjusting to physical changes
   c. adopting flexible social roles
   d. establishing satisfying living arrangements

13. Which of the following elderly persons is likely to be the happiest?
   a. a single elderly woman in good health and financially secure
   b. a married elderly couple in poor health but financially secure
   c. a single elderly man in good health but financially struggling
   d. a married elderly couple in good health and financially secure

14. About ______ percent of elderly African Americans live below the official poverty level.
   a. 27
   b. 47
   c. 67
   d. 87

15. Alvin recently retired. Currently he feels that he has mastered his role as a retiree. He has settled into a routine and is completely aware of his needs, strengths, and weaknesses. He is in the ______ stage of retirement.
   a. honeymoon
   b. stability
   c. reorientation
   d. termination

16. What is the proper sequential order for Elisabeth Kubler-Ross's stages of reaction to news of impending death?
   a. bargaining, denial, anger, acceptance, depression
   b. denial, anger, bargaining, depression, acceptance
   c. denial, anger, depression, bargaining, acceptance
   d. bargaining, anger, depression, denial, acceptance

17. Research on death and dying ______.
   a. supports neither Shneidman's nor Kubler-Ross's views
   b. supports Shneidman's views more than Kubler-Ross's views
   c. supports Kubler-Ross's views more than Shneidman's views
   d. equally supports both Kubler-Ross's and Shneidman's views

18. Allowing a terminally ill patient to die, even when the technology is present to prolong, but not save, the dying person's life, is called ______.
    a. positive euthanasia
    b. primary euthanasia
    c. negative euthanasia
    d. secondary euthanasia

19. An organized, ritualistic way of responding to death in which a community acknowledges that one of its members has died is called ______.
    a. a living will
    b. a hospice
    c. an obituary
    d. a funeral

20. In our society, which of the following people is likely to die at the youngest age?
    a. a Hispanic American
    b. a Native American
    c. an African American
    d. an Asian American

True-False Questions

21. According to Erikson, achieving ego identity is the central task of young adulthood. _______

22. The age 30 transition is more difficult for men than for women. _______

23. Men can also experience menopause. _______

24. Most elderly people live on incomes that put them below the official poverty level. _______

25. Euthanasia and genocide refer to the same practices. _______

Essay Question

26. Explain what empty-nest syndrome is and discuss what evidence there is to support or refute this concept.

Student Activities

Name ______________________________ **Date** ____________

16.1 Where Are You?

From the discussion in this chapter, where would you place your current development? In what ways is your experience consistent with the discussion and in what ways is your experience inconsistent with the discussion?

1. Current development:

2. Consistent experiences:

3. Inconsistent experiences:

Name ______________________________ **Date** ____________

16.2 Our Parents as Subjects

Consider one or both of your parents for a while. Where are they in terms of their adult development? Would they tend to nod agreeably if they were reading this chapter, or would they look puzzled or even openly disagree?

1. Try to create their reaction in your mind and describe it.

2. This might be a good time to call home and check out your attempt to empathize with either or both parents. What can it accomplish? What will they say to these questions?

   a. When in their lives did they experience the greatest amount of freedom?

   b. When did they experience the greatest physical change? How did it affect them?

   c. When did they feel most in control of their lives? If not now, how is it different now?

   d. What changes do they look forward to?

   e. What could you add to this set of questions?

Name ______________________________ **Date** ____________

16.3 Getting Ready for the Rest of Life

Support groups help us through so many of life's experiences. There are support groups in our locale for victims of diseases, former patients of various disorders, survivors of suicide, and parents who experience the loss of a child. There are also informal social supports we enjoy when lunching with colleagues, bowling with friends, or talking over the fence with a neighbor.

Where will we get support for growing older and dealing with the challenges of aging? Will we just have to laugh at ourselves as our eyes lose their focus, our waistlines fight for space, and our children's tuition bills come due? It may be that the most reliable support will come from within ourselves.

Taking Shakespeare's dictum that "nothing is either good or bad, but thinking makes it so," reword the following changes that can come with aging so that the glass is half full instead of half empty, so to speak.

> The first half of life consists of the capacity to enjoy without the chance; the last half consists of the chance without the capacity.
>
> Mark Twain

1. Please calculate your life expectancy (from Chapter 16), and imagine you discovered you have just passed the halfway point of your predicted lifespan. Will this be the half of life described by Mark Twain as the "half that consists of chance without the capacity?" How could the last half be described in positive language?

2. Suppose you are holding the newspaper at arm's length and still squinting to read the print which you feel "isn't as good as it used to be." If you give in to nature and start wearing glasses, you would be showing your age. How could this turn of events be described positively?

Activity continued on the back

3. Soon there will be no child living in your home. Growing up and moving out is creating the "empty nest." What can be positive about this?

4. Of all the challenges or changes outlined in this chapter, what one would you add to this exercise? How could you reconstruct it in a more positive light?

5. What is the next major life change you anticipate? Consider the chapter discussion relevant to your age and use it to compare or contrast this next major life change, again, viewing it in a positive light.

6. Identify one change or challenge in this chapter that you will **not** be experiencing because of your abilities, beliefs, strengths, or choices. How will it be possible to avoid this one?

Name ______________________________ **Date** ____________

16.4 Aging and Stereotypes

Television and movie scriptwriters often take advantage of stereotypes about aging, and thereby contribute to some of the myths surrounding it. Please identify an example of ageism that is perpetuated by the entertainment media, and bring your example to class to contribute to a discussion.

1. Describe your example here.

2. How is this portrayal of aging inaccurate or different from your real-life experience of older people?

3. In contrast to question 1, illustrate a case where the writer has helped provide some accurate insight.

Name ________________________________ **Date** ____________

16.5 A Fountain of Youth

As your text describes, there are many scientific efforts underway to slow down the deterioration associated with aging. Drugs such as DHEA, HGH, and melatonin are just the first wave of what may someday be true anti-aging drugs. Experts in aging believe that within just a few generations (at most) science will be able to "stretch" the human lifespan out to around 150 years, with the person feeling young and healthy virtually the entire time. Many researchers believe that within 100 years science will be able to expand human life expectancy to around 300 to 400 years, with people being youthful and vigorous most during most of their extended lives. A few extremely optimistic researchers believe that at some point we will be able to stop the aging process entirely, and while people will still die from war, accidents, crime, and some diseases, no one will die from old age. This raises some interesting questions about the impact such changes will have on society.

1. How do you think extended or unlimited aging would affect or change society?

2. What potential problems do you see this creating for society itself, and the world in general?

3. If a pill were available that would stop aging completely, would you take it? Why or why not? If you would take it, can you imagine reasons why someone else might not? What would those reasons be?

17

The Challenge of the Workplace

Chapter Outline

I. Seeking Self-Fulfillment in the Workplace

A. Extrinsic versus Intrinsic Motives for Working

II. Vocational Development

A. Stages of Vocational Development
   1. Box: What Do You Say Now? Positive Impression
B. Writing a Resume
C. How to Make a Positive Impression at an Interview
D. Developmental Tasks in Taking a Job
   1. Box: Adjustment in the New Millennium: Career - What's Hot, What's Not

III. Adjustment in the Workplace

A. Satisfaction on the Job
   1. Box: Self-Assessment: How Do You Feel About Your Work? The Job Satisfaction Index
B. How to Enhance Job Satisfaction *and Productivity:* Improving the Quality of Work Life Is Also Good Business
C. Work and Stress

IV. Women in the Workplace

   1. Box: Adjustment in a World of Diversity: Why Does Mommy Work?
A. The Workplace for Women
B. Sexual Harassment
   1. Box: What Do You Say Now? Resisting Sexual Harassment

V. Adjustment and Modern Life

A. Finding a Career That "Fits"
   1. Box: Self-Assessment: What's Your Vocational Type? Attend the Job Fair and Find Out!

Chapter Overview

Reasons for Working. Workers are motivated by both extrinsic rewards (money, status, security) and intrinsic rewards (the work ethic, self-identity, self-fulfillment, self-worth, and the social value of work).

Stages of Vocational Development. Super identified five stages of development: fantasy, tentative, realistic choice, maintenance, and retirement stages.

Developmental Tasks in Taking a New Job. These include making the transition from school to the workplace, learning the job tasks, accepting responsibility and subordinate status, and learning how to cope with coworkers, supervisors, successes, and failures.

Measures for Enhancing Job Satisfaction. Measures that contribute to job satisfaction include careful recruitment and selection, training and instruction, unbiased appraisal and feedback, goal setting, linking financial compensation to productivity, work redesign, allowing workers to make appropriate decisions, and flexible work schedules.

Stress in the Workplace. Stressors include the physical, individual, group, and organizational types. We can cope with them by evaluating our appraisal of them, enhancing our person-environment fit, and managing stress.

Improving the Workplace for Women. Women profit from more realistic career planning, maintaining employment continuity, child-care facilities, and training programs.

Sexual Harassment. One commonly accepted definition of sexual harassment consists of "deliberate or repeated unsolicited verbal comments, gestures, or physical contact of a sexual nature that is unwelcome."

Coping Styles and Work Adjustment. John Holland identified six coping styles: realistic, investigative, artistic, social, enterprising, and conventional. Persons with certain coping styles better fit, or are better adjusted in, certain occupations. For example, scientists are investigative and beauticians are realistic and conventional.

Balance Sheets and Career Decision Making. Use of a balance sheet helps us weigh the pluses and minuses of following a particular career path, and also helps us identify gaps in the information we need to make a decision.

Psychological Tests and Career Decision Making. Psychological tests measure our intelligence, aptitudes (as in music), interests, and personality traits. We can then compare our scores on these measures to those of people who are well-adjusted in various occupations.

Learning Objectives

After studying this chapter you should be able to:

1. Compare and contrast the various intrinsic and extrinsic motives for working.

2. Identify and briefly explain Super's stages of vocational development.

3. Explain what a resume and a cover letter are, and provide a detailed description of what each should, or should not, contain.

4. Summarize, in detail, the things you should do to make a good impression at a job interview.

5. Identify and discuss the various developmental tasks in taking a new job.

6. Describe the various measures that can be taken to enhance job satisfaction.

7. Identify the various sources of stress in the workplace, describe their effects, including burnout, and explain what steps can be taken to cope with workplace stress.

8. Describe discrepancies in pay and promotion for women in the workplace, and identify and explain the steps that can be taken to improve the workplace for women.

9. Discuss the types of behavior that represent sexual harassment, and explain what steps a person can take to protect himself or herself against sexual harassment.

10. Describe the six coping styles proposed in Holland's theory and explain how certain coping styles "fit" better in certain occupations than in others.

11. Explain what a balance sheet is and describe how it can be used to enhance the process of making career decisions.

12. Identify at least two psychological tests that could be useful in the career decision-making process and explain how psychological tests can help us make better career decisions.

Key Terms

extrinsic
intrinsic
the work ethic
self-identity
self-fulfillment
self-worth
Super's theory
theory Z
quality circle
flextime
burnout
the earnings gap
sexual harassment
Holland's theory
realistic style
investigative style
artistic style
social style
enterprising style
conventional style
WAIS
EPPS

Key Terms Review

Define each of the following terms:

1. Extrinsic: ____

____

2. Intrinsic: ____

____

3. The Work Ethic: ____

____

4. Self-Identity: ____

____

5. Self-Fulfillment: ____

____

6. Self-Worth: ____

____

7. Theory Z: ____

____

8. Quality Circle: ____

____

9. Job Burnout: ____

____

10. The Earnings Gap: ____

____

11. Sexual Harassment: ____

____

12. Holland's Theory: ____

____

13. Realistic Style: ____

____

14. Investigative Style: ____

____

15. Artistic Style: ____

____

16. Social Style: ____

____

17. Enterprising Style: ____

____

18. Conventional Style: ____

____

19. WAIS: ____

____

20. EPPS: ____

____

Chapter Review

1. The major reason for working is _________.

2. Three extrinsic reasons for working are:

   a. ____

   b. ____

   c. ____

3. Five intrinsic reasons for working are:

   a. ______________________________

   b. ______________________________

   c. ______________________________

   d. ______________________________

   e. ______________________________

4. The ***Dictionary of Occupational Titles*** currently lists more than _________ occupations.

5. The five stages of Super's theory of vocational development are:

   a. ______________________________

   b. ______________________________

   c. ______________________________

   d. ______________________________

   e. ______________________________

6. When you apply for a job, you usually send a _________ with a _________ _________.

7. A resume is a _________ of your job qualifications and should be kept to _________ page(s) if at all possible.

8. The six parts of a resume are:

a. ______________________________

b. ______________________________

c. ______________________________

d. ______________________________

e. ______________________________

f. ______________________________

9. A cover letter should include each of the following:

a. ______________________________

b. ______________________________

c. ______________________________

d. ______________________________

e. ______________________________

f. ______________________________

g. ______________________________

10. A job interview is a __________ occasion and a __________.

11. Five developmental tasks in taking a job are:

a. ______________________________

b. ______________________________

c. ______________________________

d. ______________________________

e. ______________________________

12. In the United States, there is usually a(n) __________ relationship between management and labor.

13. Increasing job satisfaction also increases __________.

14. Five methods for enhancing job satisfaction and productivity are:

    a. ______________________________

    b. ______________________________

    c. ______________________________

    d. ______________________________

    e. ______________________________

15. Five individual stressors on the job are:

    a. ______________________________

    b. ______________________________

    c. ______________________________

    d. ______________________________

    e. ______________________________

16. Burnout is common among people who have high levels of role __________, role __________, and role __________.

17. Five signs of job burnout are:

    a. ______________________________

    b. ______________________________

    c. ______________________________

    d. ______________________________

    e. ______________________________

18. Five suggestions for preventing burnout are:

a. ______________________________

b. ______________________________

c. ______________________________

d. ______________________________

e. ______________________________

19. Working women usually work two shifts. One in the __________ and one in the __________.

20. Working mothers are primarily concerned about their __________.

21. The average female high school graduate earns less than the average male __________ ______________________________.

22. Six measures for reducing the earnings gap are:

a. ______________________________

b. ______________________________

c. ______________________________

d. ______________________________

e. ______________________________

f. ______________________________

23. Five types of sexual harassment are:

a. ______________________________

b. ______________________________

c. ______________________________

d. ______________________________

e. ______________________________

24. Five ways to resist sexual harassment are:

a. ______________________________

b. ______________________________

c. ______________________________

d. ______________________________

e. ______________________________

25. **Matching:** Match the coping style from Holland's theory on the left with its appropriate description on the right.

_______ a. Realistic

_______ b. Investigative

_______ c. Artistic

_______ d. Social

_______ e. Enterprising

_______ f. Conventional

1. abstract in thinking, creative, and introverted; well-adjusted in research or college and university teaching
2. adventurous, impulsive, domineering, and extraverted; gravitates toward leadership and planning roles in industry and government
3. high self-control, needs for order, desire for social approval, enjoys routine, not very creative; well-adjusted in banking, accounting, and clerical work
4. concrete thinkers, mechanically oriented, enjoy using their hands; well-adjusted in farming, unskilled labor, skilled trades
5. creative, emotional, intuitive, interested in feelings; gravitate toward visual and performing arts
6. extraverted, socially concerned, high verbal ability, strong needs for affiliation; gravitate toward social work, teaching, or counseling

26. Two methods for gathering information for making career decisions are a __________ __________ and __________ __________.

27. Three types of information necessary to make satisfying career decisions are:

a. ______________________________

b. ______________________________

c. ______________________________

28. The most widely used intelligence tests are the __________ and the __________-__________.

Sample Test

Multiple-Choice Questions

1. At the turn of the century, a typical work week was from sunrise to sunset, ______ days a week.
   a. four
   b. five
   c. six
   d. seven

2. Which of the following is an extrinsic motive for working?
   a. the work ethic
   b. self-fulfillment
   c. security in old age
   d. self-worth

3. Adherents of the work ethic view life without work, even for the financially independent, as ______.
   a. justifiable
   b. in poor taste
   c. immoral
   d. unfulfilled

4. People who work because doing a job well makes them feel good about themselves and their work improves their attitude about themselves are focusing on which intrinsic motive for working?
   a. self-worth
   b. self-identity
   c. self-fulfillment
   d. the work ethic

5. Which of the following is the correct sequential order for the stages of Super's theory of vocational development?
   a. fantasy, realistic choice, tentative choice, maintenance, retirement
   b. tentative choice, fantasy, realistic choice, maintenance, retirement
   c. fantasy, realistic choice, maintenance, tentative choice, retirement
   d. fantasy, tentative choice, realistic choice, maintenance, retirement

6. Chad is in high school. He is in the process of narrowing down his career choices. He is thinking about being an artist because he has artistic talent and he likes art, but he isn't sure about many of the specifics involved in becoming a professional artist. According to Super, he is in the ______ stage of vocational development.
   a. fantasy
   b. tentative choice
   c. realistic choice
   d. maintenance

7. When you send your resume in to a company, the people screening it will most likely see it in which of the following orders?
   a. hiring officer, secretary, personnel manager
   b. secretary, personnel manager, hiring officer
   c. secretary, hiring officer, personnel manager
   d. personnel manager, hiring officer, secretary

8. Male interviewers rate men who wear cologne ______, and women who wear perfume ______.
   a. negatively, negatively
   b. positively, negatively
   c. negatively, positively
   d. positively, positively

9. Recent surveys indicate that ______.
   a. most workers are completely satisfied with all aspects of their jobs
   b. most workers are completely satisfied with most aspects of their jobs
   c. most workers are not completely satisfied with most aspects of their jobs
   d. most workers are not completely satisfied with any aspects of their jobs

10. Methods such as improved recruitment and placement, training and instruction, goal setting, and work redesign have resulted in ______.
    a. no gains in either worker satisfaction or productivity
    b. improved worker satisfaction, but no gains in productivity
    c. improved productivity, but no gains in worker satisfaction
    d. improvements in worker satisfaction and productivity

11. Which of the following is **NOT** a category of stressors in the workplace discussed in your text?
    a. physical environment
    b. individual stressors
    c. emotional stressors
    d. organizational stressors

12. Edgar is exhausted from constantly trying to be all things to all people. He tries to please everyone no matter how unsure he is of what they really want from him. He is experiencing ______.
    a. role conflict
    b. role ambiguity
    c. role overload
    d. role diffusion

13. Evidence on job commitment indicates that ______.
    a. women are less committed to their jobs than men
    b. only childless women are less committed to their jobs than men
    c. only women with children are less committed to their jobs than men
    d. women are just as committed to their jobs as men

14. The average female college graduate earns ______.
    a. the same as the average male high school graduate
    b. less than male high school graduates but more than the average male with an eighth-grade education
    c. less than males with an eighth-grade education but more than male grade-school dropouts
    d. less than the average male grade-school dropout

15. Which of the following is **NOT** a reason for the earnings gap?
    a. Women still work in traditionally low-paying occupations.
    b. Men with graduate degrees are more likely than women to gravitate toward higher paying specialties.
    c. Even in similar job areas, men are given higher-paying, more responsible positions.
    d. Women aren't physically capable of handling the manual labor required in the high-paying construction jobs held by many men.

16. John Holland's theory of vocational types identified ______ different personal styles and matching vocational fields.
    a. 3
    b. 6
    c. 9
    d. 12

17. Rita tends to be abstract in her thinking. She is creative, introverted, and would rather spend an evening playing chess or solving a mystery than going to a party. She is interested in becoming a research scientist or a university professor. According to Holland's theory, she is a(n) ______ type.
    a. realistic
    b. artistic
    c. investigative
    d. enterprising

18. Irwin has high self-control, a strong need for order, high desire for social approval, and enjoys a predictable routine. Creativity is **NOT** one of his strengths. He is in college studying to be an accountant. According to Holland's theory, he is a(n) ______ type.
    a. realistic
    b. social
    c. investigative
    d. conventional

19. A commonly used test, discussed in the text, to measure personality traits is the ______.
   a. SCII
   b. WAIS
   c. EPPS
   d. WISC

20. Within the service industry, the area that is not as "hot" for new jobs as other areas is in ______.
   a. health
   b. government
   c. education
   d. business

True-False Questions

21. Occupational prestige is central to social standing. _______

22. Increased job satisfaction decreases employee turnover and absenteeism. _______

23. Performance should not usually be linked to financial reward. _______

24. Women are less committed to their jobs than men. _______

25. The WAIS measures various areas of vocational interest. _______

Essay Question

26. Describe the various measures that can be taken to enhance job satisfaction.

Student Activities

Name ______________________________ **Date** ____________

17.1 Resources for Career Information

There are some fantastic resources waiting at your library that can provide important information about the career you have chosen or are considering. You will find the reference librarian **very** helpful and able to direct you to titles such as ***The Dictionary of Occupational Titles*** and ***The Occupational Outlook Handbook***. The latter is updated yearly and is quite complete in coverage of the nature of occupations. Both titles are widely held at libraries designated as Federal Depository Libraries and generally are available at local, regional, and campus libraries. Ask the person behind the reference desk for directions, and answer these questions about your chosen career, or what you might consider for a career:

1. What is the nature of the work? Does it seem to fit your preconceptions?

2. What work conditions are associated with the occupation?

3. How many people are currently employed in this occupation?

4. What education, training and other qualifications are required?

5. What is the outlook for this career choice? How many more people are expected to be needed in the future?

Activity continued on the back

6. What earnings and advancement opportunities are associated with this career choice?

7. What health benefits are associated with this job?

8. Is your interest in this career enhanced or reduced by this exercise? What exactly was influential?

9. Which stage of vocational development is associated with this exercise?

10. If you won the lottery, would you still choose this career? Why or why not? If not, what else would you do?

Name ________________________________ **Date** ___________

17.2 Our Work and Our Identity

The text points out the tendency for us to say "I am a _______" rather than "I work as a ______," and thus, we intertwine career with self-identity. We will be or already are sensitive at those times people ask us what our major is, what our career plans are, and what work we do.

Ask three people who are unfamiliar with your career interests to grade the "prestige" they associate with five jobs that you identify, including your first choice. Use a scale of 1 to 10, with 10 being the most prestigious job. Also ask all participants to give an example of a job they would rate a 1 and one they would rate a 10.

Follow-Up Questions:

1. Is it alarming or comforting to learn what others think of your choice? Why?

2. How much did the three judgments vary? In what ways did they vary?

3. Do the opinions of others regarding your career choice have any value to you? Why or why not?

Harcourt Brace & Company

Name ______________________________ Date _____________

17.3 Supercharging Your Formal Education

It is hard to find it in writing, but students generally know that there are courses outside their major, called electives, that are extremely useful, exciting, and valuable.

1. What courses outside your major could you describe to your class that you would highly recommend? Why are these courses valuable? What benefits do they provide?

2. Ask a friend for his or her recommendation for an elective course and the reason for the recommendation. What did the friend recommend and why does he or she recommend it?

3. Ask a faculty member for his or her recommendation for an elective course and the reason for the recommendation. What did the faculty member recommend and why did she or he recommend it?

4. Please bring these to class for sharing, and indicate which class or classes intrigue you.

Name ________________________________ **Date** ____________

17.4 What Matters on the Job?

Since most of us have work experience, we can judge the relative contribution of several of the components that influence job satisfaction or dissatisfaction. Rank each item from 1 to 10, with 1 representing the most important and 10 representing the least important. Briefly explain your rating.

1. ______ The boss
2. ______ Geographic location
3. ______ Fellow workers
4. ______ Work environment
5. ______ Hours
6. ______ Salary/Money
7. ______ Advancement potential
8. ______ Benefits (health insurance, etc.)
9. ______ Status/Prestige
10. ______ Daily tasks on the job

Follow-Up Questions:

1. This is an exercise that is also good to share with other members of your class. It probably would be useful to discover what your classmates' experiences are, especially if they are quite different from your own. For example, working nights or weekends might not be part of your experience, so the insights of others might be valuable if you are thinking of a career in a medical field.

2. Given the possible effects of criticism, goal setting, linkage of pay to productivity, work redesign, flextime, and stress at the workplace, how would you change the workplace you rated in this exercise?

Activity continued on the back

3. How would you monitor, measure, and document improvements that your recommendations could create?

18

Having and Rearing Children

Chapter Outline

I. Children: To Have or Not To Have

1. Box: Self-Assessment: Should You Have a Child?

II. Conception

A. Infertility
   1. Box: Adjustment in the New Millennium: Sperm and Egg "Donations" for Overnight Delivery?

III. Prenatal Development

A. The Stages of Prenatal Development
B. Environmental Influences
C. Chromosomal and Genetic Abnormalities
D. Genetic Counseling and Testing
   1. Box: Adjustment in a World of Diversity: Some Notes on Prenatal Care: A Tale of Three Neighborhoods

IV. Childbirth

A. The Stages of Childbirth
B. Methods of Childbirth
   1. Box: What Do You Say Now? Selecting an Obstetrician
C. The Postpartum Period

V. How to Be an Authoritative Parent (Rearing Competent Children)

VI. Issues in Childrearing

A. Breast-Feeding versus Bottle-Feeding: Does It Make a Difference?
B. The Children of Divorce

VII. Adjustment and Modern Life

A. Dealing With Day Care
B. Coping With Child Abuse

Harcourt Brace & Company

Chapter Overview

The Process of Conception. Conception takes place when an ovum is released by an ovary and fertilized by a sperm cell in a fallopian tube.

Fertility Problems. The most common fertility problem among men is insufficient sperm production, and, among women, endometriosis and blocked fallopian tubes. There are many ways of coping with fertility problems. Among them are adoption, artificial insemination, in vitro fertilization, embryonic transfer, and surrogate motherhood.

Prenatal Development. There are three stages of prenatal development. These are the germinal stage, the embryonic stage, and the fetal stage. There are also many factors that can affect prenatal maturation and development. Inadequate diet leads to lags in development, particularly motor development. Some maternal pathogens can be passed through the placenta so that the child is given congenital disease. Maternal drinking is linked to fetal alcohol syndrome, and maternal smoking is connected with undersized babies and problems in learning. Older parents put the child at risk for chromosomal disorders. Chromosomal disorders include Down syndrome. Genetic abnormalities include PKU, sickle-cell anemia, and Tay-Sachs disease.

Prenatal Diagnosis and Testing. A number of methods exist for learning whether something is wrong with the baby before it is born. These include parental blood tests, amniocentesis, chorionic villus sampling, and ultrasound.

Anesthesia During Childbirth. Many women must use local or general anesthesia during childbirth. It seems to make the newborn relatively sluggish for a number of hours after birth, but no severe long-term effects have been clearly identified.

The Lamaze Method. The Lamaze method prepares the mother and a coach for childbirth by education, relaxation exercises, and muscle strengthening exercises.

Postpartum Depression. There are three common kinds of postpartum depression: postpartum blues, which are transient and mild and affect about half of new mothers, postpartum depression, which is more severe and longer lasting, but less common, and postpartum psychosis, which is the rarest, but the most severe and may require hospitalization. Each problem may reflect the interaction of hormonal influences and concern about the mother role.

Rearing Competent Children. Baumrind found that the parents of the most competent children make demands for mature behavior, clearly communicate their values and beliefs, give their children a great deal of love, and applaud their children's accomplishments. These parents are called "authoritative" parents.

Breast- versus Bottle-Feeding. Breast-feeding is connected with fewer allergies and gives the child some of the mother's antibodies, helping fend off certain diseases. However, most children thrive with either method.

Children and Divorce. When parents get divorced it is common to see the children suffer emotional turmoil. There is often downward movement in socioeconomic status which puts further pressure on the children. Adolescents usually adjust better then younger children, and girls better than boys. Parents should not stay together for the sake of the children if they are going to fight in front of them. But if they can agree on childrearing practices and express their other disagreements in private, the children might be better off with both parents staying together.

Child Abuse. Child abuse frequently reflects current stresses and attitudes, or personal experiences, which suggest that it is "normal" to hit one's children.

Day Care. Day care apparently doesn't interfere with parent-child bonds of attachment. Day care appears to foster social skills, but day-care children are also somewhat more aggressive than children cared for in the home - possibly because they become used to competing for limited resources.

Learning Objectives

After studying this chapter your students should be able to:

1. Identify and briefly explain the various reasons to have or not to have children.
2. Discuss the various fertility problems people have and identify methods for coping with these problems.
3. Identify the three stages of prenatal development and explain what happens developmentally at each stage.
4. Specifically explain how maternal diet, drugs, and parental age affect prenatal development.
5. Briefly explain the causes and effects of each of the following: Down syndrome, Tay-Sachs disease, sickle-cell anemia, hemophilia, and PKU.
6. Identify the various prenatal tests for learning if something is wrong with the baby before it is born, and explain what each test measures and how it works.
7. Identify the stages of childbirth and explain what happens at each stage.
8. Discuss the issues involved in whether or not anesthesia should be used during childbirth and explain the various methods of childbirth.
9. Explain what the Lamaze method is, how it involves the spouse of the pregnant woman, and how it works.
10. Compare and contrast maternity blues, postpartum depression, and postpartum psychosis.
11. Compare and contrast authoritarian, authoritative, and permissive styles of parenting in terms of how they differ from each other and how they affect children.
12. Discuss the evidence on breast-feeding versus bottle-feeding. Which method is better and why?
13. Discuss the effects of divorce on children and explain why parents either should or should not stay together for the sake of the children.
14. Compare and contrast children raised in day care versus children reared at home.
15. Identify what steps parents can take to improve their chances of selecting a good day-care facility for their child.
16. Identify the various causes of child abuse and discuss the effects of abuse and neglect on children who are abused or neglected.

Key Terms

ovulation
fallopian tube
uterus
luteinizing hormone
zygote
conception
infertility
artificial insemination
pelvic inflammatory disease
endometriosis
in vitro fertilization
donor IVF
embryonic transfer
surrogate mothers
germinal stage
period of the ovum
embryonic stage
placenta
teratogens
fetal alcohol syndrome
anorexia
Down syndrome
phenylketonuria
sickle-cell anemia
Tay-Sachs disease
hemophilia
genetic counseling
amniocentesis
chorionic villus sampling
ultrasound
alphafetoprotein assay
fetoscopy
oxytocin
effaced
dilated
episiotomy
perineum
placental stage
midwife
general anesthesia
local anesthetics
Lamaze method
Caesarean section
postpartum period
maternity blues
postpartum depression
postpartum psychosis
instrumental competence
authoritative
authoritarian
permissive

Key Terms Review (Because of the number and complexity of the terms in this chapter this exercise will be divided into two parts. The first part will deal with prenatal development and problems. The second part will focus on the birth process itself.)

Key Terms Review #1

Define each of the following terms:

1. Luteinizing Hormone: ____

   ____

2. Zygote: ____

   ____

3. Conception: ____

   ____

4. Artificial Insemination: ____

   ____

5. Endometriosis: ____________________

____

6. In Vitro Fertilization: ____________________

____

7. Embryonic Transfer: ____________________

____

8. Germinal Stage: ____________________

____

9. Embryonic Stage: ____________________

____

10. Teratogen: ____________________

____

11. Fetal Alcohol Syndrome: ____________________

____

12. Anoxia: ____________________

____

13. Down Syndrome: ____________________

____

14. Phenylketonuria: ____________________

____

15. Sickle-Cell Anemia: ____________________

____

16. Tay-Sachs Disease: ______________________________

____

17. Hemophilia: ______________________________

____

18. Amniocentesis: ______________________________

____

19. Chorionic Villi Sampling: ______________________________

____

20. Alphafetoprotein Assay: ______________________________

____

21. Fetoscopy: ______________________________

____

Key Terms Review #2

Define each of the following terms:

1. Oxytocin: ______________________________

____

2. Efface: ______________________________

____

3. Dilate: ______________________________

____

4. Episiotomy: ______________________________

____

5. Perineum: ____

____

6. Placental Stage: ____

____

7. Midwife: ____

____

8. Lamaze Method: ____

____

9. Caesarean Section: ____

____

10. Postpartum Period: ____

____

11. Maternity Blues: ____

____

12. Postpartum Depression: ____

____

13. Postpartum Psychosis: ____

____

14. Instrumental Competence: ____

____

15. Authoritative: ____

____

16. Authoritarian: ____

____

17. Permissive: ____

____

Chapter Review

1. Luteinizing hormone surges about one to two days prior to __________.

2. According to the "motherhood mandate," it is traditional for women to bear at least __________ children.

3. Five reasons **FOR** having children are:

   a. ____

   b. ____

   c. ____

   d. ____

   e. ____

4. Five reasons for **NOT** having children are:

   a. ____

   b. ____

   c. ____

   d. ____

   e. ____

5. About __________ percent of couples in the United States have fertility problems; in __________ of ten cases the problem is with the man, in the other __________ of ten cases the problem is with the woman.

6. Three types of male fertility problems are:

   a. ____

   b. ____

   c. ____

7. Three types of female fertility problems are:

   a. ____

   b. ____

   c. ____

8. The most frequent cause of infertility in males is ______________________, while in females it is ______________________.

9. Four methods used to help women with blocked fallopian tubes bear children are:

   a. ____

   b. ____

   c. ____

   d. ____

10. The three stages of fetal development are the __________ stage, the __________ stage, and the __________ stage.

11. **Matching:** Match the agent on the left with its effects on a developing fetus on the right.

________ a. Alcohol

________ b. Aspirin (large doses)

________ c. Caffeine

________ d. Cigarettes

________ e. Cocaine

________ f. Narcotics

________ g. Marijuana

1. early delivery? neurological problems? birth defects?
2. addiction, undersize
3. mental retardation, addiction, hyperactivity
4. undersize, premature delivery, fetal death
5. respiratory problems, bleeding
6. spontaneous abortion, neurological problems
7. stimulates fetus, other effects uncertain

12. **Matching:** Match the disorder on the left with the symptoms on the right.

________ a. Cystic fibrosis

________ b. Down syndrome

________ c. Hemophilia

________ d. Huntington's chorea

________ e. Neural tube defects

________ f. Phenylketonuria

________ g. Retinoblastoma

________ h. Sickle-cell anemia

________ i. Tay-Sachs disease

1. a fatal neurological disorder with onset in middle age
2. a fatal neurological disorder that afflicts Jews of European origin
3. blindness caused by a dominant gene
4. a sex-linked disorder in which the blood fails to clot properly
5. a genetic disease in which the pancreas and lungs become clogged with mucus
6. a blood disorder that aflicts mostly African Americans
7. a genetic condition in which a child is mentally retarded with a characteristic fold of skin over the eye
8. a disorder in which children cannot metabolize phenylalinine
9. disorders of the brain and spine such as anencephaly and spina bifida in which part of the spine is missing or exposed

13. There is little doubt that the __________ are the ideal time (biologically) for women to bear children.

14. Five methods of prenatal testing are __________ __________ sampling, __________, __________, __________ assay, and __________.

15. During the first stage of childbirth, uterine contractions cause the cervix to __________ and __________.

16. The second stage of childbirth begins when ____.

17. When the baby's head begins to emerge from the birth canal, the baby is said to have __________.

18. The third stage of childbirth is known as the __________ stage.

19. Today, anesthesia is used in more than __________ percent of American deliveries.

20. The Lamaze method of childbirth is a form of __________ childbirth.

21. In a __________ __________, the child is delivered through surgical rather than natural means.

22. Three types of maternal depression are: __________ __________, a common, short-term phenomenon; postpartum __________, a much more serious, long-term problem; and postpartum __________, in which there is serious impairment in ability to meet the demands of daily life.

23. **Matching:** Match the parenting style on the left with its appropriate description on the right.

________ a. Authoritative

________ b. Authoritarian

________ c. Permissive

1. high restrictiveness (use of force), moderate demands for mature behavior, low communications ability and low warmth and support

2. high restrictiveness (use of reasoning), high demands for mature behavior, high communications ability, and high warmth and support

3. Low (easygoing) restrictiveness, low demands for mature behavior, low communications ability, and low warmth and support

24. Children of __________ parents have greater self-esteem, self-reliance, social competence, and achievement motivation than other children do.

25. Children of __________ parents are often withdrawn or aggressive.

26. Children of __________ parents are less mature than other children.

27. Four methods of prompting confidence in children are:

   a. ______________________________

   b. ______________________________

   c. ______________________________

   d. ______________________________

28. Five benefits of breast-feeding are:

   a. ______________________________

   b. ______________________________

   c. ______________________________

   d. ______________________________

   e. ______________________________

29. One of the major conflicts between divorced parents with children is __________ practices.

30. Divorced parents, on the whole, are significantly less likely to show __________ behaviors that foster __________ competence. They make fewer demands for __________ behavior, decline in __________ ability, and show less __________ and warmth.

31. Most investigators find that living in stepparent families as opposed to nuclear families has __________ psychological impact.

32. Children in day-care are more likely to _________ their toys, and to be _________, self-_________, and _________; but they are also less _________ and more _________.

33. Five things to consider when selecting a day-care center are:

a. ______________________________

b. ______________________________

c. ______________________________

d. ______________________________

e. ______________________________

34. Five factors that contribute to child abuse are:

a. ______________________________

b. ______________________________

c. ______________________________

d. ______________________________

e. ______________________________

35. Abused children show an alarming pattern of _________ and _________ problems.

Sample Test

Multiple-Choice Questions

1. When it is released from the ovary, the ovum enters ______.
   a. the umbilical cord
   b. the fallopian tube
   c. the uterus
   d. the cervix

2. A couple will conceive a girl if the ovum combines with a(n) ______.
   a. X-bearing sperm
   b. Y-bearing sperm
   c. Z-bearing sperm
   d. O-bearing sperm

3. A fertilized ovum is called ______.
   a. a zygote
   b. an egg
   c. an embryo
   d. a fetus

4. Each of the following is discussed in the text as a reason **NOT** to have children **EXCEPT** ______.
   a. time together
   b. dual careers
   c. mandate, not choice
   d. financial security

5. Each egg contains ______ chromosomes.
   a. 12
   b. 23
   c. 35
   d. 46

6. Jerome and Marsha have wanted children but they have been unable to conceive due to Jerome's low sperm count. In an effort to conceive, multiple ejaculations of Jerome's sperm are collected, quick frozen, and then injected into Marsha's uterus at the time of her ovulation. This procedure is known as ______.
   a. in vitro fertilization
   b. embryonic transfer
   c. donor IVF
   d. artificial insemination

7. Jerome and Marsha want to have children but have been unable to conceive due to Marsha's inability to produce ova. They submit to a procedure whereby Jerome's sperm are injected into the uterus of a female volunteer. After five days, the developing embryo is removed from the volunteer and placed within Marsha's uterus. This procedure is known as ______.
   a. in vitro fertilization
   b. embryonic transfer
   c. donor IVF
   d. surrogate motherhood

8. The prenatal stage of development from conception to implantation is called the ______ stage.
   a. placental
   b. germinal
   c. fetal
   d. embryonic

9. The membrane in the umbilical cord which allows only some substances to pass through it is called ______.
   a. the follicle
   b. the placenta
   c. the fallopian tube
   d. the ovum

10. Jerome and Marsha's newborn baby is undersized, has a smaller than average brain, widely spaced eyes, a flattened nose, and an underdeveloped upper jaw. The baby is slightly retarded, lacks coordination, and has heart problems. The baby is suffering from ______.
    a. Down syndrome
    b. Turner's syndrome
    c. Klinefelter's syndrome
    d. fetal alcohol syndrome

11. From a biological vantage point, the ideal time for women to bear children is in their ______.

a. teens
b. twenties
c. thirties
d. forties

12. Jerome and Marsha did not have their baby until they were in their late thirties. The baby is mentally retarded, lags in motor development, has a protruding tongue, and has a distinctive fold of skin over the eye. The baby is suffering from ______.

a. cystic fibrosis
b. Down syndrome
c. Huntington's chorea
d. phenylketonuria

13. Genetic defects such as hemophilia are carried on the ______ sex chromosome.

a. X
b. Y
c. Z
d. O

14. A method of visually examining the fetus by inserting a narrow tube with a lens attached into the uterus is called ______.

a. amniocentesis
b. chorionic villi sampling
c. ultrasound
d. fetoscopy

15. The placental stage of childbirth refers to the ______ stage of childbirth.

a. first
b. second
c. third
d. fourth

16. Maternity blues is experienced by about ______ of new mothers.

a. 25 percent
b. 50 percent
c. 75 percent
d. 100 percent

17. Marge recently gave birth to a baby boy. Since then, she has experienced rapid and dramatic upswings and downswings in mood, along with hallucinations and delusions. She is best described as having ______.

a. postpartum psychosis
b. postpartum depression
c. adjustment anxiety
d. maternity blues

18. In general, which of the following has **NOT** been found to be true of divorced parents?

a. They make fewer demands for mature behavior from their children.
b. They do not communicate as well with their children.
c. They show more nurturance and warmth toward their children.
d. They develop inconsistent disciplinary methods with their children.

19. Today, about ______ percent of mothers work outside the home.

a. 27
b. 47
c. 67
d. 87

20. Which of the following is **NOT** true of abused children?

a. They show more social problems and abnormal behavior patterns.
b. They are less likely to venture out and explore the world.
c. They are more likely to be depressed.
d. They are less likely to be aggressive.

True-False Questions

21. Luteinizing hormones stimulate menstruation. _______

22. Drugs and disease organisms cannot pass through the placenta during pregnancy. _______

23. Postpartum blues may last a year or more. _______

24. Many children of divorce who appear to be adjusting develop problems later on, when they are about to enter their own intimate relationships. _______

25. The majority of children who are abused do not grow up to abuse their own children. _______

Essay Question

26. Identify and briefly explain the various reasons to have or not have children.

Student Activities

Name ______________________________ Date ____________

18.1 Personal Experience

Having children can be among the most exciting experiences in your life, while at the same time being among the scariest experiences once the awesome responsibility you have taken on by having a child really sinks in. Once you get the child home you also realize how unprepared you are for many of the things with which you will now have to cope. While there are hundreds of childrearing manuals, some much more helpful than others, each child is different and no child comes with a set of "operating instructions" custom tailored to that particular child.

1. Visit your favorite library and/or bookstore. How many childrearing books can you find on the shelves or in the indexes?

2. Please identify and characterize the one that appeals to you most and explain why.

Name ______________________________ **Date** ______________

18.2 What Are the Odds?

1. What odds do you give yourself for becoming a parent? Write it as a percentage, and write down what you think the odds are for college students. Are your odds higher or lower than the odds you gave to college students in general? Why?

2. Ask several friends the same thing and write down their responses here.

3. Compare the odds given by you and your friends with the likelihood given for parenting in the United States and Canada (approximately 80 percent). Do you and others have very different ideas about the odds in general or your odds in particular? If so, why do believe your odds are different?

4. What classes on parenting, if any, are offered on your campus? Where else could you go in your community or region to enroll in such classes?

Name ________________________________ **Date** ______________

18.3 To Have or Have Not

First read the reasons presented in Chapter 18 to have or not to have children and check the items that seem to apply to you. Now take a position to have or to have not, even if only for this exercise. If you cannot decide, flip a coin.

1. Identify the strongest reason that is inconsistent with your chosen or coin-determined position. Explain why you are not influenced by that reason.

2. Write a rebuttal that challenges that reason. Explain why you are so strongly influenced by that rebuttal.

3. Now do the same for the strongest reason in support of your position. Explain why you believe so strongly in this reason.

Name ______________________________ **Date** ____________

18.4 Are You Feeling the Pressure?

Have others ever tried to influence your choice about having children? Was it strong persuasion or subtle hints? If this has not happened to you, has it happened to one of your siblings or friends?

1. Record here any influences you detect from friends, family or other sources (for you or your sibling/friend).

2. What position gets the heaviest support - not just in terms of sheer numbers, but also in terms of strengths and influence? For example, an argument from a friend may be more manipulative than an ad for Huggies, and a casual comment from a relative may be more weighty than a lecture from a confirmed bachelor professor.

Name ______________________________ **Date** ____________

18.5 In Your Judgment

Since how our parents raised us can influence how we will or would raise children and because you now have some sound basis for judging, please characterize your parents' childrearing with regard to the emphasis they placed on authoritarian, authoritative, or permissive styles.

Also, please describe the strengths or weaknesses you think you will bring to the tasks of parenting, and explain what you can do to help correct or compensate for your weaknesses.

What do you look forward to the most about having children, if you choose to have them?

Activity continued on the next page

What is your biggest fear about having children or your ability to raise children, should you choose to have them?

What are some steps you can take ahead of time to alleviate your fears or minimize the problems you anticipate?

If you choose to have children, about how old do you want to be when you have your first child? Why this age and not an older or younger age?

Answer Key

Chapter 1

Chapter Review

1. grow (4)
2. psychology (4)
3. Adjustment, personal growth (6)
4. Adjustment (6)
5. Genes, chromosomes (7)
6. clinical, healthy personality (8)
7. human genome (6)
8. Ethnic groups (9)
9. Asian, Hispanic (10)

10a. the dramatically changing ethnic make-up of the United States (9)
b. to enable students to appreciate the cultural heritage and historical problems of various ethnic groups (10)
c. to help psychologists understand how ethnic diversity concerns psychological intervention and consultation (11) or, the experiences of various ethnic groups in the United States highlight the impact of social, political, and economic factors on human development (9)

11. age, physical ability, sexual orientation (13)

12a. formulate a research question (14)
b. develop a hypothesis (15)
c. test the hypothesis (15)
d. draw conclusions about the hypothesis (15)

13. sample, population (16)
14. random (17)
15. men, women's (17)
16. Validity (23)
17. descriptive, causes (24)
18. +1.00 and -1.00 (24)
19. experimental, control (26)

20a. 5 (23)
b. 1 (19)
c. 7 (24)
d. 3 (24)
e. 2 (19)
f. 6 (26)
g. 4 (22)

21. placebo (26)

22a. plan ahead (27)
b. study a variety of subjects each day (28)
c. accept your concentration span (29)
d. cope with distractions (29)
e. use self-rewards (29)

23a. survey (30)
b. question (30)
c. read (30)
d. write (30)
e. review (30)

Sample Test

1. C, 4	6. A, 13	11. C, 24	16. A, 27	21. F, 6
2. B, 4	7. B, 14	12. B, 24	17. D, 30	22. F, 10
3. B, 8	8. A, 17	13. D, 26	18. B, 30	23. F, 15
4. C, 9	9. B, 17	14. C, 26	19. D, 12	24. F, 18
5. D, 12	10. C, 19	15. A, 26	20. B, 17	25. T, 31

26. This essay is a short-answer essay which requires you to identify the key differences between the two major approaches to healthy personality: a clinical or a healthy-personality approach. In your answer you must identify the key elements of each approach as discussed in your text. The clinical approach focuses mainly on the ways in which psychology can help people correct problems and cope with stress. Books written from this approach are frequently written from a psychodynamic or behaviorist perspective. The healthy-personality approach primarily focuses on healthful patterns of personal growth and development, including social and vocational development. Books written from this approach are likely to be written from a phenomenological perspective.

Chapter 2

Chapter Review

1. Freud (36)
2. physician (37)
3. iceberg (37)
4. conscious, preconscious, unconscious (37)
5. id, ego, superego (38)
6. eros, libido (38)
7. oral, anal, phallic, latency, genital (39-40)
8. fixation (39)
9. Jung, Adler, Horney, Erikson (40-41)
10. self (40)
11. superiority, inferiority complex (40)
12. psychosocial (41)

13a. 6 (42)
b. 8 (42)
c. 2 (42)
d. 4 (42)
e. 1 (42)
f. 7 (42)
g. 5 (42)
h. 3 (42)

14. ego identity (41)

15a. the abilities to love and work (42)
b. ego strength (42)
c. a creative self (43)
d. compensation for feelings of inferiority (43)
e. positive outcomes (43)

16. traits (43)
17. Hippocrates, yellow, black, blood, phlegm (43-44)

18. 18,000 (44)
19. extraversion, neuroticism, conscientiousness, agreeableness, openness (45)
20. behaviorist (46)

21a.	4 (48)	e.	11 (67)	i.	3 (49)	m.	6 (49)
b.	10 (48)	f.	13 (47)	j.	8 (49)	n.	9 (68)
c.	5 (66)	g.	7 (48)	k.	1 (49)	o.	2 (49)
d.	12 (66)	h.	15 (49)	l.	14 (49)		

22a. 2 (47)
b. 4 (47)
c. 1 (47)
d. 3 (47)
23. person, situational, expectancies(50)
24. observational (50)
25a. competencies (51)
b. encoding strategies (51)
c. expectancies (53)
d. emotions (53)
e. self-regulatory systems and plans (53)
26a. rich opportunities for observational learning (54)
b. learning of competencies (54)
c. accurate encoding of events (54)
d. accurate expectations and positive self-efficacy expectations (54)
e. emotions (54)
f. efficient self-regulatory systems (54)
27. existentialism (54)
28a. fully experiencing life in the present (55)
b. making growth choices rather than fear choices (55)
c. acquiring self-knowledge (55)
d. striving toward honesty in interpersonal relations (55)
e. becoming self-assertive (55)
f. striving toward new goals (55)
g. becoming involved in meaningful and rewarding life activities (55)
h. remaining open to new experiences (55)
29. biological, safety, love and belongingness, esteem, self-actualization (53)
30. self (57)
31. conditional, conditions of worth, unconditional, self-esteem (57)
32. Bokanovsky's process (58)
33a. experiencing life in the here and now (60)
b. being open to new experience (60)
c. expressing feelings and ideas (60)
d. trusting feelings and ideas (60)
e. engaging in meaningful activities (60)
f. being capable of making major changes in one's life (60)
g. being one's own person (60)
34. individualists, collectivists (61)

Sample Test

1. B, 37	6. C, 39	11. C, 44	16. D, 49	21. F, 38
2. D, 37	7. A, 39	12. A, 47	17. A, 50	22. F, 42
3. B, 38	8. B, 40	13. C, 47	18. D, 57	23. T, 49
4. B, 38	9. A, 42	14. D, 48	19. A, 62	24. F, 57
5. A, 38	10. A, 43	15. D, 48	20. C, 67	25. F, 68

26. In this question, you must first identify the two major phenomenological theorists discussed in the text -- Abraham Maslow and Carl Rogers. You should then explain that phenomenological theory generally focuses on subjective experience rather than empirical evidence in its approach to understanding the human condition. Then identify the common points expressed by Maslow and Rogers who both propose that the personal, subjective experiencing of events is the most important aspect of human nature and that, as unique individuals, we are our own best experts on ourselves. Furthermore, in discussing the elements of a healthy personality, the phenomenologists all agree that healthy people experience life in the here and now, are open to new experiences, express their feelings and ideas, trust their intuitive feelings, engage in meaningful activities, are capable of making major changes in their lives, and are their own persons. You might wish to offer brief explanations for each of the above qualities (similar to those presented in the text). Then you must brielfy contrast this approach with psychodynamic, behavioral, and social-cognitive theories.

Chapter 3

Chapter Review

1. role, person, self (72)
2. primacy, recency (73)
3. eye contact, posture, distance (74)
4. face, toward (74)
5. provocations, anger (75)
6. prejudice, discrimination (76)

7a. assumptions of dissimilarity (78)
- b. social conflict (78)
- c. social learning (78)
- d. information processing (78)
- e. social categorization (78)

8. physical, social, personal (79-82)
9. taller, slimmer (81)
10. problems, success (84)
11. values, ethics (85)
12. self-concept (85)
13. self-esteem (86)
14. ideal self (88)
15. attribution (91)
16. dispositional, situational (92-93)

17a. 5 (94)
- b. 3 (93)
- c. 4 (94)
- d. 1 (92)
- e. 2 (93)

18a. Helping nations avoid jumping to the conclusion that other nations are always to blame for their behavior. (92)
- b. Helping nations avoid jumping to the conclusion that they are never to blame for their own behavior. (92)
- c. Helping a nation recognize that other nations may tend to blame it for things that are not its fault. (93)
- d. Helping a nation recognize that other nations often see themselves as forced to act as they do. (93)

19. Any five of the following eleven choices are correct:

a. Be aware of the first impressions you make on others. (95)
b. Make your visa or resune neat and list your important accomplishments at the beginning. (95)
c. Plan or rehearse your first few remarks. (95)
d. Smile. (95)
e. Be well-dressed and appropriately dressed. (95)
f. Attend to your penmanship. (95)
g. Seek eye contact with your instructors or others with whom you communicate. (95)
h. When you talk to your instructors, or others, be reasonable and sound interested in their subject. (96)
i. When you pass someone in a race, put on a burst of speed. (96)
j. Ask yourself if you are being fair to other people in your life. (96)
k. Before you eliminate other people from your life, ask yourself if your first impression of them reflects the real person. (96)

20a. Be aware of what other people are telling you with their body language. (96)
b. Pay attention to your own body language to help make desired impressions on others. (96)
c. Pay attention to your own body language as a way of learning about yourself. (96)

21a. role reversal (97)
b. intergroup contact (97)
c. seeking compliance with the law (98)
d. self-examination (98)

22a. improve yourself (99)
b. challenge the realism of your ideal self (99)
c. substitute realistic, attainable goals for unattainable goals (99)
d. build self-efficacy expectations (100)

Sample Test

1. D, 72	6. B, 79	11. C, 87	16. D, 99	21. T, 76
2. A, 73	7. B, 81	12. C, 88	17. D, 100	22. T, 81
3. A, 75	8. D, 84	13. C, 93	18. A, 81	23. T, 85
4. B, 75	9. B, 85	14. A, 93	19. A, Append.	24. F, 88
5. A, 76	10. B, 85	15. A, 94	20. A, Append.	25. F, 94

26. To answer this question you must first specifically identify each of the three parts of the self - the physical self, the social self, and the personal self - and briefly describe what each part is or does. For example, the physical self is your body and affects you through your physical appearance and your health. It can affect the hobbies, activities, and job choices you make and may affect how others interact with you because of your outward appearance. Your social self reflects the social masks you wear in your interactions with others and the social roles you play throughout your life. Finally, the personal self is the part of you that only you know about. It is hidden from others and reflects the day-to-day experience of being you.

The second part of the question demands that you take these three parts and describe how they meld together to form the "self." In answering this, it is usually helpful to focus on the idea that you need all three parts to be effectively self-aware and effective in your interactions with others. A couple of situations in which you need more than one part to function effectively can be helpful here.

Chapter 4

Chapter Review

1. emotional appeal, fear (104)
2. central, peripheral (104-105)
3a. the nature of the message (105)
 b. the person delivering the message (105)
 c. the context in which the message is delivered (105)
 d. the audience (105)
4a. repeated exposure (105)
 b. two-sided arguments (105)
 c. emotional appeal (105)
 d. arguments that run counter to the interests of the communicator (106)
5. expertise, trustworthiness, attractiveness, similarity (106)
6. selective avoidance, selective exposure (106)
7. good (107)
8. low, high (109)
9. foot-in-the-door, lowballing (109)
10. Nazis' slaughter of the Jews in WWII (111)
11. the effects of punishment on learning (111)
12. 5, 65 (114)
13a. socialization (114)
 b. lack of social comparison (114)
 c. perception of legitimate authority (114)
 d. the foot-in-the-door technique (115)
 e. inaccessibility of values (115)
 f. buffers (115)
14. deindividuation, diffusion of responsibility (117)
15. low, high, social shyness, gender, familiarity, group size, social support (117-118)
16. bystander effect (118)
17a. the bystanders are in a good mood, or empathic (118)
 b. the bystanders believe an emergency exists (118)
 c. the bystander assumes the responsibility to act (119)
 d. the bystander knows what to do (119)
 e. the bystander knows the person in trouble (119)
 f. the person in trouble is similar to the bystander (119)
18. assertive, nonassertive, aggressive (120)
19a. self-monitoring (121)
 b. confronting irrational beliefs (122)
 c. modeling (124)
 d. behavioral rehearsal (124)
20. fogging, broken-record (124)

Sample Test

1. A, 104
2. C, 105
3. D, 105
4. D, 106
5. A, 106
6. C, 106
7. C, 109
8. A, 109
9. D, 111
10. B, 111
11. D, 114
12. C, 114
13. C, 117
14. C, 118
15. A, 118
16. A, 119
17. A, 120
18. A, 123
19. C, 124
20. B, 126
21. T, 106
22. F, 109
23. T, 115
24. F, 117
25. F, 120

26. This question requires a straightforward listing of the factors that affect the persuasiveness of a communicator as discussed in your text, and a brief explanation as to what each one is and/or how it works. The factors listed in your text are expertise, trustworthiness, attractiveness, and similarity between the speaker and the audience.

Chapter 5

Chapter Review

1. adapt, cope, adjust (130)
2a. household hassles (131)
b. health hassles (131)
c. time/pressure hassles (131)
d. inner-concern hassles (131)
e. environmental hassles (131)
f. financial responsibility hassles (131)
g. work hassles (131)
h. future-security hassles (131)
3a. correlational evidence (136)
b. positive versus negative life changes (136)
c. the need for novel stimulation (136)
d. personality differences (136)
e. the role of cognitive appraisal (136)
4. Prostaglandins (137)
5. Analgesic, prostaglandins (137)
6. endorphin (137)
7a. accurate information (138)
b. distraction and fantasy (138)
c. hypnosis (138)
d. relaxation training and biofeedback (139)
e. coping with irrational beliefs (139)
f. social support (139)
8. frustration (139)
9. emotional barriers (140)
10a. approach-approach (141)
b. avoidance-avoidance (141)
c. approach-avoidance (141)
d. multiple approach-avoidance (141)
11. Type A, Type B (141-143)
12. rapidly (143)
13a. natural disasters (143)
b. technological disasters (145)
c. noise (146)
d. air pollution (147)
e. extremes of temperature (147)
f. crowding (148)
14. noise (146)
15. Carbon monoxide (147)
16. aggressive (147)
17. crowding (148)
18. tripling effect (149)
19. self-efficacy (150)

20. commitment, challenge, control (150)
21. control (151)
22. humor (151)
23a. emotional concern (154)
b. instrumental aid (154)
c. information (154)
d. appraisal (154)
e. socializing (154)
24. pride (155)
25. pluses, minuses (156)
26a. tangible gains and losses for oneself (156)
b. tangible gains and losses for others (156)
c. self-approval or self-disapproval (156)
d. approval or disapproval of others (156)

Sample Test

1. B, 130	6. B, 137	11. C, 144	16. B, 149	21. T, 130
2. C, 130	7. C, 138	12. D, 146	17. B, 150	22. F, 137
3. D, 131	8. B, 140	13. C, 147	18. D, 151	23. T, 147
4. D, 131	9. D, 141	14. B, 147	19. A, 154	24. F, 151
5. D, 133	10. B, 141	15. D, 148	20. D, 156	25. T, 155

26. This question requires you to define frustration and conflict in a way that highlights how they are similar and/or different from each other. Whereas frustration is a feeling resulting from anything which blocks or thwarts a motive, either intentionally or unintentionally, conflict results when two opposing motives exist and the gratification of one motive necessarily prevents the gratification of the other.

Then you must identify the four types of conflict discussed in the text. Even though the question only asks you to identify each conflict (which could be interpreted to mean list them), it is a good idea to write down a one-sentence explanation of each conflict you list such as:

> approach-approach conflict: a conflict in which a person must choose between two desirable options and in choosing one option must forfeit the other option.

The other three types of conflicts are: an approach-avoidance conflict, an avoidance-avoidance conflict, and a multiple approach-avoidance conflict.

Chapter 6

Chapter Review

1. Health (162)
2. Stress (162)
3a. early identification of people at risk for disease (164)
b. rising expectations for programs that encourage people to change high-risk behavior (165)
c. growing numbers of people who are coping with chronic diseases (165)
d. a shift toward inclusion of community and public health perspectives (165)
e. the need to address health problems on a global scale (165)
4. general adaptation syndrome, alarm reaction, resistance, exhaustion (164)
5. endocrine, corticosteroids (165)
6. autonomic, sympathetic, parasympathetic (167)

7. trait, state (169)
8a. anxiety (155)
b. anger (170)
c. depression (170)
9. optimal (170)
10. leukocytes, pathogens, antigens, antibodies (170-171)
11. psychoneuroimmunology (171)
12. seven years (174)
13. seven years (176)
14. better, longer (176)
15. Headaches (176)
16. muscle tension, migraine (177)
17. dysmenorrhea, amenorrhea, premenstrual syndrome (178)
18. prostaglandins (178)
19. biological (179)
20. estrogen, progesterone, serotonin (179-180)
21. any five of the following eleven items:
a. don't blame yourself (180)
b. keep track of your menstrual symptoms to help identify patterns (180)
c. develop strategies for dealing with days that you experience the greatest distress (181)
d. ask yourself if you harbor any self-defeating attitudes toward menstruation (181)
e. see a doctor about your concerns (181)
f. develop nutritious eating habits (181)
g. eat smaller meals throughout the day (181)
h. make exercise a part of your lifestyle (181)
i. check with your doctor about vitamin and mineral supplements (181)
j. ask your doctor for a recommendation regarding pain-relieving drugs (181)
k. remind yourself that menstrual problems are time-limited (181)
22. Any five of the following items:
a. family history (181)
b. physiological conditions (182)
c. patterns of consumption (182)
d. Type A behavior (182)
e. hostility and holding in feelings of anger (182)
f. stress (182)
g. chronic fatigue (182)
h. chronic emotional strain (182)
i. a physically inactive life-style (182)
23a. weight control (182)
b. stopping smoking (182)
c. reducing hypertension (182)
d. lowering serum cholesterol (183)
e. modifying Type A behavior (183)
f. exercise (183)
24. cancer (184)
25. biology, psychosocial (185)
26a. control our exposure to behavioral risk factors for cancer (185)
b. have regular screenings for cancer (185)
c. regulate the amount of stress impacting on us (185)
d. if struck by cancer, fight it vigorously (185)
27a. get recommendations (189)
b. set up an appointment (189)
c. listen to yourself (190)

Sample Test

1. C, 162
2. C, 163
3. C, 164
4. C, 165
5. C, 167
6. D, 167
7. B, 168
8. A, 169
9. D, 169
10. C, 169
11. B, 171
12. B, 171
13. D, 172
14. A, 175
15. D, 175
16. C, 177
17. D, 178
18. B, 179
19. A, 179
20. D, 182
21. F, 164
22. T, 167
23. F, 170
24. T, 172
25. T, 176

26. In the first section of this question, even though it is not explicitly requested, you should identify the three clusters of symptoms related to menstrual problems: menstrual pain, physiological discomfort during menstruation, and premenstrual syndrome. Then you should note that the causes of most menstrual problems are biological but that beliefs and attitudes toward menstruation can heighten physiologically caused problems.

    Having done this, you should identify the suspected causes of specific menstrual problems such as: Primary dysmenorrhea: caused by organic problems such as endometriosis, pelvic inflammatory disease, ovarian cysts, etc. Secondary dysmenorrhea: linked to hormonal changes. PMS: may reflect unusually high levels of estradiol and progesterone or an imbalance between the two, as well as secretions of prostaglandins that can cause cramping and painful discomfort. Psychological factors reflecting cultural beliefs about menstruation being a period of "pollution" and "raging hormones" may increase subjective discomfort and result in greater mood changes and more missed time from work.

    In discussing the effects, you should note that the physical effects are usually pain and discomfort and that the mood changes, as discussed above, are often tied to psychological rather than purely physiological factors.

    Finally, in discussing ways to cope with menstrual distress, you need to list the methods discussed on page 166 of the text. Since the question doesn't specify how many of the methods you should list, you should ask your instructor (in a real test situation). It is possible that an instructor might want you to list all ten methods presented in the text. Most instructors would probably be satisfied with four or five. But you can never assume this. You should always ask, or write them all down if you are not sure.

Chapter 7

Chapter Review

1. nutrients (195)
2. proteins, carbohydrates, fats, vitamins, minerals (195)
3. amino, hormones, enzymes, antibodies (195)
4. carbon, hydrogen, oxygen, energy (195)
5. stamina, skin, vitamins (196)
6. organic (196)
7. anti-oxidants, free radicals (196)
8. Vitamins, calcium, fruits, vegetables (197)
9. family togetherness, caring (197)
10. “ob” (197)
11. adipose (198)
12. anorexia nervosa, bulimia nervosa (198-199)
13. taller, slimmer (200)
14. anaerobic, aerobic (201-204)
15. fitness (204)

16. metabolic, calories (204)
17. strength, upper (210)
18. slower, hemoglobin (or red blood cells) (211)
19. depression (209)
20a. feelings of physical well-being (212)
  b. improved physical health (212)
  c. achievement (of exercise goals) (212)
  d. an enhanced sense of control over one's body (212)
  e. the social support of fellow exercisers (212)
  f. the attention of researchers (212)
21. Any five of the following:
  a. before you start, seek the advice of a medical expert (212)
  b. consider joining a beginner's aerobics class (212)
  c. get the proper equipment (212)
  d. read up on the activity you are considering (212)
  e. select activities you can sustain for a lifetime (212)
  f. keep a diary or log and note your progress (212)
  g. don't try to exercise "through" severe pain (212)
  h. have fun (212)
22. wheelchairs (213)
23. flexibility, strength, cardiovascular (214)
24. one-third (214)
25. REM (215)
26. biological, psychological (216)
27. REM (217)
28. taking sleeping pills (218)
29. any four of the following five:
  a. relax (218)
  b. challenging irrational beliefs (218)
  c. don't ruminate in bed (218)
  d. establish a regular routine (219)
  e. use fantasy (219)
30a. set reasonable goals (220)
  b. improve nutritional knowledge (220)
  c. decrease calorie intake (222)
  d. exercise (223)
  e. behavior modification (223)
  f. track your progress (226)
31a. 5 (223)
  b. 8 (223)
  c. 4 (223)
  d. 6 (225)
  e. 1 (225)
  f. 9 (225)
  g. 7 (225)
  h. 3 (225)
  i. 2 (225)

Sample Test

1. D, 194	6. A, 198	11. A, 205	16. D, 221	21. T, 197
2. C, 195	7. B, 198	12. A, 215	17. B, 223	22. T, 200
3. A, 196	8. D, 199	13. A, 215	18. B, 200	23. F, 204
4. C, 196	9. B, 204	14. C, 216	19. D, 206	24. F, 215
5. B, 197	10. A, 204	15. D, 218	20. B, 211	25. F, 218

26. In answering this question you must first identify the three major concerns psychologists have regarding the use of sleeping pills for coping with insomnia:

    1. you attribute your success to the pills and risk becoming dependent on them
    2. you develop tolerance for sleeping pills and thus must increase the dose to continue to get the desired result
    3. high doses of sleeping pills can be dangerous, particularly when mixed with alcohol

    Then you must briefly describe the alternative methods psychologists use to help people cope with insomnia: lowering arousal, challenging irrational beliefs, using fantasy, and using stimulus control.

Chapter 8

Chapter Review

1a. 3 (230)
b. 7 (230)
c. 5 (230)
d. 6 (230)
e. 1 (230)
f. 8 (231)
g. 4 (231)
h. 2 (231)
2. predisposition (232)
3. Alcohol (233)
4. stomach, liver (233)
5. Native, Irish (233)
6. fattening, undernourished (236)
7. cirrhosis, Wernicke-Korsakoff (236)
8. nicotine (236)
9. seven (237)
10. hydrocarbons (237)
11. Passive (237)
12. Sigmund Freud (239)
13. pain, performance, vigilance, confidence (240)
14. unrefined, rush (240)
15. constricts, learning, memory, strokes (240)
16. elevate, hallucinations, nausea, disorientation, vomiting (242)
17. motor coordination, perceptual (242)
18. narcotics, morphine, heroin, codeine, Demerol (242)
19. morphine (242)
20. opioid, heroin (242)
21. amobarbitol, phenobarbitol, pentobarbitol, secobarbitol (243)
22. anxiety, epilepsy, blood pressure, insomnia (243)
23. internal bleeding, coma, death (243)
24. self-control, primitive (243)
25. benzadrine, hexadrine, ritalin (243-244)
26. peer, painful existence (244)
27. serotonin (245)
28. stimulant, cognitive behavior (245)
29. marijuana, LSD, PCP, mescaline (240,246)
30. tolerance, psychological, physiological (246)

31a.	5 (242)	f.	10 (239)
b.	8 (236)	g.	3 (246)
c.	9 (242)	h.	7 (240)
d.	1 (243)	i.	4 (246)
e.	6 (243)	j	2 (243)

32. Any five of the following fourteen:
  a. tell your family and friends you're quitting (248)
  b. think of specific things to tell yourself (about how quitting will help you) when you feel the urge to smoke (248)
  c. tell yourself that the first few days are the hardest (248)
  d. remind yourself that you're "superior" to nonquitters (248)
  e. start your attempt to quit when you wake up (248)
  f. go on a smoke-ending vacation (248)
  g. throw out ashtrays and don't allow smokers to visit you for a while (248)
  h. don't carry matches or light other people's cigarettes (248)
  i. sit in nonsmokers' sections of restaurants and trains (248)
  j. fill your days with novel activities that won't remind you of smoking (248)
  k. use sugar-free mints or gum as substitutes for cigarettes (249)
  l. interpret withdrawal symptoms as a sign you're winning and getting healthier (249)
  m. buy yourself presents with the cash you've saved by not buying cigarettes (249)
  n. ask your physician or pharmacist about nicotine replacement therapy (249)

33. Any five of the following fourteen:
  a. count your cigarettes to establish your smoking baseline (249)
  b. set concrete goals for controlled smoking (249)
  c. gradually restrict the settings in which you allow yourself to smoke (249)
  d. get involved in activities where smoking isn't allowed or practical (249)
  e. switch to a brand of cigarettes you don't like (250)
  f. hold your cigarettes with your nondominant hand only (250)
  g. keep only enough cigarettes to meet your reduced daily goal (250)
  h. use sugar-free candies or gum as a substitute for a few cigarettes each day (250)
  i. jog (or engage in some other form of exercise) instead of having a cigarette (250)
  j. pause before lighting up and put the cigarette in an ashtray between puffs (250)
  k. put the cigarette out before you reach the end (250)
  l. gradually lengthen the amount of time between cigarettes (250)
  m. imagine living a prolonged, noncoughing life (250)
  n. as you smoke, picture blackened lungs, coughing fits, and the possibilities of cancer and other lung diseases (250)

Sample Test

1. D, 230	6. D, 233	11. A, 240	16. C, 243	21. T, 233
2. C, 230	7. B, 233	12. A, 240	17. D, 244	22. F, 233
3. C, 231	8. C, 236	13. A, 242	18. C, 248	23. F, 234
4. B, 231	9. A, 236	14. A, 242	19. D, 239	24. T, 242
5. A, 232	10. C, 237	15. B, 243	20. A, 264	25. F, 246

26. To answer this question you must first properly identify the two psychological views regarding the causes of substance abuse, the psychodynamic view and the social-cognitive view. Then you must briefly explain the theoretical perspective of each view. Then you must present a synopsis of the biological view of the causes of substance abuse.

In your explanation of the psychodynamic view, you must mention that psychodynamic theorists see drug use and abuse as an attempt by people to control unconscious needs and impulses that they do not feel they can control without drugs. Social-cognitive theorists, however, feel that people often begin drug use on the basis of modeling the behavior of others (such as peers or parents), following the recommendations of others (usually peers), and because of positive expectancies about the effects of the drug.

The biological view emphasizes that some people may inherit genetic predispositions or sensitivities toward physiological dependence on certain substances such as alcohol, nicotine, or cocaine. These inherited tendencies do not guarantee someone will become a substance abuser, but they do increase the chances of it happening.

Chapter 9

Chapter Review

1a. unusual behavior (255)
b. socially unacceptable behavior (255)
c. faulty perception or interpretation of reality (255)
d. severe personal distress (255)
e. self-defeating behavior (255)
f. dangerous behavior (255)
2a. 4 (256)
b. 5 (256)
c. 3 (256)
d. 1 (256)
e. 2 (256)
3. observable, symptoms (257)
4. neuroses (258)
5a. computers can be programmed to ask specific sets of questions in a definite order(259)
b. clients may be less disconcerted about reporting personal matters to a computer (259)
c. use of the computer for diagnosis frees clinicians to spend more time in providing direct clinical service (259)
6. Adjustment, mildest (259)
7a. phobias (262)
b. panic disorder (262)
c. generalized anxiety disorder (263)
d. obsessive-compulsive disorder (263)
e. posttraumatic stress disorder (264)
f. acute stress disorder (265)
8. specific, social, agoraphobia (262)
9. obsession, compulsion (263)
10a. 6 (267)
b. 3 (267)
c. 7 (254)
d. 1 (267)
e. 8 (262)
f. 4 (262)
g. 9 (263)
h. 2 (263)
i 5 (264)
j. 10 (265)
11. serotonin, norepinephrine, GABA (266)
12a. dissociative amnesia (266)
b. dissociative fugue (266)
c. dissociative identity disorder (266)
d. depersonalization disorder (266)
13. conversion, hypochondriasis (269)
14. la belle indifference (269)
15. major depression, bipolar disorder (269)

16. learned helplessness (271)
17. internal, stable, global (272)
18. neuroticism (272)
19. serotonin, noradrenaline (274)
20. Schizophrenia (275)
21. grandeur, reference, persecution (275)
22. disorganized, catatonic, paranoid (276)
23. ego, id, oral (276)
24. 1, 10-15, 35 (277)
25. multifactoral (278)
26. Personality (278)
27a. 2 (279)
b. 1 (279)
c. 3 (279)
d. 4 (279)
28. arousal (280)
29. quicker, more (281)
30. stressful, social support (282)
31a. people who threaten suicide are only seeking attention (282)
b. people who fail at suicide attempts aren't really serious and are only seeking attention (282)
c. only "insane" people would attempt to take their own lives (282)
d. most people with suicidal thoughts act on them (282)
32. any five of the following seven:
a. draw the person out (283)
b. be empathetic (283)
c. suggest that measures other than suicide may solve the problem (283)
d. ask how the person intends to commit suicide (283)
e. suggest that the person go with you to obtain professional help now (283)
f. extract a promise that the person will not commit suicide before seeing you again (283)
g. do not tell the person threatening suicide that he or she is silly or crazy (283)

Sample Test

1. D, 254	6. C, 259	11. D, 269	16. B, 276	21. F, 257
2. B, 255	7. A, 262	12. A, 269	17. B, 277	22. F, 259
3. C, 256	8. A, 263	13. D, 272	18. A, 279	23. F, 262
4. B, 256	9. C, 266	14. C, 274	19. C, 281	24. T, 270
5. A, 258	10. C, 268	15. D, 275	20. A, 261	25. T, 279

26. In this question you must provide a description of anxiety disorders in general as well as a brief explanation of each of the specific types of anxiety disorders such as follows:

Anxiety disorders are characterized by nervousness, fears, feelings of dread and foreboding and sympathetic overarousal. The anxiety is either out of proportion to the threat or exists where there is no apparent threat at all. The specific types of anxiety disorders include:

1. Phobias - irrational fears of objects, situations, public scrutiny, or open spaces and crowds.
2. Panic Disorder - a recurrent experience of extreme anxiety (panic attacks) in the absence of any external anxiety-eliciting source.
3. Generalized Anxiety Disorder - persistent feelings of dread and foreboding which is "free floating," combined with sympathetic arousal which lasts for at least six months.

4. Obsessive-Compulsive Disorder - A disorder in which a person experiences either recurring thoughts or images which seem beyond control, irresistible urges to repeat an act or engage in ritualistic behaviors that serve no functional purpose, other than to relieve anxiety, or both.
5. Posttraumatic Stress Syndrome - A delayed reaction to a psychologically stressful event which is characterized by intense fear, reliving of the event, and avoidance of stimuli associated with the event.
6. Acute Stress Disorder - A reaction to a psychologically stressful event which is similar to PTSD except that it appear within two to four weeks of the experiencing of the event and the symptoms do not persist as long as those of PTSD.

Chapter 10

Chapter Review

1a. it is a systematic interaction between a client and a therapist (288)
b. it brings psychological principles to bear on the client's problems or goals (288)
c. it influences a client's thoughts, feelings, and behaviors (289)
d. it helps the client overcome psychological disorders, adjust to problems in living, or develop as an individual (289)
2. Psychoanalysis, feelings, urges, insight (289)
3. free association, catharsis (290)
4. wish fulfillment (291)
5. manifest, latent (291)
6. ego (291)
7. subjective, conscious, present (292)
8a. unconditional positive regard (292)
b. empathic understanding (292)
c. genuineness (292)
9. integrate conflicting parts of their personality (293)
10. dialogue (293)
11. conditioning, observational (293)
12. flooding, systematic desensitization, modeling (294)
13. learned, counterconditioning (294)
14. aversive (296)
15a. token economy (297)
b. successive approximations (297)
c. social skills training (297)
d. biofeedback training (297)
16a. restriction of the stimulus field (299)
b. avoidance of powerful stimuli that trigger habits (299)
c. stimulus control (299)
17a. response prevention (299)
b. competing responses (299)
c. chain breaking (299)
18a reinforcement of desired behavior (299)
b. response cost (299)
c. "grandma's method" (299)
d. covert sensitization (299)
e. covert reinforcement (299)
19. themselves, world, futures (300)

20a. selective perception (300)
b. overgeneralization (301)
c. magnification (301)
d. absolutist thinking (301)
21. activating, beliefs, consequences, irrational catastrophizing (303)
22. use any five of the folowing ten beliefs
a. you must have sincere love and approval all of the time from people who are important to you (303)
b. you must prove yourself thoroughly competent, adequate, and achieving, or you must at least have real competence or talent at something important (303)
c. things must go the way you want them to go (303)
d. other people must treat everyone fairly and justly (303)
e. when there is danger or fear in your world, you must be preoccupied with and upset by it (303)
f. people and things should turn out better than they do (303)
g. your emotional misery comes almost completely from external pressures that you have little or no ability to control (303)
h. it is easier to evade life's responsibilities and problems than to face them with self-discipline (303)
i. your past influenced you immensely and must therefore continue to determine your feelings and behavior today (303)
j. you can achieve happiness by interia and inaction (304)
23a. it is economical (306)
b. it provides a greater fund of information to draw on than one-to-one therapy (306)
c. appropriate behavior receives group support (307)
d. it reassures patients that others suffer from similar doubts, problems, and failures (307)
e. group members who show improvement provide hope for other patients (307)
f. it provides a place for group members to practice needed behavioral skills (307)
24. serious psychological, personal growth (308)
25. scapegoat (308)
26a. problems in running experiments in psychotherapy (309)
b. problems sorting out therapy effectiveness from the effects of "nonspecific factors" (309)
27. meta-analysis (309)
28. white, English (311)
29. chemotherapy (drug therapy), electroconvulsive therapy, psychosurgery (311)
30a. antianxiety drugs (311)
b. antipsychotic drugs (311)
c. antidepressants (311)
d. lithium (311)
31. depression (313)
32. stigmatize (316)
33. physical symptoms (316)
34a. interacting with clients in the language requested by them (316)
b. using methods that are consistent with the client's values and levels of acculturation (316)
c. developing therapy methods that incorporate clients' cultural values (316)
35. identity, pride, cohesion, mastery (317)
36. male dominance (317)
37. satisfied, social pressure, prejudice (318)

Sample Test

1. A, 288
2. D, 290
3. D, 291
4. D, 291
5. B, 292
6. C, 293
7. D, 294
8. C, 296
9. B, 299
10. C, 300
11. C, 302
12. B, 308
13. D, 309
14. A, 310
15. A, 312
16. D, 313
17. A, 314
18. B, 316
19. B, 317
20. A, 312
21. F, 289
22. F, 291
23. T, 300
24. T, 308
25. F, 312

26. In this question you must first identify the three major biological approaches to therapy: drug therapy, electroconvulsive therapy, and psychosurgery. Within the category of drug therapy there are antianxiety drugs, antidepressant drugs, antipsychotic drugs, and lithium. Antianxiety drugs work by lowering activity of the central nervous system. This, in turn, reduces heart and respiration rates and feelings of nervousness and tension. Problems include tolerance, sedation effects, physical dependence, and rebound anxiety.

    Antipsychotic drugs appear to work by blocking dopamine receptors in the brain. Not all patients are responsive to them, however.

    Antidepressants work by increasing the amounts of noradrenaline and serotonin available to the brain. They tend to work better when combined with psychotherapy.

    Lithium appears to work by moderating levels of noradrenaline. Its major drawbacks include memory loss and depressed motor speed.

    No one knows why ECT works, but it does help patients with major depression who do not respond to antidepressant drugs. The major problems associated with it are tied to the reluctance many have of passing an electric current through someone's brain, the fact that no one knows why it works, and loss of memory.

    Finally, psychosurgery has been used mainly in the form of the prefrontal lobotomy. It calms down agitated patients by severing neural pathways between the frontal lobes and the thalamus. It has many side effects, ranging from hyperactivity and distractibility to impaired learning, seizures, and even death.

Chapter 11

Chapter Review

1. defensive, active (322-323)
2a. use of drugs and alcohol (322)
b. aggression (322)
c. withdrawal (323)
d. fantasy (323)
e. defense mechanisms (323)
3a. 8 (324)
b. 5 (324)
c. 2 (324)
d. 3 (324)
e. 1 (324)
f. 7 (324)
g. 4 (324)
h. 6 (324)
4a. develop awareness of them through careful self-examination (325)
b. prepare thoughts that are incompatible with them (325)
c. reward yourself for effective changes in your beliefs (325)
5a. alleviating your sense of time urgency (326)
b. alleviating your hostility (328)
6a. situational reconstruction (329)
b. focusing (330)
c. compensatory self-improvement (330)
7a. gradual approach (331)
b. systematic desensitization (333)
8. irrational, frustration (334)

9a. develop a rational-emotive analysis of anger (334)
b. relaxation (337)
c. assertive behavior (337)
d. self-reward (337)
10a. meditation (339)
b. progressive relaxation (341)
11. relaxation response, metabolism (340)
12. tense their muscles, progressive relaxation (341)
13a. cognitive restructuring (345)
b. progressive relaxation (349)
c. overlearning (349)
14a. pinpoint irrational, catastrophizing thoughts (346)
b. construct incompatible, rational alternatives (346)
c. practice thinking the rational alternatives (347)
d. reward yourself for thinking rational alternatives (347)
15a. use pleasant events to lift your mood (349)
b. challenge irrational, depressing thoughts (352)
c. exercise (356)
d. use assertive behavior (356)

Sample Test

1. A, 322	6. A, 324	11. B, 333	16. B, 340	21. T, 322
2. D, 323	7. A, 325	12. D, 333	17. A, 346	22. F, 323
3. B, 324	8. B, 327	13. C, 334	18. D, 349	23. F, 337
4. D, 324	9. B, 328	14. D, 334	19. C, 352	24. F, 344
5. B, 324	10. A, 329	15. A, 339	20. C, 332	25. T, 352

26. In this question you must first list and briefly explain each of the defensive coping mechanisms (alcohol and drug use, aggression, withdrawal, fantasy, and defense mechanisms), then the active coping mechanisms (controlling stressful cognitions, coping with Type A behavior, enhancing psychological hardiness, and coping with emotional responses to stress). You may wish to list a strength and/or drawback to each coping method.

 Then you must review the strengths and weaknesses of active versus defensive coping in general. You should note that while defensive coping can buy you time to regroup and may reduce the immediate impact of a stressor, it rarely eliminates the stressor and may leave you vulnerable to future harm by that stressor or other stressors. Active coping teaches you how to change the situation (to take charge and gain control) so as to remove the stressor or to change your reaction to the stressor in a way that buffers its effects. In the long run, active coping is much more effective with far fewer costs than defensive coping.

Chapter 12

Chapter Review

1. gender roles (360)
2a. women and men have basically different psychological and sexual natures (360)
b. men are the superior, dominant gender (360)
c. gender differences and male superiority are "natural" (360)
3. breadwinners, homemakers (361)
4. Machismo, marianismo (361-362)
5. the systematic exclusion of women from science, industry, and world affairs (364)

6. verbal, visual-spatial(364)
7. small, narrowing (364)
8. more, more, more (365)
9. closer, more (365)
10. men, women (366)
11a. females are more likely to feel anxious or guilty about aggressive behavior (366)
 b. females behave as aggressively as males when they have the means to do so and believe the aggression is justified (366)
 c. females are more likely to empathize with the victim (366)
 d. gender differences in aggression decrease when the victim is anonymous (366)
12. Prenatal (366)
13. left, right (366)
14. identification (367)
15. Oedipus and Electra complexes (367)
16. observational, identification, socialization (367)
17. anxious, fight (368)
18. Gender-schema (370)
19. masculine, feminine (370)
20. Sex, social learning (370)
21. masculine, feminine, androgynous, undifferentiated (371)
22. androgynous (371)
23. femininity, femininity (372)
24. masculinity, androgyny (372)
25. 50, 35, 15 (372)
26. Sexism (377)
27. Boys, girls (378)
28. boys, girls, feminine (379)
29. math (379)
30. male, positive, anxiety (380)
31. glass, mommy (381)
32. overload, parent, worker (381)

Sample Test

1. B, 360	6. B, 365	11. A, 367	16. C, 372	21. T,364
2. C, 361	7. C, 366	12. B, 369	17. C, 377	22. T, 366
3. C, 364	8. C, 367	13. B, 370	18. D, 378	23. T, 368
4. D, 365	9. A, 367	14. A, 371	19. A, 380	24. F, 372
5. C, 365	10. A, 367	15. D, 372	20. D, 362	25. T, 378

26. In this question you must explain each of the perspectives individually with an emphasis on their common points and their areas of disagreement. The three perspectives are as follows:

Freud: believed that gender identity results from children identifying with the same-sex parent during the resolution of the Oedipus and Electra complexes. In his model, gender identity remains flexible until the age of 5 or 6, when the Oedipus and Electra complexes are typically resolved.

Social-cognitive theory: states that observational learning, identification, and socialization are all involved in the formation of gender identity and gender roles. Children identify through a broad, continuous process affected by rewards, punishments, and observations of the frequencies with which men and women engage in certain behaviors.

Gender-schema theory: states that children use gender as a way to organize their perceptions of the world. They learn that some behaviors more than others affect how they are perceived by others and they learn to judge themselves according to the traits perceived as important for their gender.

All three approaches involve some level of identification; however, for Freud, that identification is limited to same-sex parents whereas with the other theories it is a much broader, more fluid process. Freud's theory does not take into account rewards and punishments or observational learning. Gender-schema theory does not emphasize direct rewards and punishments but focuses more on the indirect rewards and punishments that are tied to how people are perceived. Both social-cognitive and gender-schema theories take into account a broader social context for the development of gender identity, although they focus on somewhat different aspects of that broader context.

Chapter 13

Chapter Review

1. friendship, love (390)
2. asset, less (391)
3. heavier, thinner (392)
4. flat, medium, large (392)
5. outgoing, expressive, negatively (393)
6. physical, warmth, assertiveness, wit, achievement, honesty (393)
7. age, health, social, reliability (395)
8. good (396)
9. disorders, more (396)
10. fear of rejection by more attractive people (398)
11. physically attractive, financial security (399)
12. similar, attitudes (399)
13. sexual, religious (399)
14. powerful (400)
15. Gay, lesbians (400)
16. three, two (401)
17. X, mother (402)
18. hormones (403)
19. genetic, male, stress (403)
20. mysterious, complex (403)
21. as well (403)
22. who lives next door and who sits next to whom, similar interests (406)
23. intimate feelings (406)
24. cliques, crowds (406)
25. the ability to keep confidences (406)
26. any five of the following twelve:
    a. they offer handy sources of social support (407)
    b. they offer a crowd of people with whom to do and share things (407)
    c. they confer prestige upon brothers and sisters (407)
    d. they offer the beginnings of a lifelong network that may be of use in obtaining jobs and climbing the corporate ladder (407)
    e. they channel social life into house and college occasions (407)
    f. joiners become part of a tradition (407)

g. they frequently provide high-quality living arrangements (408)
h. they provide social inducements to become involved in athletics (408)
i. they encourage participation in planning social occasions and managing house business (408)
j. many houses encourage studying (408)
k. upperclass members often provide valuable information about the strengths and weaknesses of various courses and professors (408)
l. many houses have superb test files (408)

27. any five of the following nine:
a. they have norms that pressure members to conform (408)
b. members who seek friends among nonmembers may face disapproval (408)
c. they may put pressure on members to date the "right kind" of people (408)
d. there is often pressure to socialize only with members of your own house, or similar houses (408)
e. sometimes, the living arrangements they provide are not satisfactory (408)
f. there may be pressure to play on athletic teams, even when you don't want to (409)
g. there may be pressure to assume planning and administrative burdens (409)
h. there may be subtle, or explicit, pressure not to study (409)
i. there may be perils related to hazing (409)

28a. 2 (410)
b. 6 (410)
c. 5 (410)
d. 7 (410)
e. 8 (410)
f. 9 (410)
g. 4 (411)
h. 1 (412)

29 intimacy, passion, commitment (410-411)
30. Romantic, companionate (413)
31. adolescence, peer (417)
32. depression, sick (417)
33. any five of the following nine:
a. lack of social skills (417)
b. lack of interest in other people (417)
c. lack of empathy (417)
d. high self-criticism concerning social behavior (417)
e. failure to disclose information about themselves to potential friends (418)
f. cynicism about human nature (418)
g. demanding too much too soon (418)
h. pessimism about life in general (418)
i. external locus of control (418)

34a. make frequent social contacts (418)
b. be assertive (418)
c. become a good listener (419)
d. let people get to know you (419)
e. fight fair (419)
f. tell yourself that you're worthy of friends (419)
g. go to the counseling center (419)

Sample Test

1. B, 389	6. C, 398	11. A, 406	16. A, 410	21. T, 391
2. A, 392	7. C, 398	12. B, 406	17. A, 414	22. F, 393
3. D, 392	8. C, 399	13. C, 410	18. B, 417	23. F, 396
4. D, 393	9. D, 403	14. D, 410	19. A, 393	24. F, 403
5. C, 396	10. B, 406	15. D, 410	20. A, 410	25. F, 410

26. This is a straightforward question in which you simply list the six styles of love discussed in the text with a brief one- or two-sentence explanation of each style. They are as follows:

Eros: romantic love; mostly sexual attraction or lust combined with an idealized view of one's partner and the feeling of being "in love"
Ludus: game-playing love.
Storge: friendship love similar to affection and attachment
Pragma: pragmatic, practical, or logical love
Mania: possessive, excited love
Agape: selfless, generous love

Chapter 14

Chapter Review

1a. attraction (424)
b. building (424)
c. continuation (424)
d. deterioration (424)
e. ending (424)
2. propinquity, positive, affiliation, propinquity, negative, affiliation (424)
3. visual (424)
4. physical, attitudinal, reciprocal positive, physical, attitudinal, reciprocal negative (424-425)
5a. the opening line (425)
b. small talk (425)
c. exchanging name, rank, and serial number (425)
d. self-disclosure (426)
e. mutuality (426)
6. successive approximations (427)
7. continuation (426)
8. dependent, inadequacy, exclusiveness (428)
9. Equity (428)
10. desirable, inevitable (428)
11a. taking action that might improve the relationship (428)
b. end the relationship (428)
12. waiting, doing nothing (428)
13a. alternative partners are available (429)
b. partners are not committed to maintaining the relationship (429)
c. there is little satisfaction in the relationship (429)
d. they expect it to fail (429)
14. Marriage (430)
15. homogamy (431)
16. the boy or girl next door (431)
17. any five of the following eleven items:
a. whether the wife will take her husband's surname, or retain her maiden name, or whether both will use a hyphenated last name (434)
b. how household tasks will be allocated and who will be responsible for what everyday activities - such as cleaning, washing, etc. (434)
c. whether or not the couple will have children, and if so, how many and at what time in the marital life cycle (434)
d. what type(s) of contraception to use and who will take responsibility for birth control measures (434)
e. how child-care responsibilities will be divided between the husband and wife (434)

f. whether they will rent or buy a place to live and whether residential decisions will accommodate the husband's or wife's career plans (434)
g. how the breadwinning functions will be divided, who will control the family finances, and how economic decisions will be made (434)
h. how in-law relations will be handled, and whether vacations will be spent visiting relatives (434)
i. what proportion of leisure activities will be spent apart from the spouse and what leisure activities will be spent together (434)
j. how sexual relations will be arranged and whether fidelity will be preserved (434)
h. how they will go about changing specific parts of their marital contract as the marriage progresses (434)

18. communication (435)
19a. affective communication (435)
b. problem-solving communication (435)
c. sexual satisfaction (435)
d. agreement about finances (435)
20. twice, minority (437)
21. curiosity, personal growth (438)
22. sex, soul mates (438)
23. monogamy (439)
24. seven, four, two (439)
25. communication, understanding, financial support (440)
26. financial, emotional (440)
27. separated, divorced (441)
28. sexiest (441)
29a. people are getting married at later ages (443)
b. more people are going for advanced education (443)
c. many women are placing career objectives ahead of marriage (444)
30. open, group, cohabitation, communes (444)
31. Cohabitation, living together (445)
32a. part-time/limited cohabitation (446)
b. premarital cohabitation (446)
c. substitute marriage (446)
33a. challenge irrational expectations (447)
b. negotiate differences (449)
c. make a contract for exchanging new behaviors (449)
d. increase pleasurable marital interactions (450)
e. improve communication skills (451)
34a. talk about talking (451)
b. request permission to raise a topic (452)
35a. engage in active listening (452)
b. use paraphrasing (453)
c. reinforce your partner for communicating (453)
d. use unconditional positive regard (453)
36a. ask questions designed to draw your partner out (453)
b. use self-disclosure (454)
c. give your partner permission to say something that might be upsetting to you (454)
37a. take responsibility for what happens to you (454)
b. be specific (454)
c. Use "I" talk (454)
38a. evaluate your motives (454)
b. pick a good time and place (455)
c. be specific (455)
d. express dissatisfaction in terms of your own feelings (455)
e. keep complaints to the present (455)
f. try to phrase criticism positively (455)

39a. ask clarifying questions (455)
b. paraphrase the criticism (456)
c. acknowledge the criticism (456)
d. negotiate differences (456)

40a. try to see the situation from your partner's perspective (456)
b. seek validating information (456)
c. take a break (456)
d. tolerate differentness (456)
e. agree to disagree (456)

Sample Test

1. A, 424	6. D, 429	11. D, 437	16. A, 444	21. T, 427
2. B, 424	7. D, 430	12. B, 439	17. C, 445	22. F, 430
3. C, 425	8. C, 431	13. D, 440	18. D, 451	23. F, 435
4. B, 426	9. A, 431	14. D, 441	19. B, 427	24. T, 444
5. C, 427	10. A, 435	15. A, 444	20. C, 442	25. F, 448

26. Your book lists ten different suggestions (pages 383-385) on how to make requests when trying to improve marital communication. You need to list each of these and provide a one- or two- sentence explanation for each one. For example:

> Be specific: Don't make general statements like "Be nicer to me," because your partner may not understand what that involves or that he or she is currently behaving in a way that is not "nice." It is much more effective to make specific statements focused on specific behaviors such as "Please don't cut me off in the middle of a sentence."

Chapter 15

Chapter Review

1. orgasm, strength (462)
2. masturbation (462)
3. incest (462)
4. wife (463)
5. sex (463)

6a. 3 (463)
b. 9 (463)
c. 7 (463)
d. 6 (464)
e. 8 (464)
f. 4 (464)
g. 5 (465)
h. 2 (463)
i. 1 (464)
j. 10 (465)
k. 11 (465)

7. clitoridectomy (465)
8. testes (466)
9. testes, testosterone (466)
10. scrotum (466)
11. urine, sperm (466)
12. loose erectile (466)
13. excitement, plateau, orgasmic, resolution (467)
14. refractory, orgasm, ejaculate (469)

15. estrogen, progesterone (469)
16. organizing, activating (469)
17. estrogen, progesterone, testosterone (470)
18. psychological (471)
19. pheromones, vomeronasal (472)
20. acquaintances (472)
21. anger, dominance (474)
22. rapists, victims (474)
23a. women are responsible for rape if they dress provocatively (475)
b. women say no when they mean yes (475)
c. all women like men who are pushy and forceful (475)
d. rapists are crazed by sexual desire (475)
e. deep down inside, women want to be raped (475)
24a. 1 (477)
b. 3 (477)
c. 5 (477)
d. 6 (477)
e. 8 (478)
f. 2 (478)
g. 4 (479)
h. 7 (479)
25. 2, 56 (480-484)
26. immune, opportunistic (484)
27. blood, semen, vaginal, cervical, breast milk (484)
28. white blood (or CD4) (484)
29. Male-female sexual intercourse, gay males, drug abusers (484)
30. blood, saliva, urine (8485
31. triple (485)
32a. 1 (483)
b. 2 (483)
c. 3 (482)
d. 8 (482)
e. 4 (482)
f. 7 (483)
g. 5 (482)
h. 6 (483)
33. pill (486)
34a. 3 (486)
b. 6 (487)
c. 9 (488)
d. 5 (488)
e. 1 (488)
f. 8 (488)
g. 10 (489)
h. 11(489)
i. 4 (489)
j. 7 (490)
k. 2 (490)
35. sterilization (491)
36. any five of the following fifteen suggestions:
a. establish signals and arrangements with other women in an apartment neighborhood (492)
b. list only first initials in the telephone directory or mailbox (492)
c. use dead-bolt locks (492)
d. keep windows locked and obtain iron grids for first-floor windows (492)
e. keep entrances and doorways brightly lit (492)
f. have keys ready for the front door or car (492)
g. do not walk alone in the dark (492)
h. avoid deserted areas (493)
i never allow a strange man into your apartment or home without checking his credentials (493)
j. drive with the car windows up and the doors locked (493)
k. check the rear seat of the car before entering (493)
l. avoid living in an unsafe building (493)
m. do not pick up hitchhikers, including women (493)
n. do not talk to strange men on the street (493)
o. shout "Fire!" not "Rape!" (493)

37. any five of the following seven suggestions:
   a. avoid getting into secluded situations until you know your date well (493)
   b. be wary when a date attempts to control you in any way (493)
   c. be very assertive and clear concerning your sexual intentions (493)
   d. when dating a person for the first time, try to date in a group (493)
   e. encourage your college or university to offer educational programs about date rape (493)
   f. talk to your date about his attitudes toward women (493)
   g. discuss items from the questionnaire on attitudes that support rape with a man you are considering dating (493)
38. any five of the following eleven suggestions:
   a. refuse to deny the prevalence and harmful nature of AIDS (497)
   b. remain abstinent (497)
   c. engage in a monogamous relationship with someone who is not infected (499)
   d. be selective (499)
   e. inspect one's partner's genitals (499)
   f. wash one's own genitals before and after contact (499)
   g. use spermicides (499)
   h. use condoms (499)
   i. consult a physician about medication (499)
   j. have regular medical checkups (499)
   k. when in doubt, stop (499)

Sample Test

1. A, 462	6. B, 467	11. C, 478	16. A, 487	21. T, 462
2. D, 463	7. C, 469	12. A, 479	17. D, 488	22. F, 466
3. C, 464	8. D, 471	13. D, 480	18. B, 491	23. F, 469
4. C, 464	9. B, 473	14. D, 482	19. C, 465	24. F, 474
5. A, 466	10. B, 477	15. D, 484	20. C, 478	25. F, 480

26. This question requires you to provide an overview (which should include some statistics) on the frequency of rape in the United States, who commits rape, and who gets raped. For example, 70,000 rapes were reported in 1990, but since only about one in five rapes is believed to be reported, about 350,000 may have actually occurred. Only one in five is perpetrated by a stranger; most rapes are committed by acquaintances. Many more cases of forced rape occur within marriages and some people consider those to be rape. Date rape is also a problem. Surveys indicate 9% of college women may be victims, although there is still much controversy in these cases as to exactly what constitutes rape.

    While sex may be one reason men rape women, most experts see it as an expression of anger at women or an attempt to physically dominate women. Many rapists have long histories of violent offenses and appear to use violence as a source of sexual arousal. Many rapists may also be encouraged by cultural myths that imply that when a woman says no, she is really playing "hard to get" and "wants to be dominated," so she really means yes. Or they may be responding to cultural pressures to be a "real man" which means using physical force to dominate others, including women. Other myths, such as the myth that "only bad girls get raped" create an atmosphere where the victim is often either not believed or is perceived as having "asked for it" and therefore her charges are not taken seriously or are almost impossible to prosecute effectively, particularly in cases of date rape. This may result in the offender "getting away with it" which discourages women from prosecuting and may encourage men to continue sexually aggressive behavior by confirming that what they have done is acceptable.

Chapter 16

Chapter Review

1. twenties (506)
2. intimacy, isolation, ego integrity (506)
3. earlier, maintain (506)
4a. selecting and courting a mate (507)
 b. learning to live contentedly with one's partner (507)
 c. starting a family and becoming a parent (507)
 d. rearing children (507)
 e. assuming the responsibilities of managing a home (507)
 f. beginning a career or job (507)
 g. assuming some civic responsibilities (507)
 h. establishing a social network (507)
5. individuation, autonomy, social relationships (509)
6. age 30, settling down (509)
7. questioning (509)
8. stable, gradual, minor (510)
9. Menopause, climacteric, menstruation (or ovulation) (510)
10. any five of the following ten myths:
 a. menopause is abnormal (511)
 b. the medical establishment defines menopause as a disease (511)
 c. after menopause, women need complete replacement of estrogen (511)
 d. menopause is accompanied by depression and anxiety (511)
 e. at menopause, women suffer debilitating hot flashes (511)
 f. a woman who has had a hysterectomy will not undergo menopause afterward (511)
 g. menopause signals an end to women's sexual interests (511)
 h. menopause brings an end to a woman's child-bearing years (511)
 i. a woman's general level of activity is lower after menopause (512)
 j. men are not affected by their wives' menopause (512)
11. calcium, D (512)
12. strength, energy, sex, prostate, cardiovascular (513)
13. verbal, speed, visual-spatial (513)
14a. general health (514)
 b. socioeconomic status (514)
 c. stimulating activities (514)
 d. marriage to a spouse with a high level of intellectual functioning (514)
 e. openness to new experience (514)
15. generativity, stagnation (514)
16a. facilitating our children's transition from home life to "making it" in the outside world (514)
 b. developing engrossing leisure activities (514)
 c. relating to one's spouse as a person (514)
 d. assuming important social and civic responsibilities (514)
 e. maintaining satisfactory performance in one's career (514)
 f. adjusting to the physical changes that attend middle age (514)
 g. adjusting to aging parents (514)
17. midlife crisis (515)
18. dreams (515)
19. 35, 40 (516)
20. more, more, more (517)
21. empty-nest, mellowness, confidence, stability (519)
22. 65 (519)
23. six or seven, dimmer (520)

24. more, less, more, less (521)
25. infants, children (524)
26a. calorie restriction (524)
 b. vitamins (524)
 c. hormones (525)
 d. telomerase (525)
 e. playing with genes (525)
27. free-radicals, antioxidants, C,E, carotene (524)
28. melatonin, DHEA, human growth (525)
29. telomerase (525)
30. retain control over their lives (523)
31. programmed sensescence (523)
32. wear-and-tear (523)
33. hippocampus, acetylcholine (523-524)
34. ego integrity, despair, let go (526)
35a. coming to value wisdom more than strength and power (526)
 b. coming to value friendship and social relationships mmore than sexual prowess (526)
 c. retaining emotional flexibility so that we can adjust to changing family relationships and the ending of a career (526)
 d. retaining mental flexibility so that we can form new social relationships and undertake new leisure activities (526)
 e. keeping involved and active and concerned about others so that we do not become preoccupied with physical changes or the approach of death (526)
 f. shifting interest from the world of work to retirement activities (526)
36a. adjusting to physical changes (526)
 b. adjusting to retirement and to change in financial status (526)
 c. establishing satisfying living arrangements (527)
 d. learning to live with one's spouse in retirement (527)
 e. adjusting to the death of one's spouse (527)
 f. forming new relationships with aging peers (527)
 g. adopting flexible social roles (527)
37. financial security, health (527)
38a. reshaping one's life to concentrate on what people find to be important and meaningful (527)
 b. a positive outlook (528)
 c. challenging oneself (528)
39a. the preretirement phase (529)
 b. the honeymoon phase (530)
 c. the disenchantment phase (530)
 d. the reorientation phase (530)
 e. the stability phase (530)
 f. the termination phase (530)
40. denial, anger, bargaining, depression, acceptance (531)
41. hospice (534)
42. Euthanasia (535)
43. living will (535)
44a. separation of the dead from the living (535)
 b. visitation (535)
 c. ritual (536)
 d. the procession (536)
 e. committing the body to its final resting place (536)

Sample Test

1. A, 506
2. B, 506
3. A, 506
4. A, 507
5. C, 509
6. B, 510
7. A, 511
8. C, 515
9. A, 519
10. B, 523
11. D, 525
12. A, 526
13. D, 527
14. C, 529
15. B, 530
16. B, 531
17. B, 531
18. C, 535
19. D, 535
20. B, 520
21. F, 506
22. F, 509
23. F, 512
24. F, 529
25. F, 535
26. This question requires you to define the concept of "empty-nest syndrome," explain its origins, and discuss the evidence for or against it. It was a concept originally aimed at traditional female homemakers who devoted their lives to raising their children only to find them grown up and "leaving the nest" by the time these women had reached middle adulthood. This supposedly left them with a profound sense of loss, emptiness, and depression.

    In general, the research is mixed regarding empty-nest syndrome today. While some women ***and men*** experience some problems when the children leave home, there is no evidence that it is as devastating for most people as the concept suggests. Many women and men find that with the children gone, they have more time for themselves and each other and their happiness and life satisfaction surge upward.

Chapter 17

Chapter Review

1. economic (542)
2. there are numerous possible correct answers to this, but the three presented in the text are:
   a. the paycheck (542)
   b. fringe benefits (542)
   c. security in old age (542)
3. any five of the following eight:
   a. the opportunity to engage in challenging, stimulating and satisfying activities (543)
   b. the opportunity to broaden social contacts (543)
   c. the work ethic (543)
   d. self-identity (543)
   e. self-fulfillment (543)
   f. self-worth (543)
   g. social values of work (543)
   h. social roles (544)
4. 20,000 (544)
5. any five of the following six:
   a. fantasy (544)
   b. tentative choice (545)
   c. realistic choice (545)
   d. maintenance (545)
   e. career change (545)
   f. retirement (545)
6. resume, cover letter (545)
7. summary, one (934)

8a. a heading (546)
b. a statement of your job objective (546)
c. a summary of your educational background (546)
d. a summary of your work experience (546)
e. personal information (546)
f. a list of references (546)

9a. explanation of the purpose of the letter (548)
b. explanation of how you learned about the opening (548)
c. comparison of your qualifications and the job requirements (548)
d. statements of desired salary and geographic limitations (548)
e. request for an interview or other response to the letter (549)
f. statement that references will be sent upon request (549)
g. thanks for the prospective employer's consideration (549)

10. social, test (549)

11. any five of the following ten tasks:
a. making the transition from school to the workplace (552)
b. learning how to carry out the job tasks (552)
c. accepting responsibility for your job tasks and functions (552)
d. accepting your subordinate status within the organization or profession (552)
e. learning how to get along with your coworkers and supervisor (552)
f. showing that you can maintain the job, make improvements, and show progress (553)
g. finding a sponsor or mentor to "show you the ropes" (553)
h. defining the boundaries between your job and other areas of your life (553)
i. evaluating your occupational choice in the light of supervisor appraisal and measurable outcomes of your work (553)
j. learning to cope with daily hassles on the job, frustrations, and successes and failure (553)

12. adversarial (553)

13. productivity (559)

14. use any five of the following nine suggestions:
a. improved recruitment and placement (559)
b. training and instruction (559)
c. use of constructive criticism (559)
d. unbiased appraisal of worker performance (560)
e. goal setting (560)
f. financial compensation (560)
g. work redesign (561)
h. work schedules (561)
i. integration of new workplace technology (561)

15a. work overload (562)
b. boredom (562)
c. conflict about one's work (562)
d. excessive responsibility (562)
e. lack of forward movement (562)

16. conflict, overload, ambiguity (985)

17. any five of the following eight:
a. loss of energy and feelings of exhaustion, both physical and psychological (563)
b. irritability and shortness of temper (563)
c. stress-related problems, such as depression, headaches, backaches, or apathy (563)
d. difficulty concentrating or feeling distanced from one's work (563)
e. loss of motivation (563)
f. lack of satisfaction or feelings of achievement at work (563)
g. loss of concern about work in someone who was previously committed (563)
h. feeling that one has nothing left to give (563)

18. any five of the following ten suggestions:
  a. establish your priorities (564)
  b. set reasonable goals (564)
  c. take things one day at a time (564)
  d. set limits (564)
  e. share your feelings (564)
  f. build supportive relationships (564)
  g. do things you enjoy (564)
  h. take time for yourself (564)
  i. don't skip vacations (564)
  j. be attuned to your health (564)

19. workplace, home (565)

20. children (567)

21. grade-school dropout (567)

22a. more realistic career planning (568)
  b. providing employers with accurate information about women in the workforce (568)
  c. heightening awareness of the importance of women's careers in dual-career marriages (568)
  d. maintaining employment continuity and stability (568)
  e. increasing job flexibility and providing child-care facilities (568)
  f. recruiting qualified women into training programs and jobs (568)

23. use any five of the following ten:
  a. verbal abuse or harassment (570)
  b. unwelcome sexual overtures or advances (570)
  c. pressure to engage in sexual activity (570)
  d. remarks about a person's body, clothing, or sexual activities (570)
  e. leering at, or ogling, someone's body (570)
  f. telling unwanted dirty jokes in mixed company (570)
  g. unecessarily touching, patting, or pinching someone (571)
  h. whistles and catcalls (571)
  i. brushing up against someone's body (571)
  j. demands to engage in sexual activity that are accompanied by threats concerning someone's status as a worker, or a student (571)

24. use any five of the following eight suggestions:
  a. impart a professional attitude (570)
  b. discourage harassment and promote the kind of social behavior you want (570)
  c. don't get into a situation alone with a harasser (570)
  d. keep a record of the incidents of harassment to document the problem (570)
  e. put the harasser on direct notice that you recognize the harassment for what it is and you want it to stop (570)
  f. confide about harassment to reliable friends, school counselors or advisers, or parents or relatives (570)
  g. find out where you can file a complaint and get it acted on (570)
  h. see a lawyer (570)

25a. 4 (574)
  b. 1 (574)
  c. 5 (574)
  d. 6 (574)
  e. 2 (574)
  f. 3 (575)

26. balance sheet, psychological tests (572-573)

27a. intellectual and educational appropriateness (576)
  b. intrinsic factors (576)
  c. extrinsic factors (576)

28. WAIS, Stanford-Binet (573)

Sample Test

1. C, 542
2. C, 542
3. C, 543
4. A, 543
5. D, 544
6. B, 545
7. B, 546
8. A, 549
9. C, 553
10. D, 559
11. C, 562
12. B, 563
13. D, 565
14. C, 567
15. D, 568
16. B, 574
17. C, 574
18. D, 575
19. C, 573
20. B, 555
21. T, 544
22. T, 559
23. F, 560
24. F, 565
25. F, 573

26. Your text presents nine different strategies for enhancing job satisfaction (pages 899-904). In your answer you need to identify each of the nine and present a brief (one- to two-sentence) explanation for each strategy. For example:

    Use of constructive criticism: Criticism is sometimes necessary for people to correct mistakes and improve the quality of their work. But it is important that criticism be given constructively, focused on improving someone's performance, rather than destructively, focused on hurting the person or tearing them down. Constructive criticism can make workers feel that you are helping them, whereas destructive criticism destroys morale and can create conflict.

Chapter 18

Chapter Review

1. ovulation (580)
2. two (581)
3. use any five of the following nine reasons:
   a. personal experience (582)
   b. personal pleasure (582)
   c. personal extension (582)
   d. relationship (582)
   e. personal status (582)
   f. personal competence (582)
   g. personal responsibility (582)
   h. personal power (582)
   i. moral worth (582)
4. use any five of the following thirteen reasons:
   a. strain on resources (582)
   b. increase in overpopulation (582)
   c. choice, not mandate (582)
   d. time together (582)
   e. freedom (582)
   f. other children (582)
   g. dual careers (582)
   h. financial security (582)
   i. community welfare (582)
   j. difficulty (582)
   k. irrevocable decision (582)
   l. failure (582)
   m. danger (582)
5. 15, four, six (581)

6a. low sperm count (581)
b. low sperm motility (581)
c. damaged sperm (581)
7a. lack of ovulation (581)
b. endometriosis (581)
c. obstructions or malfunctions of the reproductive tract (581)
8. low sperm count, lack of ovulation (581)
9a. in vitro fertilization (583)
b. donor in vitro fertilization (583)
c. embryonic transfer (583)
d. surrogate motherhood (583)
10. germinal, embryonic, fetal (585)
11a. 3 (587)
b. 5 (587)
c. 7 (587)
d. 4 (587)
e. 6 (587)
f. 2 (587)
g. 1 (587)
12a. 5 (588)
b. 7 (588)
c. 4 (588)
d. 1 (588)
e. 9 (588)
f. 8 (588)
g. 3 (588)
h. 6 (588)
i 2 (588)
13. twenties (587)
14. chorionic villi, amniocentesis, ultrasound, alphafetoprotein, fetoscopy (589-590)
15. efface, dilate (592)
16. the baby first appears at the opening of the birth canal (592)
17. crowned (593)
18. placental (593)
19. 90 (594)
20. prepared (594)
21. Caesarean section (595)
22. maternity blues, depression, psychosis (595-597)
23a. 2 (597)
b. 1 (598)
c. 3 (598)
24. authoritative (598)
25. authoritarian (598)
26. permissive (598)
27a. be reasonably restrictive (598)
b. don't hesitate to demand mature behavior (598)
c. explain why you make certain demands on your children (599)
d. frequently express love and caring (599)
28. any five of the following eight benefits:
a. breast milk is tailored specifically to human digestion (599)
b. breast milk contains all essential nutrients in their most usable form (599)
c. breast milk varies in nutritional content according to the changing needs of the infant (599)
d. breast milk contains antibodies that can prevent problems such as ear infections and bacterial meningitis (599)
e. breast milk helps protect against diarrhea and childhood lymphoma (a form of cancer) (599)
f. breast milk is less likely than formula to give rise to allergic responses and constipation (599)
g. breast milk even reduces the likelihood of obesity in later life (599)
h. breast-feeding is even healthful for the mother, reducing the risk of early breast cancer, ovarian cancer, and the hip fractures that result from osteoporosis following menopause (600)
29. childrearing (600)
30. authoritative, instrumental, mature, communications, nurturance (601)

31. little (601)
32. share, independent, confident, outgoing, compliant, aggressive (604)
33. select any five of the following eleven factors:
  a. Is the center licensed? (604)
  b. What is the ratio of children to caregivers? (604)
  c. What are the qualifications of the center's caregivers? (604)
  d. How safe is the environment? (605)
  e. What is served at mealtime? (605)
  f. Which caregivers will be responsible for your child? (605)
  g. What toys, games, books, and other educational materials are provided? (605)
  h. What facilities are provided to promote the motor development of your child? (605)
  i. Are the hours offered by the center convenient for your schedule? (605)
  j. Is the location of the center convenient? (605)
  h. Do you like the overall environment and "feel" of the center? (605)
34a. situational stress (606)
  b. a history of child abuse in at least one parent's family of origin (606)
  c. acceptance of violence as a way of coping with stress (606)
  d. failure to become attached to the children (606)
  e. rigid childrearing attitudes (606)
35. personal, social (606)

Sample Test

1. B, 580	6. D, 583	11. B, 587	16. B, 595	21. F, 580
2. A, 580	7. B, 583	12. B, 588	17. A, 597	22. F, 586
3. A, 580	8. B, 585	13. A, 589	18. C, 601	23. F, 595
4. C, 582	9. B, 585	14. D, 590	19. C, 603	24. T, 600
5. B, 581	10. D, 586	15. C, 593	20. D, 606	25. T, 606

26. While the question does not ask for a specific number of reasons for or against, your text presents nine reasons for having children and thirteen reasons for not having children. This is more than most instructors would ask you to present in a single essay, so you should ask your instructor how many items they want for each side of the question. Most instructors will probably want about four or five reasons for having children and four or five reasons for not having children. In that regard, pick any five from each category (pages 940-942) and provide a one- or two-sentence explanation for each one you present.